MODERN AFRICA

Modern Africa
A Social and
Political History
Third Edition

Basil Davidson

Longman
London and New York

Longman Group Limited
Longman House, Burnt Mill,
Harlow, Essex CM20 2JE, England
and Associated Companies throughout the world.

*Published in the United States of America
by Longman Publishing, New York*

© Longman Group UK Limited 1993, 1989
This edition © Basil Davidson 1994

First published 1983
Second edition 1989
Third edition 1994
Fourth impression 1995

ISBN 0 582 21288 X PPR

British Library Cataloguing-in-Publication Data

A catalogue record for this book is available from the British Library.

Library of Congress Cataloging in Publication Data

Davidson, Basil, 1914–
    Modern Africa: a social and political history/Basil Davidson. – 3rd ed.
        p.   cm.
    Includes bibliographical references and index.
    ISBN 0-582-21288-X
    1. Africa — History — 1884–1985.   2. Africa — History — 1985
I. Title.
DT29.D384   1994
960′.3—dc20   93–3815
                                                                            CIP

Set by 15 in 10/12 Monophoto Bembo

Produced by Longman Singapore Publishers (Pte) Ltd.
Printed in Singapore

Contents

List of maps

Preface

I have written this book chiefly for students and others who are preparing for a variety of intermediate and senior level examinations, and who need a general but reliable understanding of the modern history of Africa.

Designed for use with more detailed national or local histories, it presents these histories within the framework of an all-African overview of events, movements, ideas, dates and personalities between about 1914 and 1990.

But while the book concentrates on the wide range of subjects and themes required for full examination coverage, I hope that teachers, college students and other readers will find here a useful and stimulating narrative and synthesis.

Carrying this history to the threshold of the 21st Century, I have again enlarged *Modern Africa* in this Third Edition, and brought it up to date from previous editions.

Basil Davidson

Under Foreign Flags: 1914–1930

PART ONE studies changes and developments in the years 1914–1930. Among questions examined in its chapters are:

Chapter One   The Early Years of the Twentieth Century
● What was the colonial partition?
● How did the First World War (1914–1918) affect Africans?

Chapter Two   Colonial Africa: to 1930
● How did the colonial systems work?
● Who paid for them, and how?
● What did the colonial systems do to African land, labour, and trade?

Chapter Three   African Responses: to 1930
● What was colonial 'pacification'?
● Who were the early leaders of anti-colonial protest?
● What were the Ethiopianist and other religious movements?
● What was the migrant labour system, and how did it work?
● Who were the 'educated few', and why were they important?

Chapter Four   Key Ideas for Progress
● Who began the Pan-African movement, and why?
● How did the ideas of modern nationalism begin and spread in Africa?
● What was the National Congress of British West Africa, and what is the African National Congress of South Africa?
● What was the policy of 'assimilation'?
● How did nationalism take shape in North Africa? Who were the early leaders of Islamic nationalism?
● What were the *Salafiyyah*, the *Wafd*, the *Destour*, the *Etoile Nord-Africaine*?

CHAPTER ONE

The Early Years of the Twentieth Century

THE HERITAGE OF HISTORY

Africa is probably the oldest continent. Most of it consists of ancient rocks which have changed little in structure since they first took shape some 200 million years ago. Still larger than the Africa of today, that most ancient continent has been named Gondwanaland. Huge fragments then broke away from Gondwanaland and became India, Australia, and South America. This is the explanation of the theory known as 'continental drift'.

Whether or not this theory is right, Africa can certainly claim to be the birthplace of mankind. Science in the past half-century has shown that the earliest ancestors of ourselves evolved in Africa, and, from Africa, spread around the world in developing the various branches of mankind that we know today.

Africa's own civilisations are seen to have developed from the onset of the Neolithic or New Stone Age some 10,000 years ago. Their most important region of early development was the vast plainland of the Sahara before it began drying to a desert. From the plainland of the green Sahara, as it then was, the black peoples multiplied and spread, eventually creating the great civilisations of Pharaonic Egypt and the Nile Valley.

Elsewhere, across the vast tropical and southern regions of the continent the black peoples of ancient times progressed from one phase of development to another. They introduced cattle. They invented methods of growing food-crops under tropical conditions. After about 500 BC they began smelting and forging iron for tools. They tamed their difficult continent. At the same time they evolved their own religious and social beliefs, methods of self-government, and ways of keeping the peace.

3

All this has had to be done against the problems of an often very hostile ecology and climate. Not only is Africa big – so big that the whole of the USA could be contained within it several times over – but Africa is also a continent of great natural variation. Most of it stretches between the latitudes of 35° North and 35° South of the Equator. Within this huge area there are countless differences of rainfall, soil fertility, plant and animal life; and each of these differences has challenged the survival of mankind. That survival has required a constant self-adjustment. Nothing has been easy; nothing has been guaranteed.

But a new challenge to the black peoples, a different kind of challenge offering new opportunities but bringing new dangers, began some 500 years ago. That was when the 'outside world' – largely, the European 'world' – first reached the African scene in a direct and frequent way. This new contact with Europe brought gains to Africa as well as to Europe, especially in the exchange of goods and ideas. But it also brought the long and painful tragedy of the trans-Atlantic trade in Africans captured into slavery and sent to the Americas. This was helpful for the development of the Americas, but very bad for the development of Africa. And this slave trade lasted more than 300 years.

Another challenge followed. By the middle of the nineteenth century the leading countries of Europe lost interest in exporting African labour to the Americas. Now they wanted to be able to use African labour in Africa itself. For that purpose they needed to take control of the black people's continent. So Europe invaded Africa, took possession of Africa, and divided Africa into colonies of Europe.

The period of invasion, lasting some twenty years, was more or less completed by 1900. There followed a longer period, between sixty and ninety years, of direct European rule, called colonial rule. This was a time of profound upheaval for all of Africa's peoples. It brought irreversible changes. Nothing would ever be the same.

The colonial period began to come to an end in 1951. But the process of 'decolonisation', of Africa's struggle to win freedom from foreign rule, has had to be long and difficult. Many colonies were able to become independent states during the 1960s. Yet only in 1990 did Namibia cease to be a colony of racist South Africa, while the black majority of South Africans continued to suffer the persecutions of *apartheid*.

All this is the history of Modern Africa. It is a history of great human dramas: of conflict and courage, sorrows and setbacks, stubborn progress. These dramas of the black peoples have lain at the very heart of the world we know.

We investigate this history step by step, and begin with the colonial partition.

PARTITION OF AFRICA

Partition means 'dividing up' or 'sharing out'; and colonial means 'foreign rule' or 'foreign settlement' or both. The colonial partition was the sharing out of Africa among strong empire-building powers such as Britain, France and Germany; and several weaker ones such as Portugal, Italy, Belgium and Spain.

For a long time during the nineteenth century, these powers quarrelled over the shares of Africa that each wanted to get. But in 1884–85, at a conference in Berlin (then capital of a German empire) they agreed to invade and take Africa without fighting each other. They marked out 'spheres of interest'. Then each invaded the continent within its own 'sphere'.

Many African peoples tried to defeat these invasions. But the Europeans were too strong in technology and organisation, especially in the use of rifles and machine-guns; and the partition was almost complete by about 1900. Most of the colonial frontiers – the frontiers, today, of independent African states – were fixed on the map by the end of 1901. Only Ethiopia, and in a lesser way Liberia, continued to rule themselves.

That is how the colonial systems or empires came into existence: seven of them until 1918, when Germany's system was ended, and then six. These systems differed greatly in detail, as we shall see. Sometimes, wherever kings or chiefs were willing and able to work with colonial government, the systems operated by what was called 'indirect rule'. Otherwise, the colonial governments ruled 'directly' through their own white officials and African servants.

But all systems, in essential ways, operated with the same assumptions and for the same purpose. Each of them was racist and exploitative. They used colonial power to treat Africans as inferior to Europeans, justifying this by a whole range of myths about a supposed 'white superiority'. The purpose of using colonial power in this way was to make Africans serve the interests of European colony-owners.

These systems brought some gains as well as many losses, for their history was a contradictory process. We study it in three main periods. First, from the First World War of 1914–18 to the great economic depression which began in 1929–30. Secondly, through the 1930s to the end of the Second World War of 1939–45. Thirdly, through the struggles of modern nationalism to the end of the colonial empires. After that, in the fourth part of this book, we consider the years of Africa's regained independence.

Before 1914

The colonial powers partitioned Africa by agreement with each other. But they still had to invade and occupy the colonies thus marked by the lines on the map. They did this by crushing African resistance wherever it appeared. At first, European troops were used, as well as troops from other colonies such as India and the West Indies. After 1900, African troops under European officers did most of this work.

Military occupation was far advanced by 1914. Even so, colonial rule by military force was often weak or incomplete; large areas remained outside its control. Yet the colonial systems were now in place; and the time was ripe to make them produce wealth for their owners. At this point, however, there came a mighty interruption.

THE FIRST WORLD WAR, 1914–1918

The colonial powers managed to keep the peace between each other in Africa. But they could not keep it in Europe. In 1914 a vast and terrible conflict broke out between Britain, France and Russia on one side, and Germany with Austria-Hungary on the other. This spread through Europe and killed millions.

Each power drew upon its colonies for men and money. For the first time on any scale, Africa was pulled into the quarrels of the outside world. The consequences were many and deep. They were military, social and economic, and political.

On the military side, African men were taken into the European colonial armies either as soldiers or as porters and servants. Sometimes this was done by enlarging colonial regiments already in existence, such as the British West African Frontier Force, the French *Tirailleurs*, the German *Schütztruppen*, the Belgian *Force Publique*. Men joined for the wages that were paid, or in obedience to orders imposed on them by their chiefs.

Yet these small colonial forces were not enough. Huge French losses on the 'Western Front' in France (so called to distinguish it from the 'Eastern Front' in Russia) soon led the French government to demand more African troops, and conscription (forcing men to join an army) then began. Much the same was done by the British on a smaller scale, especially in East Africa, to obtain porters and other service personnel needed in Britain's war against the Germans in Tanganyika (the mainland country of modern Tanzania).

Armies of men vanished into the jaws of this monstrous war. From first to last, the French raised about 211,000 troops from their West and Equatorial colonies, some 270,000 from their North African colonies, and about 40,000 from Madagascar. Exactly how many of these died has never been found out. But it is generally accepted that about 200,000 Africans lost their lives in French war service.

For the British forces, Nigeria provided some 17,000 fighting men and 58,000 service personnel; many were sent to East Africa, where about 1,000 were killed. The Gold Coast (Ghana) raised some 10,000 men with losses on the same scale; Sierra Leone and The Gambia also played their part. The greatest African losses were in the British campaign against the Germans in Tanganyika. Upwards of one million East Africans were forced to become porters for the British. Of these, perhaps as many as 100,000 were killed by military action, hunger or disease. The Germans, Portuguese and Belgian colonial authorities also relied on 'call-up' of African troops and porters, at times in large numbers and often by force. As with much else in the colonial period, overall figures of African losses through one or other form of war service have remained a matter for dispute; but it seems unlikely that total African losses were less than 300,000 men. The true figure may have been higher still.

BROADER CONSEQUENCES OF THE WAR

Colonial governments were obliged to give money, as a contribution to war expenses, to their respective home governments in Europe. This scarcely applied to the German colonies, which were quickly taken over by Britain, France and Belgium (and by South Africa in the case of Namibia), or, like Tanganyika, were cut off from Germany. But most of the British and French territories had to provide money from taxation. Even as small a territory as The Gambia provided £10,000 out of its total budget for 1914 of £122,225.

The war was a profoundly disturbing influence as well as an expensive one. Many rural communities were shaken or undermined. Countless families were deprived of active men taken for war service. Others tried to evade recruitment by hiding themselves or moving to another territory. There was frequent armed resistance to war service in several of the territories of French West Africa; and clashes with the colonial authorities were many. Natural disasters such as the spread of epidemics combined with food shortages to spread hunger and death. All this was a prelude to the great rural poverty of later years.

There were long-term consequences of a different kind. Especially in British West Africa, such African traders who had managed to remain active in the export market were squeezed out of business. British firms took advantage of war conditions to strengthen their hold on export-import trade. They took over, for example, the share of that trade formerly held by German firms. The war years were in fact the period in which a handful of major British trading companies secured control of all big-scale business; and much the same was true of French companies in the French territories. In this important respect, the war years completed the dispossession of Africans that the colonial conquests had begun.

As a political result, the colonial 'share out' was revised. Germany, in losing the war, lost its colonies: one in East Africa (Tanganyika, with Ruanda/Urundi); one in South-West Africa (Namibia); two in West Africa (Kamerun – or Cameroun as it was afterwards called – and Togo). Each of these was attacked by the powers allied against Germany, and chiefly by the British. German resistance lasted longer in Kamerun, and was ended only in February 1916. But in Tanganyika a skilful German commander, General Paul von Lettow Vorbeck, fought a guerrilla war against the British and their allies until the war in Europe ended. By so doing, he forced the British into a major military effort, during which, as we saw, tens of thousands of Africans lost their lives.

These four German colonies were divided among the victorious powers as 'mandated territories' of a newly born League of Nations. The British took Tanganyika and the northern part of Kamerun, adding the latter to their Nigerian colony. The French took the rest of Kamerun. Togo was divided between France and Britain. The white South Africans got hold of South-West Africa (Namibia), while the Belgians added Ruanda/Urundi to their possessions. In theory, these 'mandated territories' were not colonies or protectorates; they were 'territories in trust'. These words were supposed to mean that the European rulers of these territories were 'guardians' but not owners. In practice, for most of the people concerned, there was to be little or no real difference.

The overall effect of this first world war was to strengthen the colonial systems of the victorious powers. These powers now felt that they owned Africa. They believed that this ownership would last for ever, or at least for as long as anyone could think ahead. Here and there, as in Nigeria, the colonial power embarked on less repressive methods of rule; elsewhere, it was often the reverse.

Generally, the colonial rulers now set themselves two tasks. The first was to transform military occupation into civilian methods of rule. The second was to find new and more rewarding ways of drawing profit from the colonies. This second aim was made all the stronger by the economic crisis into which Britain, France and other colonial powers were plunged by the cost of the war.

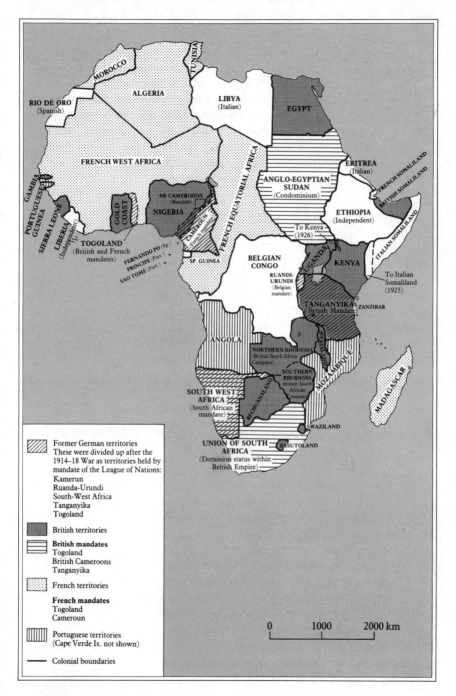

Map 1 Colonial boundaries in Africa in 1919

Meanwhile the United States of America, although at that time a growing world power, had yet to develop a direct concern with events in Africa. This concern would not appear until the aftermath of the Second World War. But the USA was already a haven for young Africans who wished to secure access to a better education than they could find at home; some of them afterwards made important political careers. Among these were Kwame Nkrumah and Kamuzu Banda. Some African-Americans, notably Marcus Garvey and W.E.B. Du Bois, were already famous names in several African countries.

CHAPTER TWO
Colonial Africa: to 1930

Many hundreds of states and communities of earlier times lost their independence to the various European colonial powers. Most lost it completely. A few, as in Northern Nigeria, managed to keep some local power to govern themselves. But their power was small, and always under colonial control even when this was called 'indirect'.

Another great change had come to them. All were gathered into some fifty colonies marked out by frontiers that were new. Few of these frontiers took any account of the interests or convenience of the African populations thus enclosed. Many of the colonial frontiers cut through the territory of former states or united communities, leaving one part in one colonial system and another part in another colonial system.

The Somali people, for example, were divided into four colonial systems: those of Britain (Somaliland), Italy (Somalia), France (Djibouti) and Ethiopia (Ogaden). Some Makonde of East Africa were in (German, then British) Tanganyika; others were in (Portuguese) Mozambique. A majority of the numerous Mandinka of West Africa were included in the French system, but others were in neighbouring (British) Sierra Leone and The Gambia. Many Hausa were in (British) Nigeria, while others were in (French) Niger.

So the immediate results for Africans under colonial rule were loss of power on one hand, and new kinds of disunity on the other.

FROM MILITARY TO CIVILIAN RULE

After the First World War of 1914–18, the victorious colonial powers continued to crush resistance and put down protest. This was misleadingly

11

called 'pacification', or 'making peace'. Very destructive of African law and order, this violent process was largely completed during the 1920s.

As their systems of repression succeeded, the colonial powers moved from military to civilian forms of rule. They kept their colonial armies, now manned by African soldiers, under European command. But they handed the tasks of government to non-military officials, while, at the same time, building police forces (again composed of Africans with European officers) so as to make sure the officials were obeyed. In short, they organised colonial civil services.

These civilian governments were various kinds of dictatorship, sometimes mild and at other times harsh. All power was placed in the hands of top governors who received orders from their national governments in Europe, but who, on the spot, could usually decide as they wished. Under the top governors were sub-governors; and under these were regional and provincial officers (sometimes called 'residents' in the British system); and under these again were local or district officers. These political officials were flanked by other services: for public works, health, education, and so on.

The officials were never many. By the 1930s, for example, the vast colonial area of French West Africa was divided into 118 *cercles* (districts), each governed by a French *commandant* (district officer). About 40 million Nigerians, in 1938, were governed by some 380 British political officials with another 1,163 in service departments (such as public works, education, health).

All these officials were Europeans. With very rare exceptions, the racist nature of colonial rule made sure that no Africans could reach positions of responsibility in the colonial services. Only as late as 1942 was there a first departure from this rule, when two African assistant district officers were appointed in the Gold Coast (Ghana).

A big consequence flowed from this situation. Being few and all European, the officials had to work, in practice, through a multitude of African interpreters, policemen, servants, or local chiefs appointed by colonial government. This meant that most people were governed in the details of everyday life by puppets or clerks who might abuse their positions, take bribes, act as bullies or otherwise serve their personal interests. That did not happen everywhere, but it happened often. In this important way, the colonial systems were not only systems of repression; they were also systems of corruption.

One reason why the officials were never many was that they and their services had to be paid for. Each colony was run by the rule that the cost of colonial government must not be allowed to cut seriously into colonial profits, or prove a burden to European taxpayers in Europe. Very few Africans had asked for colonial rule, but all Africans had to pay for it.

They had to pay for it by taxes in money; and this was widely resented. 'Taxation troubles' were many; often they were violent. There were various methods of raising taxation-money. One way was to make each family-head, or worker, pay an annual amount. Another was to make each hut-owner pay a tax. A third was to tax imports and exports. Colonial officials found it difficult to get this necessary money, but they persisted. For example: in the second half of the 1920s (1924–29) Kenya's Africans paid a total of £553,000 in personal taxes, a large percentage of all the money that they earned. By 1930 about two-fifths of all the money for government in Nigeria was being paid by direct and personal taxation of Africans, mostly farmers; the rest came from import-export taxes (customs and excise).

Some of this taxation money was used to pay the salaries and other costs of European officials and their families. Some of it was used for the benefit of the colonised populations. The richer colonial powers, such as Britain and France, built clinics, brought in doctors, and began to combat malaria and epidemic diseases. All the colonial powers built primary schools and trained teachers, although some left this primarily to Christian missionaries, mostly European. These were among the gains of colonial rule. These gains could never be large because, mostly, they had to be paid for by personal taxes on Africans. And that money was never enough to spread their gains very far (see also pp. 16–17 in this chapter and Chapter 5, p. 53); European companies in Africa paid few taxes, or even none at all.

Many officials were honest and hard-working, and with goodwill towards the peoples they governed. But all had to work within the rules of the colonial systems. The most important of these rules applied to land, labour, and trade.

ECONOMIC CONSEQUENCES

Land and labour

Though they all operated in the same ways basically, there were two kinds of colony: those with many European settlers, and those with few or none. We shall call them 'settler colonies' and 'non-settler colonies'. For Africans, it was generally much better to be in the second kind of colony than the first. This was because the interests of European settlers were placed, by the colonial powers, before the interests of Africans.

With a few exceptions, notably in Ivory Coast, West Africa remained free of European settlers apart from businessmen and others who were long-term residents rather than settlers. The reasons for this lay partly in the climate, believed to be bad for Europeans, but even more because local Africans, as in Nigeria and Ghana, successfully resisted the sale of land to settlers. Elsewhere on the continent few colonies had no settlers. By the 1920s these Europeans formed important minorities, still small in numbers but large in influence, in British East Africa, Central and Southern Africa; in South Africa, white settlers already had full control of government. Settlers became numerous in the Portuguese colonies of Mozambique and Angola; in the Belgian Congo (Zaire); in some parts of Italian Africa (notably Eritrea); and in French North Africa and Madagascar.

We may note here that other kinds of settler communities also appeared on the scene. Small numbers of Lebanese came to West Africa, and Greeks and others to other colonies. Much larger numbers of people from the Indian sub-continent also came to East Africa. Of these, about 32,000 were Indians brought to Kenya and Uganda as 'indentured labourers', or contract workers, so as to help in building the railway from Mombasa, on the coast, to the shores of Lake Nyanza (then called Lake Victoria by the Europeans). About 6,000 of these 'indentured labourers' stayed in East Africa after work on the railway was finished.

Most of these Asian newcomers, apart from the railway workers, were welcomed by the colonial authorities as useful middle-men in local trade and enterprise.

Meanwhile, a much larger immigration of Indians had begun in the British South African territory of Natal where the growing and harvesting of sugar required cheap labour in large quantity. In 1872 the number of Indian 'indentured labourers' in Natal was about 5,000; by 1886 the total had risen to 30,000 and to 60,000 by 1899. Thereafter the number of Indians continued to rise, although the practice of 'indentured labour' was gradually discontinued. In 1974 the total number of Indians in South Africa, mostly in Natal, was about 700,000 (or 2.8 per cent of the country's whole population). All were subject to the pains and penalties of South Africa's system of racist discrimination (made worse still, as *apartheid*, after 1946); and most had to work for white employers for very low wages and in bad living conditions. In short, they suffered in the land of their birth just as the Africans suffered.

Wherever settlers came from Europe, increasing quantities of the best land were taken from African farmers and sold to the settlers at give-away prices. The worst cases occurred in South Africa and Algeria. Already by 1914, a large part of the fertile land of northern Algeria had been taken by European settlers; and the total of such land continued to

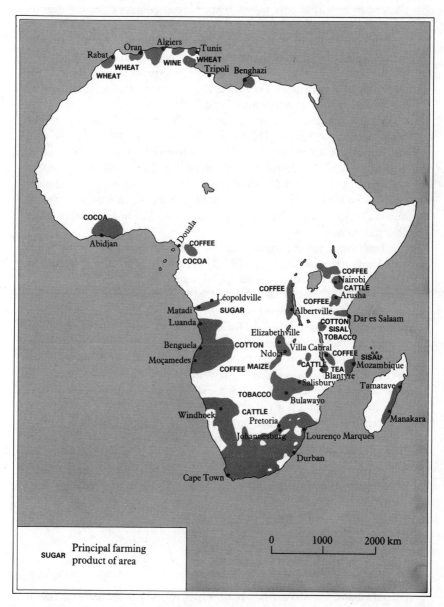

Map 2 Areas of principal European farming settlement in Colonial Africa

grow in size until the 1950s. In South Africa a government law of 1913 went even further. This law turned over about nine-tenths of all land to European ownership, so that South Africa's big African majority was allowed to own land only in one-tenth of their country. (See the map on p. 172.)

This taking of land occurred in all the settler colonies. As early as 1920, for example, a big part of the fertile, high plateau country of Angola was in European ownership. Over two million hectares of the still more fertile highlands of Kenya were likewise sold or given to European settlers by the British colonial government.

Yet the settlers could do nothing with their land, in any of the colonies, without labour. They would not do field-work themselves; so the labour had to be provided by the colonised peoples, who seldom wanted to work for Europeans. Working for themselves, as farmers or craftsmen, Africans could generally provide comfortably for their family needs and often more besides. Not yet having the use of modern forms of money, they saw no advantage in going to work for money-wages. They preferred to stay at home.

The colonial rulers therefore had to make Africans leave home. They found several ways of doing this. They began, in all the colonies, by simple methods of force. Often using their appointed 'chiefs' or 'headmen', or by sending out their colonial police, officials caused men to be rounded up and brought to work wherever they were needed. Most of the early railways were built by directly forced labour; so were most of the roads. Sometimes the cost was heavy in lives. That was the case, for example, with the French railway built from the equatorial coast at Pointe Noire to the big inland lake, then called Stanley Pool, where the town of Brazzaville took shape. Some 127,250 'fit adult males' from a host of local villages were forced to build this railway between 1921 and 1932; even by 1928, no fewer than 10,000 had died on the job from hunger or disease.

Other large systems of forced labour were used in the Portuguese colonies and in Italian Somalia; but smaller systems existed everywhere. They lasted for many years. In the French empire, for example, forced labour ended only in 1946, but continued in the Portuguese colonies until the 1960s.

THE PURPOSES OF NEW TAXATION

Forced labour, like slavery before it, was of course very wasteful of life. It was also strongly resisted. More peaceful methods were found, especially after the First World War. Mostly, these were by way of taxation. African men were made to pay taxes in money which they could get only if they worked for wages: that is, only if they worked for Europeans. In Kenya, for example, Africans were for long forbidden to grow cash crops on their own land. This was to stop Africans from winning a share of the market for cash crops, and so earning enough money to pay taxes without having to work for Europeans.

This whole process of turning farmers into wage-workers was described by an African trade unionist in 1929. 'First the white man brought the Bible,' said the Zimbabwean J. H. Mphemba. 'Then he brought guns, then chains, then he built a jail, then he made the native pay tax.'

Taxes paid for colonial government. They also forced Africans into the labour pool. Either village men went to work for wages, or else the police came for them. Largely by this method, the Southern Rhodesian (Zimbabwean) mining industry was manned, through the 1920s, by upwards of 40,000 African workers each year.

These men suffered much. Their wages were very low, their conditions of work very bad. Between 1900 and 1933 more than 30,000 African workers lost their lives in Southern Rhodesian mines: some 3,000 by accidents, and 27,000 by diseases caught at work.

Similar methods of getting labour for colonial needs spread all over the continent. They removed great numbers of men from rural life. They often ruined rural stability and peace. There were officials who protested; but they spoke in vain against the huge labour demand from foreign mining companies and settler plantations. All this was one of the major factors of African impoverishment contributing to the famines of the 1970s and after.

EXPORT CROPS AND FOOD

A different situation came about in all those non-settler colonies, chiefly in British West Africa and parts of French West Africa, where African farmers could produce crops for the export market. Here, men could mostly stay at home in their villages, or work for neighbours. These farmers were rapidly successful in growing crops for export, notably cocoa, groundnuts, palm kernels, cotton, and afterwards coffee. Unhampered by settler interference, they showed skill and enterprise. They moved with the times. They took every chance to grow and sell more.

That was a gain brought by the colonial systems: it joined these farmers to expanding markets in the rest of the world. But it was a gain with several big handicaps. One of these handicaps had to do with the prices for which these farmers could sell their export crops. The prices were fixed by foreign companies which controlled the export trade. Such companies made their profit from the difference between the low prices they paid to local African suppliers and the much higher prices for which they sold these crops in Europe or America. Supported by colonial governments, the companies made this price-difference as big as they could.

Several consequences followed. First, the profits made by foreign companies from this price-difference did not stay in the colonies. They were sent back to Europe. So the skill and enterprise of successful farmers was turned into a way of transferring wealth from colonies to countries overseas. The more that Africans produced, the bigger was this transfer. That was one of the chief reasons why gains brought by colonial systems were repeatedly cancelled out, or turned into losses, by the way those same systems worked in practice. We shall look at these trends more closely in later chapters.

Secondly, even the most successful farmers often got into debt because their costs of production were not covered by the prices they were paid. Their debt was made worse by the general lack of any proper facilities for borrowing money from banks. Even the Gold Coast's cocoa farmers, though producing most of the world's cocoa in those times, were often in debt, largely because they had no access to cheap credit.

Another consequence was long-term. The more that farmers turned to export crops, the less food could they grow for local use. Because of this, local food shortages began to be felt as early as the 1930s. For the same reason, such food shortages would afterwards become much worse. Continuing on the same lines, even though independent, many African states today have to import expensive foreign food because their farmers do not grow enough food at home. Here was another way in which the colonial systems set a pattern of export that was bad for the majority of producers in Africa.

THE CONTRADICTIONS OF 'PROGRESS'

Certainly, when our century began, the methods and organisation of African production and business greatly needed modernising. Those ways had served well in the days before modern machinery and methods of finance. Nobody anywhere produced better cloth, for instance, than the weavers of West Africa; but they produced it on hand-looms. African miners produced all the gold used for the basis of European currencies and credit after the middle of the fifteenth century; but they produced it by hand-methods in shallow mines or by panning the rivers. African traders used many things for money, such as brass manillas, salt bars, and above all, cowrie shells; but they seldom used coins or banknotes.

The greater strength of the colonial powers came from the fact that their own countries had already carried out this work of modernisation. All of them had passed through an industrial revolution – in other words, their hand-production had given way to machine-production. So what did their coming to Africa do for the modernising of Africa?

The answer again is contradictory. It did something, but not much; and each gain tended, in practice, to be cancelled out by a larger loss. The colonial period brought in, for example, the use of coins and notes. These went quickly into common use. Even as early as the ten years of 1901–1911, British West Africa (but chiefly Nigeria) imported silver coins (made in England) to the value of nearly £3.5 millions; and in 1911 the use of rods and manillas, as forms of money, could be officially ended.

That was a gain: it helped trade to expand. But in settler colonies this use of coins led to the labour system we have seen earlier, leading in turn to rural poverty. In non-settler colonies, where farmers could prosper by growing crops for export, the advantage of using coins for money was reduced by the colonial take-over of all big business, again with the results we have seen above. Banks were founded, but Africans were given no share in owning or running them. Shipping lines expanded, but they were always foreign. Great wholesale businesses were launched, but not by Africans.

It was the same with machine technology. Railways were built, but by European engineers; in most of the settler colonies, even the engine drivers were always European. Deep mines were dug for the first time, but always by foreign companies using African labour and foreign technicians. Huge profits were made from these mines, but the lion's share of the profits went always back to Europe or America; in this way too, colonial development meant the transfer of wealth from Africa to countries overseas.

We may briefly sum up. Generally, the colonial systems aimed success-fully at taking wealth out of Africa: by means of cheap mining labour; by paying prices to export crop farmers that were lower than prices on the world market; and by controlling all big business. They brought in modern technology, but they transferred to Africans no technical skills of any importance. They did not modernise Africa's means of production and trade. They introduced no industrial revolution; nor did they have any wish or interest to introduce one.

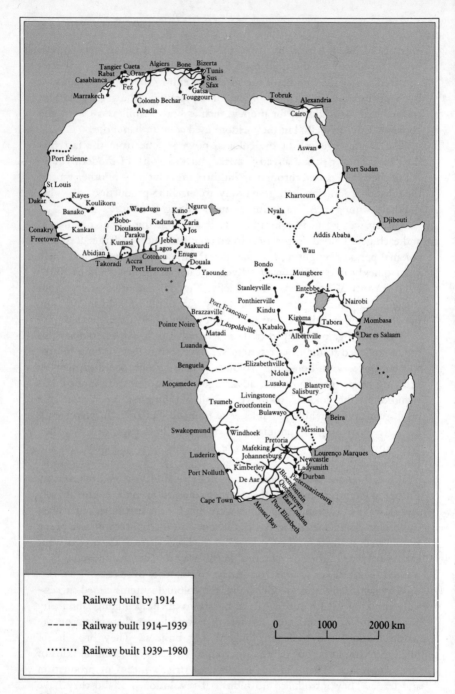

Map 3 Railways in Africa, with dates of construction

On the contrary, they set up patterns of working and earning, based on the aim of wealth-transfer abroad, that were bound to leave great problems for independent Africa to solve.

CHAPTER THREE

African Responses: to 1930

How did the people of those days respond to colonial rule and its demands? Of course the answers of Africans varied from colony to colony, and from one colonial system to another. Their first need was to study and understand their new rulers. Their next need was to make the best of things.

Most chiefs – whether they were real ones appointed by their peoples, or false ones appointed by the colonial authorities – found that they could defend their positions by serving the new rulers. Some chiefs, as in parts of Nigeria or Uganda or Kenya, even found that they could improve their positions. Many traders, though kept out of business, found that they could still make a living in small business, even sometimes a better living. Many farmers went into export crops with good results for themselves. Generally, people welcomed the chance of modernisation wherever this appeared. There was now an opportunity, though still a small one, of sending children to primary school, and even, in rare cases, to secondary school.

One big response, in short, was adjusting to the system: what historians have called 'accommodation'. Having resisted the colonial invaders in vain, Africans naturally looked for ways of getting a place inside the new systems, or even of turning these systems to African advantage. Some of these ways of accommodation, as we shall see, were to lead on to the later rise of modern nationalism and its way of escape from foreign rule. Broadly, ways of adjusting were sought by all who had the chance to do that.

But the great majority of people, above all in the settler colonies, had no such chance. They were too poor or powerless to join the social groups, or the 'better-off classes', for whom accommodation could offer something useful. The new ways of working and earning kept them fixed in their poverty and ignorance; the gains of colonial rule passed them by. For them, the choice was a hard one: to give in, or to revolt.

'PACIFICATION' IN PRACTICE

Many responded by revolt. They continued their resistance of former years, but now with new reasons for their action. They protested against forced labour, against their loss of land to settlers, against colonial taxation and much else. Such protests were sometimes peaceful; at other times they resorted to violence in reply to the violence of the colonial systems.

To all these protests, whether violent or not, the colonial powers replied with some form of 'pacification'. No year in this period passed without campaigns of 'pacification' in one region or other, and often in several. These campaigns were designed to repress, or to frighten.

If there was a violent protest to repress, many troops or armed police were used. If there was only a threat or fear of violent protest, a show of force was put on. Troops were marched about. An official circular of the Belgian Congo government laid it down, in 1924, that 'military promenades are one of the best ways of preventing any idea of revolt, of making the natives carry out their legal duties, and of keeping up habits of work among them'. The wording of that circular is interesting. It shows that the colonial powers, in this case the Belgian Congo government, were always thinking that Africans might revolt. It uses the word 'natives', meaning Africans, as a term of colonialist contempt. And it speaks of the need to keep up 'habits of work', as though Africans never worked when left to themselves.

What the 'legal duties of natives' and their 'habits of work' could really mean, in those colonial years, may be seen from another example, that of Italian Somalia. In 1930 an Italian official wrote home to his government, in Italy, that these 'duties' had become too heavy. This worried official reported that methods of forced labour in Somalia were 'a good deal worse than slavery'. If a man were a slave, he said, his master would care well for him; otherwise, if the man died from overwork, his master would have to buy another slave. But forced workers cost nothing. 'So when a Somali native dies after being given to an employer, or becomes unfit for work,' wrote this official, 'the employer simply asks the government to give him another.'

Those years saw countless protests and revolts against such treatment. Often they were small, 'lost in the backlands', barely noticed even in the colonial records. But sometimes they were big protests and long wars. These were revolts, led by outstanding men, against more than bad treatment. Beyond that, they were revolts aimed also at winning back independence.

EARLY ATTEMPTS AT ANTI-COLONIAL LIBERATION: TWO EXAMPLES

In 1899, seeing his country invaded by foreign powers, a young but learned Muslim of Somalia sent out a call for war against them. Raising 5,000 men, at first with only 200 rifles, the Sayyid Muhamad Abdille Hasan began by attacking British colonial forces. He also tackled the Italian invaders (in Somalia) and the Ethiopian invaders (in Ogaden). He began to build a united new Somali nation, even though several Somali clans refused to follow him.

Only in 1920 were the Sayyid and his 'Dervish Army' (so called after the somewhat earlier revolt of the *Mahdia* in the eastern Sudan) finally defeated. With the First World War at an end, the British sent fresh troops against him, and aircraft to bomb his fortress-capital at Tale. But the Sayyid had launched the new and powerful idea of Somali unity. He was for long afterwards remembered as the founder of an independent Somalia.

In that same year of the Sayyid's defeat in Somalia, another Muslim leader took the same road in northern Morocco. Abd al-Krim al-Khattabi (the Writer or the Learned) launched a revolt against Spanish colonial rule. He won a great battle at Anual, defeating some 60,000 Spanish troops with only 3,000 of his own, and set about founding a free republic in the north Moroccan mountains of the Rif.

Abd al-Krim's plan was to unite the Berber-speaking clans of that Moroccan region, put an end to the social inequalities of their way of life, introduce modern education and other services, and prepare for Moroccan independence in the modern world. He went some way to realise his plan before he and his republic were overwhelmed, in 1926, by a combined Spanish and French army of some 800,000 men. So he too was not forgotten. A judgment on him by the French army's intelligence service, in 1925, spoke for what the world has remembered of this extraordinary man:

> Abd al-Krim is not a warrior trying to be a king. He is not a *Mahdi* come to renew Islam. He is a nationalist seeking to liberate the territory. He is a patriot aiming to throw off a foreign yoke.

With men such as the Sayyid Muhamad and Abd al-Krim, we can see that protest and revolt went beyond a response to bad colonial treatment; these men went beyond an effort to win back the old independence of the past. They looked forward to a new kind of independence, moving with the times. So the political effects of the colonial systems were already, even in those early years, beginning to have their counter-effects. The banners of anti-colonial liberation, of what would afterwards become national liberation, were beginning to wave in the winds of political development.

The notion that people should free themselves by going forward to new ideas rather than going back to old ideas made progress as the 1920s passed by. Other important personalities show this. So it was that Harry Thuku, a clerk in the colonial administration of Kenya, led new forms of protest and political organisation in those same years. He and others formed a group in 1921, which they called the Young Kikuyu Association; and it is in this Association that historians have found some of the origins of Kenya nationalism: of the aim and programme that Kenya's various peoples should become united as a *nation*.

Other thoughtful men followed the road of peaceful political organisation in those years, and in many colonies. Their plan was to build national unity by political work, and to use this unity in order to free their peoples from foreign rule. We shall come back to this important subject.

INDEPENDENT CHURCHES AND RELIGIOUS PROTEST MOVEMENTS

To combat the colonial invasions, people had asked for the help and guidance of ancestral spirits, and of priests who spoke for those spirits. Some of these priests had become the leaders of anti-colonial rebellions, as in the great rising of the Shona and Ndebele against British invasion of their country, Southern Rhodesia (Zimbabwe), in the 1890s.

But now, after some twenty years of colonial rule, people looked more often for new kinds of spiritual guidance. Many in Africa south of the Sahara turned to the Christian teachings of European missionaries. Then they often found that these missionaries were also part of the colonial systems to which the missionaries preached submission and obedience. This led Christian Africans to form new churches of their own, or else – as in South Africa – to join independent church communities already in existence.

This movement for independent churches was another form of anti-colonial protest. It had begun long before in South Africa, colonised by settlers in an earlier time. Its leaders were inspired by the Bible message that 'Ethiopia will stretch out its hands to God': meaning by Ethiopia not just the country of that name but all the lands of black people. Many Ethiopianist churches were founded in the far south of the continent. They drew multitudes of believers, for they preached the truth that God was not part of the colonial systems, but was for the salvation of everyone. From South Africa the same movement spread elsewhere: to Central, East and West Africa.

After 1920, the various trends of the independent church movement became still more important, and suffered more persecution. They gave people fresh hope and confidence outside the ideas of obedience to colonial rule; and the colonial authorities therefore feared them. Notable among the new churches founded in these years was the Church of Jesus Christ on This Earth, launched in 1921 by Simon Kimbangu in the Belgian Congo (Zaire). In joining this church, people of the Belgian Congo expressed spiritual resistance to colonial rule, and were sorely persecuted by the Belgian authorities.

Another independent movement, a little older, was the Church of the Children of Israel founded in South Africa by Enoch Mgijima. Like the followers of Kimbangu, those of Mgijima had to face colonial persecution. In 1921 their congregation refused to move from land which the racist government of South Africa had marked out for Europeans only. South African troops killed 163 and wounded 129 of these peaceful African Christians.

Religious protest took many shapes. Their aim was not to form political organisations, or to move towards the ideas of nationalism. Protesters wanted, in a religious way, to get rid of 'the evil of the times'. But since this evil was often identified with colonial rule, their aim was also anti-colonial. An important case was the movement known usually as Watchtower, originally launched in central Africa in the 1890s but active later in a number of colonies. Often its members refused to pay colonial taxes, or broke other colonial laws. So the colonial authorities set out to suppress them, and found this difficult.

Watchtower had several offshoots. One of them was the Watchman's Society founded by Kenon Kamwana of Nyasaland (Malawi) in 1937. It was directly anti-colonial. 'We are the children of God,' Kamwana told his followers, 'and must therefore pay no attention to the laws of the *boma* [colonial government] . . . People must not be afraid to break government laws.'

All these independent Christian responses were an aspect of African protest against the colonial systems, and above all against the colonial belief that God wanted white people to rule over black people.

Such responses were not only Christian by inspiration. There were continued examples of spiritual resistance to colonial rule by Africans who remained true to their own religions. Also, large movements of Muslim protest occurred south of the Sahara as well as north of it. They tried to give people fresh self-confidence in the face of colonial conquest and repression. In Senegal, for instance, a movement called the *Muridiyya* took shape through the teaching of Ahmadou Bamba (1850–1927). Bamba himself did not directly challenge colonial rule, but the effect of his teaching was to cause his followers to challenge it. The French exiled Bamba to Gabon and then to Mauritania, and allowed him to return to Senegal only under house-arrest. Another movement of Muslim spiritual protest was the *Hamalliyya* in French Sudan (later Mali) led by Sheikh Hamallah (1883–1943).

NEW SOCIAL GROUPS, OR CLASSES-IN-THE-MAKING

It would be wrong to think of this period only in terms of protest or revolt. There was much of both, for the colonial systems were instruments of conquest and repression. But they were more than that, they were also instruments of social reorganisation. This was in line with colonial needs, and Africans had to adjust to it as best they could. Produced by industrialised countries, the colonial systems changed many ways of working and living. They brought into existence new social groupings, as well as the beginnings of the social classes into which industrialised peoples were divided.

This social reorganisation went much further after 1930, and again after 1940. But it was already at work before 1930. We have seen part of it in the 'forcing out' of African labour for colonial mines and plantations.

This 'forcing out' of labour created a new social grouping of men who worked for money-wages and who, increasingly, had no other means of livelihood. Consider one example. Africans had mined tin on the Jos Plateau (of central Nigeria) for more than 2,000 years. Using handicraft methods, they were independent producers who combined their mining with farm work. Then foreign companies, using machinery, took over the Jos mines after our century began. In 1910 there were 50 such companies in Nigeria employing 15,000 miners; and, by 1928, Nigerian tin-miners totalled nearly 40,000. But most of these men had ceased to be independent producers. They had become wage-workers.

The same happened wherever foreign companies dug deep mines: for gold in South Africa, for copper in Northern Rhodesia (Zambia), for coal

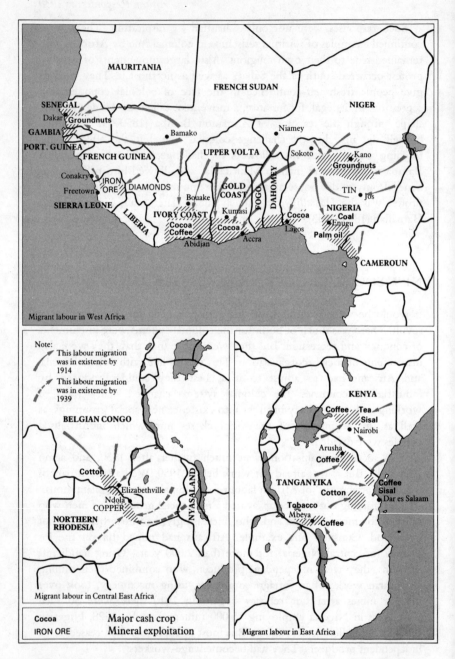

Map 4 Patterns of labour migration in Colonial Africa. Only the main migrant-labour flows are shown. (For southern Africa, see p. 163.)

and other minerals elsewhere. Huge numbers of wage-workers were employed. Nearly always they were workers brought from another place, or another colony, employed on contracts for a year or more at a time. In short, they were *migrant workers*.

As a new social group, which had never existed before on any such scale, migrant workers did not form a new, integrated class of workers, or what industrialised countries call a working-class. As migrants, they had one foot in the wage-work of the mines or plantations, but another foot in their villages at home. Here was what we have seen earlier: Africans were brought into the modern economy of machinery and wages, but they could not share in the gains of that economy except as low-paid labourers. They were not taught technology, or even to read and write. Yet they ceased to be independent farmers. We shall see later what the further consequences were. Here we should note their importance for the future.

Another new social grouping, or class-in-the-making, came into existence wherever – mostly in West Africa – African farmers went into the production of export crops. Using modern kinds of money and capital investment, farmers growing export crops (such as cocoa or groundnuts), began to buy land and pay wages to workers. Gradually, new forms of inequality appeared within African society itself. Here was another development of importance for the future.

The colonial towns were small as yet. Their big expansion came after the middle 1930s. But already, in these towns, there was a group of people who possessed some wealth in houses or trade, and another and larger group which possessed little or nothing. The inequalities of modern city life were already on the scene: small as yet, but growing.

The 'educated few'

Another emerging social group, also very small in the 1920s, was composed of persons who could benefit from modern education. This was still very difficult. In all British West Africa there was only one post-secondary college, at Fourah Bay in Sierra Leone, and one or two secondary schools; Yaba College in Nigeria was not fully opened until 1934. The opportunities in French West and Equatorial Africa were smaller still. British East and Central Africa had no single school, able to take students through 'school certificate', until Uganda's Makerere College started to do that in 1933. Opportunities were somewhat wider in Egypt and Tunisia; while in South Africa a higher college for African students, Fort Hare, was opened in 1916.

In practice, for any kind of higher education, students had to go to

Europe or America. A few managed to do this in the 1920s, just as a few had managed earlier. Understandably, they became a privileged social group. Most went into government jobs in junior civil-service grades (senior grades being for Europeans only). Some began to think hard about their countries' future. Often as lawyers or other professionals, they could look closely into the colonial systems, and find out how these systems worked. They studied these systems. They began to ask themselves what could be done to change them.

It was largely through this group, the 'educated few' or the 'intellectual élite', that the ideas of nationalism, and the struggle for political advance empowered by those ideas, now began to be known and accepted.

CHAPTER FOUR
Key Ideas for Progress

In those days, thinking about the future, educated Africans saw two big obstacles to any progress. One of these was raised, and always built higher, by the racism of the colonial systems. The Africans, this racism insisted, are inferior. They have made no history. They have created no civilisation. They cannot rule themselves: we superior Europeans must do it for them.

These assertions were not truths but myths which buttressed colonial rule. Africans had made history, and built civilisations, and ruled themselves, through countless years before any colonial ruler came upon the scene. Yet these myths, however surprising this may seem today, were widely believed in those early decades of our century. That was partly because the colonial rulers were far advanced in machinery and modern technology, and they consequently claimed that they had 'invented everything'. Partly it was because children in colonial schools were taught this same racist lesson. Africa's own development was never mentioned or discussed.

Here was one obstacle to progress: a steady and continual downgrading of African brains and skills, of Africa's real achievements. There was a second obstacle. This was raised by the division of Africa's peoples into some fifty colonies. In nearly every one of the colonies, many ancient communities or states suddenly found themselves inside the same colonial frontier, and part of the same colony. But although thus thrown together, they were still divided – by their own history, but also by the divisive methods of colonial government.

On the one hand, few of these many states and communities had ever felt the need to combine together in the past. On the other hand, the colonial systems tried hard to prevent them from combining now. Unless they did combine together now, who was going to listen to any big demand for change? Yet how were they to find common ground?

We shall return to this subject in the context of modern tribalism and nationalism (see Chapter 7). Meanwhile, in the 1920s, two powerful ideas began to circulate, the one aimed against the first obstacle, the other against the second obstacle. The first idea was Pan-Africanism. The second idea, linked to the first, was national union or nationalism.

THE PAN-AFRICAN MOVEMENT: ORIGINS AND EARLY AIMS

'Pan' is a Greek word meaning 'all'; so Pan-African means 'all-African'. But the first form of the Pan-African movement was not directly concerned with Africa. It was concerned with the black communities, of African ancestry, who lived in North America and the Caribbean (West Indies). These black people had come from many African peoples and cultures. But they had lost their languages and cultures during the time of slavery. Liberated from American slavery, they were united by remaining the victims of American and colonial racism. They were united, we can say, by their colour and by their sufferings.

Some of these black people, during the last century, came to believe that they could become free and equal only if they left America. But where, then, should they go except to the homeland of their ancestors? A 'Back to Africa' movement developed; and this was how Liberia came to be founded by black people from the USA. The same idea developed further: into the idea that all black peoples should unite in defence of their common interests, and against racism.

So the first form of this movement was, really, a 'Pan-Black' or Pan-Negro movement which took shape outside Africa. Yet the Pan-African movement, even in this early form, also stood for the defence of Africans in Africa. One of the actions of the first Pan-African congress, held in London in 1900, was to protest to Britain's Queen Victoria against racist rule in South Africa and Rhodesia.

That first congress was attended by 32 delegates. Of these, eleven were from the USA and ten from the West Indies, but only four directly from Africa. Yet its proceedings raised high the claims of African equality and achievement; and its importance was well marked by educated persons in Africa, notably in West and South Africa. The Nigerian *Lagos Standard*, a newspaper that was owned as well as edited by Africans, hailed the congress of 1900 as 'an event in the history of race movements which, for its importance and probable results, is perhaps without parallel.'

Leading spokesmen for the liberating ideas of Pan-Africanism were soon on the African scene. Among them was the West Indian and later Liberian diplomat, Edward Wilmot Blyden (1832–1912). During the 1920s, powerful help for the same ideas was given by two outstanding men across the Atlantic. One of these was the Jamaican Marcus Moziah Garvey (1887–1940), who in 1914 founded an organisation in New York, called the Universal Negro Improvement Association, and whose influence was felt widely across Africa. Another was the Afro-American William Burghardt DuBois (1868–1963), a great student of African history who eventually became a citizen of Ghana.

This movement could do nothing to change the colonial systems, for it had no power. Yet it played a useful part in telling the world about Africa's problems under colonial rule. It spoke up for colonised Africans at a time when few of these could make their voices heard through colonial walls of silence. A second congress was held in Paris, in 1919, where the victorious powers of the First World War were holding their peace conference. A third congress took place in London and Brussels in 1921; a fourth in London and Lisbon in 1923; and a fifth in New York in 1927.

But by this time, the middle of the 1920s, the ideas of the Pan-African movement were developing towards a new form. This was that Africans must find their own way towards unity and freedom. Afro-Americans could help with support and solidarity, but the problems were different; they could not lead Africa. Any sound plan for African progress, declared a leading Gold Coast thinker, Kobina Sekyi (1892–1956) in a book written during 1925, 'must be controlled and directed from African Africa and thoroughly African African.'

In this new form, the 'Pan-Black' or 'Pan-Negro' idea grew into a much more directly Pan-*African* idea. This would reach its full development only with the sixth Pan-African congress, held in Manchester (England) in 1945, when leading African nationalists combined in new demands for African independence. And that was the congress which then led on to the Organisation of African Unity (see Chapter 20). Meanwhile this revised form of Pan-Africanism was accompanied, during the 1920s, by the second idea we have noted above: the idea of *national union*.

NATIONAL UNION

The politics of *national union* had already captured the centre of the stage in the political world of the white peoples. That was during the last years of the eighteenth century and the early years of the nineteenth. Before that, the concepts of nationality and nationhood – of nationalism – had been vague and unimportant. Like other peoples, the white peoples had united round power-centres represented by kings and priests, clans and local loyalties. But the economic revolution in England, producing the system of capitalism, and the political revolution in France, greatly reinforcing the system of centralism, combined to give nationalism a new and mighty force.

The great political upheavals and changes of the nineteenth century all duly followed: above all, in its exemplary power, the emergence of the United States of America; in Europe, the national unification of Italy and afterwards of the Slav peoples of central and southern Europe; in Latin America, the rise of post-colonial republics.

By 1900 it seemed that nationalism would carry all before it. But its liberating power could be terribly reversed into disaster. This was fully displayed during the First World War, when the nations of Europe killed each other's citizens in millions. And yet it could still be said that nationalism was 'the force of the future.' Compared with nationalism, the opposing power of international socialism proved weak and ineffective. All this helped to set the African scene after the First World War.

In Africa, the ideas of nationalism were not quite new in the 1920s. They had taken shape some years earlier among the educated few of British West Africa, especially in the towns of Cape Coast (in the Gold Coast/Ghana), Lagos (in Nigeria), Freetown (in Sierra Leone), and Bathurst (Banjul in The Gambia). These men had more freedom than Africans in other colonies. Though barred from senior government jobs, they were able to discuss politics without much fear of the colonial police. They could and did publish newspapers of their own.

These men studied Europe, and saw that the basis for the independence of European peoples was that they were organised into nations: into states, that is, whose peoples had a single national loyalty and accepted a single national culture. In fact, many European states had various loyalties and cultures. But each had one that was dominant, and this was the basis of their nationhood.

Now the idea that the various peoples in a colony could become free only if they combined together as a nation, like the Europeans, had already been heard in earlier years. Influential in promoting this kind of idea, for example, was the Aborigines' Rights Protection Society, founded in the Gold Coast in 1897. In 1911 another Gold Coast thinker, S.R.B. Attoh Ahuma, published an important book called *The Gold Coast Nation and National Consciousness*. He called for Africans to be proud of their heritage and history. He argued that they must found modern nations.

Attoh Ahuma, like other early thinkers of this kind, was caught in a contradiction. He stood for African progress. But he shared the contempt of educated persons for the people of the rural areas. This early idea of national union, in other words, expressed no confidence in the ability of Africans to grow from their own historical roots and cultures. It taught that Africans must follow the lessons of European history, and copy European ways of organisation. But this, in fact, was just what the colonial rulers were also teaching.

'Let us help each other to find a way out of Darkest Africa,' wrote Attoh Ahuma in his book of 1911. 'We must emerge from the savage backwoods, and come into the open where nations are made.' That was the opinion of nearly all the educated persons of those days; and it was understandable. To become educated to a high level, they had to live in Europe and learn in European languages. Home again, they tended to live like Europeans, losing touch with their own peoples. They became what Kobina Sekyi, in a play of 1915, called 'social hybrids': persons 'born into one race, and brought up to live like members of another race.' Such was the 'been-to-Europe' fate in those times.

Yet these 'social hybrids' of the 1920s, mostly in British West Africa, played an important part. They found the common ground on which different peoples, gathered within a single colony, could make progress towards independence: the common ground, that is, of national union. They said that Africans must become nations. But they also said more, and this, too, was to be important. They said that Africans must become nations by adopting the British system of government, and not by adapting the systems formed in Africa's own history. As the Nigerian historian E.A. Ayandele has written, 'it was they who conceived the modern Nigeria which embraced the myriads of states and kingdoms of the pre-colonial era.'

FOUNDERS OF MODERN NATIONALISM: WEST AFRICA

A new move towards the development of nationalism came in 1920. Forty-five members of what the Gambian historian J. Ayodele Langley has called 'the lawyer-merchant class' in British West Africa – the spokesman of the educated few – gathered at the Accra Native Club (in the Gold Coast) during March. There they founded the National Congress of British West Africa (NCBWA), with sections in each of the four colonies (Nigeria, Gold Coast, Sierra Leone, The Gambia).

The aims of this congress combined the idea of national union with that of Pan-Africanism. As to the first, its leaders believed that they must press the British to allow them to join colonial parliaments, then known as 'legislative councils'. These were mostly advisory bodies in each colony, and had no power. But the men of the NCBWA believed that these legislatures could be made to develop into democratic parliaments, and, in time, into national parliaments.

At the same time, the NCBWA leaders argued that educated Africans must combine their efforts *across* colonial frontiers. They pressed the Pan-African idea. Their president, the Gold Coast lawyer J.A. Casely Hayford, told the third NCBWA conference:

> As there is an international feeling among all white men, among all brown men, among all yellow men, so must there be an international feeling among all black folk.

Even at its first conference in 1920, the NCBWA demanded progress towards 'a united West Africa' of the four British colonies.

Active in these discussions, besides Casely Hayford and other Gold Coasters, were well-known Nigerians such as the Reverend Patriarch Patrick Campbell, the medical doctor Richard Savage, the newspaper editor Thomas Horatio Jackson, and Prince Bassey Ephraim of Calabar. Dr Herbert Bankole-Bright was in this respect the leading Sierra Leonian, while E.F. Small was prominent among Gambians.

Not all the lawyer-merchant class agreed. The Nigerian lawyer Sir Kitoyi Ayasa rejected the congress policy on the grounds that 'we have a Yoruba nation and a Hausa nation, but so far we have no Nigerian nation.' He thought the NCBWA was going much too fast. So did the British, who rejected all the congress demands. The NCBWA went on having occasional meetings till 1933, but gradually the 'four-colony union' idea was forgotten. In sum, the NCBWA failed to make any progress. But it pointed the way, clearly, to the further development of the ideas of nationalism.

The chief weakness of the NCBWA was that its members were all privileged 'hybrids' who were against calling on the mass of people for any support. They wanted small steps, small reforms, which would ensure that they would become the leaders of the nations they talked about. They wanted to be junior partners with the British in the hope that one day they could become equal partners. The time had yet to arrive when nationalism would have mass support, and demand full independence. Then, as we shall see, the British would have to listen; and so would all the other colonial powers.

Little or nothing was heard of these ideas of national union, during the

1920s, in British East and Central Africa. There, the educated few barely existed as yet; while the European settler minorities, slowly growing stronger, took it for granted that they, and not the African majorities, were going to dominate the future of those countries.

THE AFRICAN VOICE IN SOUTH AFRICA

Here the key date was 1910. In that year the British imperial government in London withdrew Britain's political power from South Africa, and gave all this power to the two white minorities, those who spoke English and those who spoke Afrikaans (a local language descended from the Dutch language of the earliest white settlers). This was done by an Act of Union. The four countries of earlier South Africa (Cape Colony, Natal, Orange Free State, Transvaal Republic) were combined into one country, the Union of South Africa.

The whites of the four former states disagreed in many ways, but they were firmly united against the blacks: against, that is, the African majority and the two minorities of Coloureds (persons of mixed origin) and Asians. The Afrikaner (Boer) whites were severely racist by doctrine, habit and tradition. The English-speaking whites were in practice just the same, or else, if they were new immigrants, soon became so. Handed all local power in 1910, these two white communities competed with each other for the spoils and benefits. But they at once agreed with each other in passing laws, for the whole Union, which reduced or eliminated rights and opportunities for black people.

Their chief idea was to drive Africans into labour-service for white farms, white industries, and white families. One of the harshest of these new racist laws was the Land Act of 1913. It denied Africans any right to own land in nine-tenths of the whole country, even though the Africans, at that time, outnumbered the whites by four to one. With other laws of the same kind, this Land Act was a big reinforcement of the South African racist system which, becoming ever worse, would later develop into *apartheid* (see Chapter 16).

African farmers and chiefs protested in vain, for the whites had all the power and used it without mercy. Protests by educated Africans were also made. These were the work of a small number of men who had managed to secure some modern education through missionary colleges, or overseas; and above all in the USA, where they found friends and supporters. They included John Tengu Jabavu, John Dube, Pixley Seme, Solomon Plaatje and others. Meeting in 1912 at Bloemfontein, in the Orange Free State province of the newly formed Union, they launched the South African Native National Congress. Still free to organise in public, they wanted this congress to speak for a united African voice, against the united white voice, in all the four countries of the Union. So this congress was another early combination of the ideas of unity and nationalism.

The white rulers paid no attention. They went on building up their racist system. Here, too, educated men among the black communities had yet to call for mass support; like those of the NCBWA, most were moderate and cautious. In 1923 they changed the name of their organisation to the African National Congress of South Africa (ANC). The ANC was able to hold out against growing persecution; in spite of its organisational problems and, at that time, its political immaturity, it proved to be another 'parent of the future'.

THE POLICY OF 'ASSIMILATION'

Africans had to face a somewhat different form of racism in the French colonial empire. At least in British West Africa, the British always said that they had a 'mission' to lead Africans to independence, though by immensely slow steps. The French also said that they had a mission: not, however, to lead Africans to independence, but to lead them towards becoming citizens of France. On this French view, it would never be wise or acceptable that Africans should once again have independent states of their own; they could only become part of 'greater France.' They could not rebuild their civilisations in the modern world; they could only join French civilisation.

This was called the policy of 'assimilation', or 'being absorbed.' It meant that African people, to become free, had to become black French people. In practice, assimilation was impossible for nearly all Africans in the French empire. Throughout French West Africa in 1926, for example, there were more than 13 million Africans. But fewer than 50,000 of these were French citizens, and most of that small percentage were in the single colony of Senegal. All the rest were 'natives' (*indigènes*) subject to forced labour and other racist laws; as late as 1945, the number of assimilated West Africans was still below 100,000. The assimilated number was even smaller in other French colonies in Africa.

Yet these small groups of black French citizens were important. They were the ones who could get some modern education, and develop new ideas about the future. Because of the French policy of assimilation, they began to demand a bigger chance for Africans to become French citizens;

only much later did they start to think about demanding national independence. They made no progress in the 1920s or even later. They had much less freedom than educated persons in British West Africa. Their position was more like that of Africans in the British settler colonies of East and Central Africa.

The history of African newspapers underlines this. Thanks to missionary schools, British West Africa had gifted editors and journalists who were able to use their skills. Even by 1900, Sierra Leone had known as many as 34 African newspapers at one time or other; the Gold Coast had had 19, Nigeria 7. The best of these papers continued to appear. They were a big part of city life, they contained a lot about politics, and were often critical of colonial rule. But in French Africa, as in British East and Central Africa, there were few or no independent African newspapers. Editors and journalists in those colonies risked stiff punishment, and sometimes suffered it, whenever they wrote critical articles.

In the other African empires, the ideas of nationalism, or of any kind of progress for Africans, made even smaller gains; mostly, there were no gains. The Belgians ran their vast Congo colony as a stiff dictatorship. The Portuguese, Italians and Spanish did the same. All of them talked of having a mission to help Africans. But their words were even emptier than those of the British and French.

The Portuguese colonialists, for example, repeatedly claimed to be doing a great deal to 'civilise Africans'. But as late as 1970 the number of blacks in their colonies who were treated as 'civilised', because they had the status of assimilated persons, was less than one in every three hundred in Guiné (now Guinea-Bissau); while the numbers of 'civilised blacks' were not much greater in Angola or Mozambique. All the rest were treated as the objects of unlimited colonial exploitation. Even the few assimilated Africans were arrested, beaten, or exiled whenever they launched any serious anti-colonial protest.

NORTH AFRICA: ISLAM AND NATIONALISM

Colonial rule came to North Africa at different dates, and not as any direct result of the 'share-out' conference in Berlin of 1884–85. The French invaded Algeria as early as 1830, and took control of Tunisia in 1881. The British were in full command of Egypt by 1890, and, as a result of their defeat of the Mahdia, they were ruling the Sudan soon after. In 1912 the French assumed control of Morocco, while in 1911 the Italians launched a long and bitter invasion of Libya.

These invaded peoples kept strong links with Islam in the Middle East. It was from there too that they took their new ideas about self-defence by national union. Those ideas were the creation of several important Islamic thinkers such as Jamal al-Din (1838–97), who was born in Iran but known as al-Afghani. He was a founder of the idea of Pan-Islam, of the cultural and political unity of Muslims everywhere. Another was an Egyptian follower of al-Afghani's, Muhamad Abduh (1849–1905). A third was a Syrian, Muhamad Rashid Rida (1865–1935), who became one of the founders of Arab nationalism in the Middle East.

Their teachings spread into Libya and the three countries of the Maghrib (Tunisia, Algeria and Morocco), and were welcomed by patriotic Muslims. But with colonial rule both new and strong, these patriots found it hard to know what best to do. Two schools of thought developed.

One school believed that the best course was to reform Muslim society by strong reliance on the traditional teachings of Islam, notably those of the predecessors or founders of Islam, and especially of the Prophet Muhamad and his companions. Using early Muslim principles, together with later concepts of banking, law codification and education, the thinkers of this group generally believed that specifically Islamic ideas and methods would enable their peoples to meet the challenge of the modern world. This traditionalist reform movement was often called the *Salafiyyah* (after *salafun,* 'predecessors'). Its modern and sometimes extremist form, in the 1980s, became known as 'fundamentalism'.

A second school of thought, which eventually became much stronger than the first, was no less loyal to Islam; but its thinkers believed that their effort could succeed only by adopting secular (non-religious) ideas and methods of organisation. They urged that the oppression of imperialist nations could be thrown off only by forming anti-imperialist nations, and, therefore, by launching anti-imperialist movements and parties of nationalism.

These two groups were both opposed to colonial rule. But their difference of opinion about how best to oppose it continued for many years. This difference made national union more difficult.

As time went by, the secular trend won wider support. Western forms of politics began to emerge. As early as 1906, three political parties were formed in Egypt. But the first strongly nationalist party appeared there in 1918. This was the *Wafd*. A party of Egypt's lawyer-merchant class, more numerous than elsewhere, the *Wafd* called for negotiations with Britain to end the country's colonial situation.

For their part, the British wanted to keep military and economic control over Egypt. But they had no interest in governing the country;

they were ready for Egyptians to do that. So they partly agreed with the *Wafd*. In 1922 they recognised Egyptian independence, but stayed in power behind the scenes. The *Wafd* continued to lead Egyptian politics, but there was no weakening of British control until the 1950s (see Chapter 10).

Other North Africans watched these political moves. What could they do to follow them? Little or nothing in Libya, because colonial war continued there right down to 1932. This war had begun with Italian invasion in 1911. At first the Italians fought the Turkish forces of the old Ottoman empire, but these Turks withdrew from Libya in 1912. Then the Italians found themselves faced with a new and more powerful Libyan armed resistance, organised by such patriots as Ahmad Sharif and Umar al-Mukhtar, and by the *Sanussiya* – originally a movement of Muslim religious inspiration, founded long before by Sidi Muhammad al-Sanussi. Under the leadership of Sharif and Mukhtar the resistance of the *Sanussiya* and of other Libyans was overcome by the Italians only in 1932, and after years of ruthless warfare.

Things went differently in Tunisia next door. Shortly before 1914, educated persons in Tunisia formed the Young Tunisian Party, and later pressed for a share with the French in governing Tunisia. In 1920 they and others formed a new party, the *Hizb al-Hurr al-Dasturi*, or *Destour* as the French called it. Its aim was to persuade the French to allow Tunisia to return to its constitution (*Dastur*) of 1860, under which the educated few could have some political power in a parliament. To this the French paid no attention. Also, the French ignored demands for better wages and conditions put forward by Tunisian workers organised in new trade unions. But effective Tunisian protests were to come later.

Algeria's situation was still more difficult. Most of Algeria was governed as part of the 'home country' of France, but strictly in the interests of the white settlers in Algeria. These settlers persecuted the Algerians by an unrelenting racism like that of the whites in South Africa. They believed that Algeria could never be anything except a region of France, and should continue to be governed by French people in the interests of French people.

Trying to improve their situation, Algerian leaders were divided on what best to do. In this period of the 1920s, most agreed with Sheikh Ben Badis. Although an Algerian patriot, Ben Badis believed that Algerians must accept French rule at least for a time of 'guardianship.' 'The Algerian nation,' he said in 1925, 'is weak and insufficiently evolved. It feels a vital need to come within the protecting wing of a strong and civilised nation.' That nation was France. This was really just what leading nationalists in West Africa were also saying then. Let us try to make progress, they were saying, but for the time being we shall have to do it under British colonial leadership.

Not all Algerian spokesmen agreed with Ben Badis. The Amir Khaled al-Kader, descendant of a great Algerian leader of the 1830s, spoke for the independence of Algeria. But the Amir was ahead of his time; he had to end his life in exile.

A more important trend took shape, across the Mediterranean, among Algerian migrant workers in France. Even by 1926, because there was no work for them at home, these numbered about 18,000. They were badly paid, lived poorly, and needed to combine in self-defence. In 1926 a young Algerian nationalist, Messali Hadj (1898–1974), began to lead this self-defence movement. He formed the *Étoile Nord Africaine* (*North Africa Star*) in France, and the *Étoile* soon had thousands of Algerian members. For North Africa, this was the first big anti-colonial party whose leaders and most members did not belong to the lawyer-merchant class. They were workers with revolutionary ideas. Soon their demands went beyond better conditions; soon they were demanding Algerian independence. They began to take their ideas and demands back to Algeria, and to spread them there. A tremendous struggle lay ahead, although it unfolded only many years later.

Morocco was allowed to keep its own king and local officials when the French seized control in 1912. But it was not long before the French were taking all the big decisions in governing Morocco, and most of the small decisions too. Their control was shaken, in 1920–26, by Abd al-Krim's war of independence in the Rif mountains (see p. 24). After that, they brought Morocco under tighter French control (as the Spanish also did in their northern zone). There was no effective political resistance at this time by Morocco's educated class. Yet here, too, new struggles lay ahead.

SUMMARY
Resistance and Adjustment

During the 1920s, the colonial systems were fully installed. 'Pacification' was completed. Military government was displaced by civilian government.

Many continued to resist colonial government and taxation: sometimes by revolt, often by new movements of religious protest, or else by moving across colonial frontiers. Many others thought it more sensible to adjust to the system and make the best of things. Most chiefs did that; so did persons who served colonial government as appointed 'chiefs', 'headmen', police, interpreters, soldiers. Especially in non-settler colonies, farmers found they could make money or at least survive, by growing crops for export in line with colonial policies.

All these trends began to make big changes in African ways of earning a living. Old ways of life began to break down. New ways of life began to be looked for. There was now a bigger demand for modern education. People wanted their children to understand this modern world from which the colonial systems had come. But schools, as yet, were few. For most children there was no chance of going to school. Yet the demand persisted.

New ideas about politics, about Africa's future, began to circulate: especially, the ideas of Pan-Africanism and of national union, or nationalism. But as yet, with exceptions here and there, only the educated few of the lawyer-merchant class had these ideas. As yet, there was little or no thought of trying to win mass support for nationalism.

PART TWO

Colonialism under Strain: 1930–1945

PART TWO is about the years 1930–45. Among the questions it answers are:

Chapter Five Colonial Systems and the Great Depression
- What was the colonial economy? How did it differ from African economies before the colonial period?
- What was the Great Depression? Why did it mark a turning-point?
- In what ways did the 1930s differ from the 1920s?
- Where did colonial governments find their revenue, and how did they spend it?
- What was 'imperial protection'?
- When did Italy invade Ethiopia? With what results?

Chapter Six The Second World War, 1939–45
- What happened in the Second World War? How did it affect Africa?
- What was the Atlantic Charter?
- When and where was the United Nations founded?
- Did the UN help African progress?
- What was the influence of Asian nationalism?
- When was Israel founded? The Arab League?

Chapter Seven Towards Modern Politics
- What is meant by the term 'modern tribalism' in the colonial period?
- How and why did 'modern tribalism' develop?
- What were tribal unions? Why were they formed?
- Did tribal unions lead on to modern parties? If so, how and why?
- When did new political parties of 'mass politics' begin to appear?
- What was the importance of the Nigerian Youth League? The West African Youth League? The Gold Coast (Ghana) 'cocoa hold-up'?
- The importance of New-Destour and the *Istiqlal*? The Kikuyu Central Association?
- What were African reactions to Italy's invasion of Ethiopia?
- What was WASU? The *Union Inter-Coloniale?* The League Against Imperialism?
- What was the NCNC? The *Ashiqqa?*

Chapter Eight Colonialism in Crisis
- Why was colonialism in crisis by 1945?
- What was 'the flight to the towns'?
- What were the effects of migrant labour by 1945?
- How and why did mass political movements evolve?
- What part was played by African trade unions?

CHAPTER FIVE

Colonial Systems and the Great Depression

If you had been living in the 1920s, you would easily have thought that Africans could never again be free to run their own countries. Only Ethiopia and Liberia had their own governments: everywhere else, the colonial systems were strong and growing stronger. All resistance had failed; only the various ways of accommodation (of 'adjusting') seemed to remain. But even accommodation was far from easy; in the settler colonies, it was still more difficult.

Yet the fifteen years from 1930 to 1945 developed in fact towards a very different outcome. For this was the period when the seeds of a new independence, planted by the hands of early nationalists, began to grow into the harvest of political renewal that came later.

Two major developments encouraged this political renewal. One was the Great Depression, when everywhere in Africa the ways of working and earning, as the Sierra Leonean economist Cox-George has said of his own country, 'suffered a complete slump, touching every sector'. The second development, evolving partly from the first, was the rise of a new political resistance. Sharpened by the economic crisis, this new political resistance began to look for mass support, and, gradually, was going to find it.

THE COLONIAL ECONOMY: A DEPENDENT ECONOMY

Africa's economic dependence on the outside world of markets and market-prices had begun to take shape, long before colonial times, with the major growth of the Atlantic slave trade after about 1650. Looking

47

back, we can see that Africa's export of captive labour, as slaves, was in fact an early kind of colonial export. And so it is from around 1650 that we should date the origins of modern African dependence on the 'world system' of trade and wealth-transfer. But this early growth of dependence, before colonial times, had been partial and often indirect: many African communities and countries had not been drawn into it.

Away from the coast in the vast interior, states and communities continued to depend on themselves and on their neighbours. Slumps or booms in Europe, Asia, or America made little or no difference to them. Their exports were small, as were their imports. At a simple level of life, they could continue to provide for their own needs. Troubles in the outside world could barely touch them.

But now, by the 1920s, all this was changed. Great numbers of men were now pressured into working in mines opened by foreign companies. In this way, Africa became a vital source of minerals for the world overseas. Even as early as the five-year period from 1925 to 1929, African colonies together with white-ruled South Africa produced 56 per cent of all the gold used in the world; 16.4 per cent of the manganese; 12 per cent of the platinum; and much other mineral wealth.

It was the same with farming. Great numbers of men were now pressured, as migrant workers, into producing crops for settlers or on foreign-owned plantations: again for export. Other large numbers, mostly in the non-settler colonies, had become involved in cash-crop production. By 1929, for example, locally produced cotton provided 80 per cent of all Uganda's exports. Cocoa provided 79 per cent of all Gold Coast exports. Groundnuts represented 98 per cent of The Gambia's exports. Cloves were 61 per cent of Zanzibar's exports. What colonial development really meant in these 'mono-crop colonies' – and there were others like them – was that they were being turned into producers for the overseas market. Before the colonial period, Africa had acted as a reservoir of cheap labour – of enslaved labour – for the outside world. Now, in Colonial times, African labour was used increasingly for 'on-site' production in Africa itself. This brought more and more of Africa's communities, above all of Africa's rural communities, into the service of non-African interests.

So in one way or other, Africa's workers and traders and their families were dependent, now, on the outside world. As long as that world prospered, they could make a living. But if the outside world failed to buy these products which Africa's farmers produced for export, or bought less of them, or paid lower prices for them, then Africa's livelihood must at once suffer.

This dependence went on during the 1920s; and it was deepened, all the time, by the colonial transfer of wealth from Africa to the outside

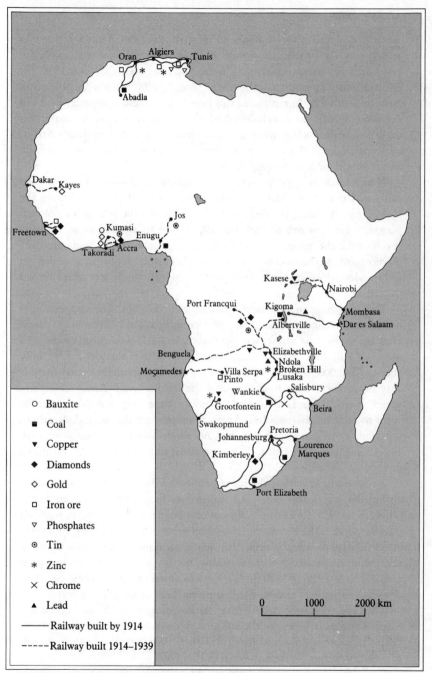

Map 5 Mineral exploitation in Colonial Africa, up to 1939. The chief railway systems linking the mining areas with the coast are also shown

world. Most profits were not used to strengthen the African economies which produced them; they were used to strengthen western European and north American economies. In the years between 1886 and 1934, for example, foreign companies invested some £ 200 million in producing African diamonds. In return for this investment, these companies paid out dividends (profits to shareholders) of £ 80 million in those 48 years. But these dividends (except when paid to white shareholders in South Africa) all went overseas. This was African wealth, but it did not stay in Africa, and it did not help to develop Africa.

Dependence and wealth-transfer continued hand-in-hand. It has been calculated that about half of all the profits of mineral exports from the Gold Coast (Ghana), between the early 1920s and the end of the colonial period, were sent out of the country, mostly to Britain. Here was one reason why the people of the Gold Coast, for example, had only one government higher-secondary school (Achimota College, founded in 1924). Money which could have paid for other schools was taken abroad instead.

That also happened in other mineral-rich colonies. The copper mines of Northern Rhodesia (Zambia), recovering in about 1935 from the Great Depression, became immensely profitable. In 1937, their profits were well over £ 4 million. But of these profits, Northern Rhodesia kept only about £540,000, by way of taxation, while a much larger total (in one way or another) went to Britain and the British South Africa Company which 'owned' the land where the mines were. The rest of the profits went to overseas shareholders. At the same time, in that period, Northern Rhodesia's African population had no single secondary school because, the colonial authorities said, the country was too poor to be able to afford one.

As in southern Africa, the more profits that were made by the mining companies, the lower were the wages that they paid to African mine-workers. In 1929, for example, the starting wage paid to an African working underground in the Northern Rhodesian copper mines was 30 shillings for every 30 days of work; but in 1940, when the mines had become far more profitable, that starting wage was only 22s 6d. Surface workers had been paid 17s 6d in 1929; in 1940 their wage was down to 12s 6d. These very low wages were another means of enlarging the flow of wealth overseas.

Thus the economic dependence of the colonies on the outside world formed one main aspect of the colonial systems, and wealth-transfer from Africa to countries overseas formed another. We shall discuss the methods of wealth-transfer overseas in detail in Part Four.

For most of the colonial systems, the 1920s were a time of economic expansion. Exports grew, profits rose. Then, quite suddenly at the end of the 1920s, the 'developed' countries of western Europe and North America hit serious trouble in the form of the Great Depression. The colonies were dragged helplessly into the same trouble.

1929: ECONOMIC COLLAPSE

It began far away. The scene of the first big drama was the New York Stock Exchange, the most important market-place in the USA for the buying and selling of company shares. Signs of economic crisis in western Europe prompted fear that the price of shares was about to collapse. This led to panic selling, and collapse soon followed. 'Golden America' plunged itself into years of hardship. More than 3,000 American banks failed by the end of 1931. Soon after, more than 12 million American workers were out of jobs, while Western Europe followed the same downhill path.

World trade slumped, because many exports could not be sold and many imports could not be bought. The consequences for Africa were disastrous. In 1929 the total value of the export-import trade of the four British West African colonies was £ 56 million; by 1931 it had collapsed almost by half to £ 29 million. The same disaster hit Britain's East and Central African colonies: in 1929 the value of their export trade stood at £ 40 million; in 1931 it was down to £ 21 million. The fourteen French West and Equatorial colonies (including the two 'mandated territories' of Cameroun and Togo) met the same hard fate. Their total export–import trade fell from £ 30 million in 1929 to less than £ 18 million in 1931; while the trade of the Belgian Congo fell by more than half in those two years. Other colonies suffered in like measure.

As trade collapsed, so did prices. The Belgian Congo was again typical. By 1932 the money paid to cotton-producers had fallen by about two-thirds. For some crops it was worse still: the money paid to Belgian Congo rubber producers fell by 90 per cent between 1929 and 1932.

The collapse did not end soon. Again taking the fairly typical Belgian Congo figures, palm-oil fell by 1934 to less than one-fifth of its 1929 value, and cocoa to little more than one-quarter of its 1929 value. To this general collapse of prices—and therefore of the money to pay producers and workers—there was only one exception. The price of gold scarcely fell at all, because, it was believed, gold would never lose its value. Those who suffered least, in consequence, were the big South African mining companies. But even this did not help South Africa's black mine-workers. Because of white South Africa's racist laws and attitudes, their wages were pushed even lower than before.

Though at its worst in the early 1930s, the Great Depression continued for several more years; in some colonies, it lasted until the early 1940s. It bit deeply into everyday life. It was so severe that historians have called it a turning point in our century, and we can easily see why.

Before the Great Depression, the colonial powers believed that they had found all the solutions to the problems of ruling Africa, and making money out of Africa, for countless years to come. Afterwards, they were increasingly worried about the future. And although the Great Depression did not in itself begin to end colonial rule, it helped to create tensions which led to the Second World War. And that terrible war, however unintentionally and paradoxically, really did mark the onset of an entirely new chapter in Africa's history.

Colonial stand-still

The world economic collapse meant that the 1930s, in contrast with the 1920s, were years of colonial standstill or retreat: in production, in prices, and in trade. There were exceptions where new mines were found: the deep mining of Northern Rhodesian (Zambian) copper, for example, began only at the end of the 1920s and expanded greatly in later years. But such exceptions were few.

As wages and prices fell, and unemployment spread, there came another fall, this time in the taxation money that governments could get from Africans, and from export–import taxes. Having less money coming in, they had less money to spend. What were they to cut?

There were two big items they could not cut very much, and which they tried hard to avoid cutting. The first of these annual budget items was the money that the colonial governments had to pay, in interest, on sums of capital they had borrowed overseas, each from its own home government or private lenders, in order to finance such things as railway rolling-stock, lines of rail, and other imported things. The amount of this annual interest payment varied from colony to colony. But a big effort always had to be made to pay it.

The second item in the annual budget of each colony that each colonial government wanted to cut as little as possible, or not at all, was the money spent on European officials, police, troops, and the like. So the chief cuts had to come from other items. Among these were the social and cultural benefits that had sometimes come with colonial rule in terms of education, health services, and public works such as the provision of better roads. The extent of these cuts varied from colony to colony. But it can be said with confidence that cuts of this kind were made in all colonies, and often they were severe.

COLONIAL BUDGETS: GOVERNMENT SPENDING IN THE 1930s

The depression in trade continued through the 1930s, but began to ease, in most territories, after about 1935. By that time, however, the spending pattern of colonial governments was firmly established, even if it became possible, here and there, to restore some of the cuts in social services imposed during the worst years of the depression.

This spending pattern varied from one colony to another, but its main characteristics can usefully be summarised. The table on p. 54 shows in an approximate way how a number of colonial governments allocated money to their principal forms of expenditure. The figures are each a percentage of total expenditure for each colony for the 1936–37 financial year.

These percentages are only a rough guide, for each colonial system estimated its expenditure in different ways. Yet it can still be seen that the cost of colonial government was high: whether in salaries paid to European officials and in the organisation of colonial civil services, or in the always high cost of police and security services. Funds available for social services had to be correspondingly low

'Colonial economic development'—the third column in the table—had a strictly limited meaning. Mostly, it meant money spent on railways, harbours, and other facilities needed by foreign companies, chiefly mining companies: the physical 'infrastructure', in other words, by means of which these companies could realise their profits. These facilities had mostly to be built by the colonial government, often using forced labour, because foreign companies naturally preferred not to invest their own money in building them. If there was now, in the 1930s, the beginnings of a communications revolution in Africa, this was primarily for the benefit of colonial interests. Any gain to Africans was incidental.

For such incidental gains, moreover, the colonised peoples had to pay an often stiff price. This price was partly in forced labour and in taxes to colonial government. But it was also in the payment, by government, of debt-interest to foreign lenders. In the Belgian Congo, for example, only 12 per cent of government revenue was spent on education and other social services during the year we are examining, 1936–37. But in the same year the Belgian Congo government was paying, to foreign lenders, about 40 per cent of all its revenues. This was in respect of debt-interest to foreign lenders for railways and other facilities needed to export the produce of the Congo's foreign-owned mines and plantations. About 20 per cent of the Nigerian annual budget was spent in the payment of

Annual budget expenditure on main items: 1936/37*

	Government (civil service, police, etc.) %	Social services (education, health, etc.) %	Colonial economic development %
N. Rhodesia (Zambia)	40.6	21.9	9.4
Kenya	38.9	22.0	14.5
Nigeria	29.3	17.8	11.5
Gold Coast (Ghana)	31.6	28.0	16.3
French West Africa (1937)	20.0	16.0	24.0
French Equatorial Africa (1937)	20.0	11.0	13.0
Belgian Congo (1935)	24.0	12.0	17.0

* *Source:* Lord Hailey, *An African Survey*, 1945, pp. 1433, 1453, 1456.

debt-interest in that same year, and more than 16 per cent of the Northern Rhodesian (Zambian) budget.

Colonial economic development, in other words, seldom meant the development of the colonised peoples. Largely, it meant the development of the means by which foreign companies could increase their profits.

Methods of taxation

We need to think a little more about taxation, in addition to the general principles outlined in Chapter 2. Government money, or revenue, came from three sources. One was the taxing of foreign companies. This was the smallest source: not because the profits were small, but, as we have seen, because most of the profits were sent, untaxed, overseas. The second source was the taxing of exports and imports (customs and excise). The third source, and usually the biggest, was the taxing of people. We have already seen how this began. By the 1930s, the system was long in use in all colonies. Some official figures for 1934 give an idea of how matters now stood: see table on p. 55.

Generally, taxes on Africans rose during the Great Depression and after, even though conditions of life were harder than before. So did taxes on non-Africans, chiefly on white settlers; but these taxes remained far lower than any such taxes in Europe. Besides this, the amounts of money spent on education and other social services for the settlers and their children were always more, and often much more, than the amounts spent on helping Africans. Here was another reason why there could be very few educated Africans in any of the settler colonies.

Taxation revenue: 1934*

		Tax from Africans	Tax from non-Africans	% of annual budget revenue
Nyasaland (Malawi)	£ Sterling	129,562	18,970	43.0
Kenya	£ Sterling	544,480	116,495	32.5
Nigeria		775,010	32,633	18l5
French Equatorial Africa	French francs	37,298,300	1,185,000	57.0
Belgian Congo	Belgian francs	80,709,434	19,764,683	28.8

* *Source:* Lord Hailey, *An African Survey*, 1945, p. 547.

Education in settler colonies

A few figures may illustrate this point. In Kenya during 1935, for example, 1,889 European children were in school, paid for by 29.2 per cent of government education money. There were 7,995 Asian and 'mixed-origin' children at school; they got 23.5 per cent. But a total of 100,720 African school children got only 47.3 per cent of the education budget. Taxes paid by Kenya Africans were bringing in nearly five times' more money to government, as the table above shows, than taxes paid by Europeans. But African schoolchildren still got less than half the education budget.

The position in South Africa was still more unfavourable to black students. In 1935, in the former Boer republics of Transvaal and Orange Free State, white students got 92.2 and 93.4 per cent of all public education money, while little more than six per cent was spent on educating the far bigger black population. In the once-liberal Cape province, the big black majority got only 13.4 per cent of public education money, and the similarly big black majority in Natal province got only 15.14 per cent.

Elsewhere, the position varied with the size of settler communities. In Uganda, with few settlers, African children (in 1936) got 89.3 per cent of public education money. In Tanganyika (mainland Tanzania, without Zanzibar) there were more settlers, but African students (all in primary school) still got 77.3 per cent. In British West Africa, without settlers, all public education money went to Africans; and the position was about the same in the French non-settler colonies. Even so, there was little money

55

for secondary education, and, outside Sierra Leone, none for university education.

In this brief analysis of colonial budgets, we have seen how the benefits of colonial rule could never be large, and how the crisis of the Great Depression in the 1930s made them smaller still. There were conscientious colonial officials who regretted this cutting into social services, but they could not prevent it.

Some other results of the Great Depression need to be looked at.

'Imperial protection'

This had to do with tariffs and quotas: with what became known as 'imperial protection', or the effort by each colonial empire to defend its interests and profits against rival empires.

Tariffs are import taxes. Their aim is to raise the price of imported goods, so that locally-produced goods suffer less from foreign competition. Quotas are government restrictions on the quantity of goods that are allowed to be produced or manufactured. Their aim is to prevent prices being lowered by an over-supply of goods.

Each of the colonial powers had always protected their colonial gains and profits; and the poorest colonial powers—the Portuguese, Spanish, Italians—had naturally done it most of all. They treated their colonies as 'private estates of the motherland.'

Much excellent cotton, for example, was grown in colonial Angola. But none of it could be processed there. All of it had to be sold, as raw cotton, to buyers in Portugal, and at prices fixed in Portugal. There it was turned into shirts and cloth. Then these cotton goods were sold back to Angola, once again at prices fixed in Portugal; and the Portuguese government, at the same time, prevented any foreign competitors from selling cotton goods to its colonies. The Portuguese in Portugal, in other words, were able to buy cheap and sell dear in a 'closed' market, and make high profits in Africa, by means of government protection. Here again we see colonial dependence and wealth-transfer going hand in hand.

The Belgians in the Congo had to operate a more 'open' market, because the Congo, by treaty, was supposed to be a free-trade zone. The French treated all their colonies as parts of a greater France, but were strong enough to open their colonies, in a limited way, to foreign competitors. The British, whose free-trade attitudes came from British strength in earlier times, were generally more open in operating their colonial markets.

Now the Great Depression struck these markets. Reacting to it, the colonial powers all participated in a trade war against each other. Tariffs were raised and multiplied. Prices of imported goods therefore tended to rise, even though most people had less money to spend. This hit the colonial peoples especially hard, for few of them had any savings; at the same time unemployment grew fast.

Yet it is likely that the colonial peoples suffered more from quotas than they did from tariffs. Both tariffs and quotas had the same aim, as we have seen: it was to keep up the selling price of goods, especially of manufactured goods. But while tariffs were trade-war weapons, quotas were the outcome of agreement between rival empires. These empires agreed, for instance, to limit the amount of sugar that was produced so as to protect the level of its selling price. In 1937, to follow the same example, a sugar-restriction agreement was imposed on the British East African colonies. The agreement greatly affected Uganda, which was to be allowed to export, in 1938, only one-third of the quantity of sugar exported two years earlier.

Quotas therefore worked in a contradictory way. They helped producers to keep up their selling prices. But they cut down the number of producers who got any price at all; and they made consumers pay more, just when consumers were getting poorer every month.

Other aspects of 'imperial protection' prevented Africans, on a bigger scale than before, from buying goods in the most favourable world markets: from buying, for example, cheap Japanese shirts instead of less cheap European shirts. In fact the whole system of international trade was in a mess, and none of the colonial powers knew how to sort things out. Their own peoples suffered much from this; colonised peoples suffered even more.

Aid for development: origins

More important in later years, another colonial policy also took shape. Because of its great importance after 1945, and again after the coming of independence, we should understand its origins and how it began. This policy was called 'aid for development.' Later, aid for development was going to be presented as a means of helping to develop Africa for the benefit of Africans. At the beginning, however, it was presented quite differently—and, in the opinion of later critics, more honestly. It was presented as a way of developing colonies for the greater benefit of their overseas owners. The basic idea, very new at the time, was that colony-owning countries should not only take money out of their colonies; they should also invest a little of their own taxpayers' money there, so that colonies could produce more profits for traders and share-holders.

The British led the way, in 1929, with a Colonial Development and Welfare Act, the first of later ones of the same kind. British taxpayers' money was to be lent to Africa (against payment of debt-interest) for 'development and welfare.' But then at once the Great Depression came, and only some £6.5 million was lent during the 1930s. Most went into mining equipment and in helping hard-pressed colonial governments to balance their budgets; very little went into social services.

This, once again, was 'aid for colonial expansion'. Besides, being in the form of loans, it had to be paid for by taxing Africans. Colonised peoples, in other words, were again providing taxation money in order to enable more wealth to be sent overseas. Between 1930 and 1940, for example, Britain made development grants to Northern Rhodesia (Zambia) which totalled £136,000. But in those same ten years the amount of money received by Britain from Northern Rhodesia, by way of taxes on Northern Rhodesia's booming copper mines, was probably not less than £2,400,000. So which country was being developed: Britain or Northern Rhodesia?

French aid policy was not much different. One ambitious plan may be noted. The French wanted to irrigate more than one million hectares of land in the middle Niger (Mali) region, so that African farmers could use the land in order to grow cotton for export. The scheme cost (in francs) more than one million pounds by 1937, but was a failure. The farmers of the middle Niger region did not take to it; they believed that cotton-growing would not benefit them. The plan provided for about 1.5 million cultivators. But by 1940 only some 12,000 were actually at work there.

Such schemes could succeed if African farmers approved of them. This was already shown by the Gezira cotton scheme in the (British-governed) Anglo-Egyptian Sudan, today the Republic of Sudan. It arose in 1913 from a demand by British cotton-manufacturers for a bigger supply of long-staple cotton. Sudanese farmers of the Gezira region found that cotton-growing would suit their interests. So they went into it in a big way. Sudanese exports of raw cotton continued to expand; and the Gezira scheme remains today a central part of the country's economy (see also Chapter 19). We should note that while growing cotton for export has benefited Sudanese farmers, the value added to raw cotton by manufacture has likewise benefited foreign (non-African) manufacturers.

Generally, aid for development continued to be aid for colonial exploitation.

NEW CONFLICTS BETWEEN THE IMPERIAL POWERS

Huge and threatening events were meanwhile on the way. Out of the disaster of the First World War, there had come in Italy an especially aggressive system called fascism. Out of the disaster of the Great Depression, there now came in Germany a still more aggressive system of the same kind, called nazism. Both were severe forms of dictatorship. Both were violently racist. Both were committed to achieve their aims by force.

All this prepared new European disasters. The collapse of the international capitalist system, early in the 1930s, now became linked to the collapse of peace between the big powers; soon enough, the Second World War began. Before it began, however, there was a prelude which greatly concerned Africa. Fascist Italy invaded Ethiopia, the African empire ruled by Haile Selassie.

Italy invades Ethiopia

In the Horn of Africa, the colonial partition had given Italy command of a large part of the country of the Somalis. Italy had also seized land along the southern part of the Red Sea, and turned this into its colony of Eritrea. Having done that, Italy proceeded to claim neighbouring Ethiopia as its protectorate, or semi-colony. When the Ethiopian emperor Menelik rejected this claim, Italy went to war but was crushingly defeated by the Ethiopians at Adua in 1896. After that defeat, Italy recognised 'the absolute and unreserved independence of the Ethiopian empire as a sovereign and independent state.' Peace followed, but Italy kept its Eritrean colony.

However, early in the 1930s, Italy's fascist government under its leader Benito Mussolini began shouting for revenge for the defeat of 1896. Claiming that Italy must also have her 'place in the African sun', Mussolini prepared for war.

The first hostilities were provoked by Italian aggression at a place called Walwal in the Ogaden province of the Ethiopian empire. Mussolini demanded that the Ethiopian emperor Haile Selassie must humble himself and pay compensation. The emperor refused, and, seeing the Italians making ready for war, appealed in January 1935 to the world security organisation, the League of Nations, for help to keep the peace.

But the League's help proved worthless, for the League was divided between pro-fascist and anti-fascist powers, with the former stronger than the latter. Despising League protests, Mussolini's bombing planes attacked Adua and Adigrat on 3 October, 1935, and Italy's invading armies followed, entering Ethiopia through Eritrea. Once more Ethiopia asked in vain for League protection. The League condemned the aggression; and 50 member-states, on 18 November, backed a scheme to apply sanctions against Italy. But the scheme failed to include a ban on oil supplies to Italy, while the British government, which controlled Egypt, also refused to close the Suez Canal to Italian ships carrying reinforcements to Italy's invading armies.

Abandoned by the outside world, the Ethiopians fought on alone. But their only well-organised military force was an imperial guard of some 25,000 men, armed with out-of-date weapons. Against this, the Italians sent in very strong forces and took the capital of Addis Ababa on 5 May, 1936. The Emperor Haile Selassie went abroad to find support, but guerrilla resistance continued. The people fought the invaders, and were sometimes led by local chiefs organised in an Ethiopian Patriotic Association.

By 1937 the Italians could claim to have conquered the country, and in 1938 their claim was accepted by the western powers. Mussolini's government boasted that 'Italy has at last got an empire of her own.' Italian farmers were sent out to settle on Ethiopian land. Italian businessmen began to take over Ethiopian trade.

Yet Italy's triumph was brief. As we shall see in the next chapter, the Second World War restored Ethiopia to independence in 1941, and returned Haile Selassie to his throne. Lasting only about five years, Italy's colonial occupation had several more durable effects. Partly for military use, the Italians built some useful roads; against that, their occupation was disturbing and sometimes brutal.

More widely, this painful invasion of Africa's oldest state, made when colonial invasions were supposed to be a thing of the past, aroused great protests throughout the continent. Such protests could not oust the Italians, but they were among the roots of a stronger movement of anti-colonial nationalism which would now emerge in many colonies (see pp. 76–77).

CHAPTER SIX

The Second World War, 1939–1945

Like the First World War, the Second was a breakdown of civilisation in Europe which brought terrible destruction. Millions died on the battlefields, or in their homes, or in nazi-fascist death camps. Cities were destroyed. There seemed no end to the tale of horror. Those who had claimed to be civilising Africans once more seemed to have failed to civilise themselves.

THE COURSE OF THE WAR

Nazi Germany began the war in September 1939 when it attacked and invaded Poland. Then Nazi Germany went on to invade Belgium, Holland, France and (unsuccessfully) Britain, and later, in June 1941, the USSR. Fascist Italy joined Germany in June 1940, and completed the subjection of France. Imperialist Japan joined the nazi-fascist 'Axis' in December 1941, when its air force disabled the American fleet at Pearl Harbor in the Pacific island of Hawaii. Japan then invaded most of southeast Asia as far as the borders of India, and brought many countries into a new but short-lived Japanese empire.

Until late in 1942, the Axis powers won most of the battles. Then the Allies (Britain, USA and USSR, with some smaller partners) began to score big victories. Fascist Italy collapsed in September 1943. Nazi Germany fought until May 1945, though at a terrible cost to the German people. Then the Allies occupied the whole country, with the British and American and small French armies coming from the west and big Soviet armies from the east, and between them they smashed the nazi system. Imperialist Japan held out until American atom bombs were dropped on Hiroshima and Nagasaki in August 1945, and then surrendered.

AFRICAN INVOLVEMENT

No part of Africa was untouched by this hugely destructive conflict, but fighting occurred only in two regions: the Horn, and North Africa.

As in the First World War, Africans had to pay in men, labour, and loss of trade. Large numbers were asked or were compelled to serve in the forces of Britain and France. Of some 80,000 African troops in the French armies inside France, perhaps as many as a quarter were lost during Germany's invasion of May 1940. They were killed in action, were murdered after capture by the racist nazi troops, or died of bad treatment in prisoner-of-war camps.

Fighting on after the collapse of France in 1940, Britain raised still larger African forces. From its East African colonies, as well as from Somaliland, Nyasaland (Malawi), and both Rhodesias (Zimbabwe and Zambia), a total of 280,000 men were recruited, mostly by conscription although many volunteered in the cause of freedom; and a large part of these were organised in fighting brigades. Tanganyika provided 86,000 of these soldiers, of whom 2,358 were killed in action or died on active service; while Kenya provided 75,000, with comparable losses.

Demand for soldiers from British West Africa was smaller, but still large. The four western colonies provided 167,000 fighting men, organised in seven brigades: three Nigerian, two Gold Coast, one Sierra Leonian and one Gambian. Most of these West African brigades were then brought together as 81 (West Africa) Division and 82 (West Africa) Division; all but one of the brigades saw active service on the battlefield.

As part of the British army, these African troops drove the Italians out of Somalia, and then destroyed the last of the Italian fascist armies in East Africa in bitter fighting across Ethiopia and Eritrea. Ethiopia was restored to independence, while short-term British military governments were installed in Somalia and Eritrea, pending post-war decisions about the future of those two countries. A leading part was played by the African brigades, for it was the soldiers of 'the Gold Coast, Nigeria and the [East African] King's African Rifles', proudly reported the Nigerian *West African Pilot*, quoting the British commander-in-chief, 'who broke the backbone of Italian resistance on the entire Kenya and Somaliland fronts after a series of brilliant attacks' across the Juba river and right up through Somalia and Eritrea. Having done that, these and other African formations went on to fight the Japanese invaders of Burma. Altogether, Africans in British colonies were organised in four Divisions of the British army, as well as in various transport and other service units; and the battle honours on their regimental standards, when they brought them home in 1945, were many.

Some Africans also served in North Africa. Here the British in Egypt had to defend their positions from powerful Italian forces advancing across the plains of the Western Desert (chiefly, of the Cyrenaica region of Libya); and these Italians were soon joined by German forces. For nearly two years the tide of battle swung back and forth in rapid tank warfare. But the British forces won the upper hand late in 1942. They drove the nazi-fascist armies out of Libya into Tunisia. Other British and American armies meanwhile landed in Algeria; very soon, nazi-fascist resistance in Tunisia was completely broken. This ended the war in Africa.

THE AFRICAN WAR EFFORT AND ITS EFFECTS

Outside the armed forces, again as in the First World War, farming and other labour was conscripted on a big scale, and with much the same destructive results. Village people in the British and Belgian colonies were organised or forced into a massive effort to increase production for export. In French West Africa, blockaded by the British because its French colonial rulers had sided with nazi Germany, village people were likewise forced into higher production for the internal market, since there could be no imports.

This long and forced 'war effort', as the colonial governments called it, was severe in its effects on rural peoples. Coming on top of previous years of forced or migrant labour, the strain of these war years deepened rural poverty, further interfered with farming and family life, and drove ever bigger numbers of rural people to seek relief in towns. From about 1940, the numbers of town-dwellers began to grow from few to many.

Like the First World War, the Second forced Africans in many colonies into a huge labour effort to produce more raw materials for export. This greatly reinforced the colonial pattern of export-dependency and wealth-transfer. Europe's economic control became even stronger than before.

But that same 'war effort' in labour and production had other effects. It upset rural stability. It undermined family life. It opened the door to a deeper rural poverty. In the settler colonies, as we shall see, the war brought more power to settler communities, thus preparing sharper conflicts. By 1945 the colonial governments were facing social problems which they soon found they could not solve. In this important respect, the war weakened colonialism.

Many of its political effects also weakened the colonial systems; and here we should notice another important difference from the consequences of the First World War. That war of 1914–18 had come too soon after the shock of the colonial invasions and conquests for Africans to grasp its full meaning for themselves, while the major colonial powers, as we have seen, came strengthened out of that war. Now it was different.

The experience of the Second World War gave a new spur to anti-colonial protest. It brought a new force to the call for anti-colonial change. War experience helped to develop a better political understanding of the colonial systems. It raised political consciousness. One cause of this was the anti-nazi, and therefore anti-racist, nature of the war on the Allied side. Another cause was the promise of the Atlantic Charter (see pp. 65–66).

A Zimbabwean writer has told the following story about a British officer in 1940 who was trying to convince an African to enlist:

> 'Away with Hitler! Down with him!' said the British officer.
> 'What's wrong with Hitler?' asked the African.
> 'He wants to rule the whole world,' said the British officer.
> 'What's wrong with that?'
> 'He is German, you see,' said the British officer, trying to appeal subtly to the African's tribal consciousness.
> 'What's wrong with his being German?'
> 'You see,' said the British officer, trying to explain, 'it is not good for one tribe to rule another. Each tribe must rule itself. That's only fair. A German must rule Germans, an Italian, Italians, and a Frenchman, French people.'

Having told this story, that Zimbabwean writer commented:

> But the extremely wary British officer did not say, 'A Briton, Britons'. What he said, however, carried weight with the Africans who rallied in thousands under the British flag. They joined the war to end the threat of Nazi domination.

Having joined the war to end nazi domination, many African servicemen began to see that the war should make an end of colonial domination as well. They fought as equals alongside white soldiers. They won battles in distant lands, and this made nonsense of the colonial-white claim to superiority. Many learned to read and write; not a few received technical training. They deepened their understanding. They welcomed the ideas of freedom. They wrote letters home to say so. They contributed to African newspapers. Here are two examples.

Early in 1945, a Nigerian serviceman wrote from India to the prominent Nigerian nationalist leader Herbert Macaulay:

We all overseas soldiers are coming back home with new ideas. We have been told what we fought for. That is 'freedom'. We want freedom, nothing but freedom.

A little earlier a Gold Coast serviceman sent a satirical poem to the *African Morning Post*, of Accra, which printed it. In a parody of Psalm 23 he wrote:

The European merchant is my shepherd,
And I am in want;
He maketh me to lie down in cocoa farms;
He leadeth me beside the waters of great need;
The general managers and profiteers frighten me.
Thou preparedst a reduction in my salary
In the presence of my creditors.
Thou anointest my income with taxes;
My expense runs over my income
And I will dwell in a rented house for ever!

These ideas about colonial injustice and inequality were reinforced by another experience of the war. Colonial whites had always claimed that Europeans would defeat non-Europeans. Now the war showed Europeans as defeated by the Japanese, but then the Japanese in turn were defeated, and partly by African soldiers. This taught lessons, even if the colonial powers failed to learn them. The Gambian historian J. Ayodele Langley has written that 'the anti-Japanese war was to unleash a decade of nationalism and revolution in South-East Asia and Africa'.

The war made colonial Africa still more dependent in the economic field. But it weakened the social and political control of the colonial governments. Besides this, it greatly weakened the principal colony-owning powers, Britain and France.

INTERNATIONAL BALANCE OF POWER

The Atlantic Charter and the United Nations [UN]

The colonial powers were weakened for a variety of reasons. First, the French were utterly defeated in 1940, and France had to endure four harsh years of German occupation, with great loss of wealth and prestige. The British won the war, but had to fight for their victory to the last man and the last penny. They came out of the war much poorer than before.

65

Secondly, the USA and then the USSR became 'super-powers' in the post-war world. Neither had an interest in strengthening the British and French colonial systems. On the contrary, if with very different political ideas, both had an interest in weakening British and French rule. Each wished to expand its own trade and influence.

Thirdly, the colonised peoples of Asia began to demand their independence. By the end of the war it was clear that Britain would have to give independence to Burma, India, and Ceylon (Sri Lanka). The growing strength and success of Asian nationalism became an encouragement to African nationalism.

But African nationalism – meaning, essentially, the demand for anti-colonial change and even for independence – had already moved ahead in response to the Atlantic Charter of 1941. This was a solemn declaration by President Roosevelt of the USA and Prime Minister Churchill of Britain. It promised that after the Allies won the war they would 'respect the right of all peoples to choose the form of government under which they will live'.

Did this promise apply to the colonised peoples as well as to Europeans, such as the French, who were then under German control and government? Churchill at once tried hard to say no to this question: he had no intention, he said in November 1942, of liquidating the British empire. But Roosevelt insisted that the promise applied to everyone; and in this he was supported by progressive political parties and persons in Britain. If it was wrong for Germans to govern and control Frenchmen, how could it be right for other Europeans to govern and control Africans or Asians? No such question had ever been asked before in Europe, save by a few radicals or revolutionaries; now it was hard to avoid.

On that question, leaders of African opinion had no doubts. Hearing of the Charter by radio and newspaper, they hailed it as a promise of freedom after the war. And they were again encouraged by British wartime propaganda in colonial-controlled broadcasts and newspapers. These often said that the great conflict was a war for freedom. They said it not only in English but also in African languages such as Swahili. They claimed that the war was *vita vya uhuru*, 'war for freedom.'

In these ways, the war began as one thing and developed into a different thing. It began as a conflict between Europeans. But it developed into more than that: it became, at least to some extent, an anti-colonial and anti-racist war as well. Some good came out of the evil.

Then there was a further development in the same direction. This was the foundation of the United Nations, in place of the discredited League of Nations, at San Francisco in the USA during April–June 1945. In line with the Atlantic Charter, and with the (differently motivated) policies of the USA and USSR, the Charter of the UN was anti-colonial. Its principles called for progress towards ending colonial rule.

The UN made little immediate difference. The old League 'mandated territories' (the former German colonies) were relabelled as UN 'trusteeship territories'. But there was one useful new rule. Each colonial power, against tough opposition by all of them, had to make annual reports on each of its colonies; and this rule put those powers on the defensive. At the same time, colonised peoples could send delegations to the UN to state their grievances. Gradually, the UN could and did become a force for anti-colonial progress. Later, its General Assembly gave a world-wide platform to the spokesmen of newly independent nations (see also Chapter 20).

India, Pakistan, Sri Lanka, Burma

Rising Asian nationalism gave new confidence to emergent African nationalism. The independence of new Asian states soon added to that confidence.

India became independent of the British empire, as the two separate states of India and Pakistan, in August 1947. Ceylon achieved its freedom in the following November, when it changed its name to Sri Lanka. Two months later, in January 1948, the Burmese became independent in the republic of the Union of Burma. A new China emerged in 1949. Other Asian peoples took the same road, although some of them, notably those of the former French colonies of Indo-China (Vietnam, Laos, Cambodia), still had to suffer years of colonial warfare.

All this was part of the background to Africa's post-war struggles for independence.

Israel and the Arab League

In May 1948 another independent state emerged, though in different circumstances. The British had recognised the right of Jews to have a national home in Palestine; and this became the independent state of Israel. One chief reason for their doing this was to give security to Jews who had survived the mass killings of nazi-occupied Europe, where some six million Jews were gassed to death, or murdered in some other way, by the nazis.

But the Jewish national state of Israel was created at the direct and painful expense of the Arab people of Palestine. Most Palestine Arabs lost homes and land. Against this injustice, a newly formed alliance of Arab states, including Egypt, launched a long campaign of protest and opposition. They called for the world to recognise the rights of Palestine Arabs.

Created some years earlier, in 1944, this alliance was the Arab League (see also p. 256). Later, the League was joined by newly independent Arab-speaking and Muslim countries in Africa, including Libya, Sudan, Tunisia, Morocco, Algeria, and also by non-Arab but Muslim Somalia. So the cause of the Palestinian people also became an African cause and this common interest was to be deepened, in later years, as Israel became ever more powerful in advancing its national interests. Confrontation between the states of the Arab League and an expanding Israel was to lead to repeated warfare.

CHAPTER SEVEN

Towards Modern Politics

The years between 1930 and 1945 may be called 'the middle colonial period'. These 'middle years' were sandwiched between the early period of conquest and 'pacification', and the later period of colonial withdrawal. We have looked at their main features. For a majority of Africa's peoples, they were years of loss rather than gain. First, there was the Great Depression, lasting through most of the 1930s. Then came the Second World War with all its misery for many communities.

But these experiences taught useful lessons. What did the European rulers really want in Africa? What were they trying to do? Not many Africans had been able to say. Many more now understood. As the answers to such questions came clear, so did the answers to another set of questions. How best could Africans defend themselves? How could they turn to their own advantage what the colonial rulers were doing, or trying to do?

The answers to this second set of questions led to what we have called accommodation, or 'adjustment'. This took many forms, including various kinds of anti-colonial resistance. Africans tried to defend and advance their interests when armed resistance had failed. One result, taking shape above all in these 'middle years', was the formation of modern tribes.

FROM COLONIAL TRIBALISM TO MODERN NATIONALISM

Africans had worked out their own ways of community life, of living together and governing themselves, through many past centuries. They had created a very large number of different communities or states. Some of these were famous empires or big states whose kings ruled over several or many communities. Others were states whose kings ruled over a single community. Many communities had no kings or chiefs, but independent village governments led by groups of elders.

Each of these old communities had its own territory, language, beliefs and loyalties. Various kinds of political structure held them together: largely, the strength of kinship, of family-ties, together with beliefs that bound each people to its rulers, or to their ancestral shrines and spirits. Age-grades were another 'cement' that could unite men and women of a community's various families or family-groups.

When the colonies were made, the new European rulers understood little or nothing about this long and complex development of African political units. They simply thought that Africans lived in 'tribes', even though nobody knew just what the word 'tribe' was supposed to mean. How could these unknown 'tribes' be controlled as cheaply as possible? As the European rulers saw things, this was now the big problem.

The problem arose, as we have seen, partly because tax money was never enough to pay for many colonial officials. It was solved partly by using African interpreters, clerks, and so on. But it was also solved by using Africans who were chiefs, or men ready to serve as appointed 'chiefs', and then giving orders through them. Each 'tribe', the new rulers now said, must have its own chief. If no chief could be found, then it was necessary to invent one.

This system ran into difficulty whenever communities would not accept 'invented chiefs'. Sometimes it ran into continuous trouble, as in Eastern Nigeria where the British made use of so-called 'warrant chiefs'. These were invented chiefs who were supposed to rule over Igbo communities who did not have chiefs. But the colonial policy of inventing chiefs remained in force, notably among the numerous communities of British East Africa.

Gradually, in many regions, this invention of chiefs had success; and two results followed. One was the combining together of several neighbouring communities under a single chief, or 'paramount' as he was often called. The other was the treating of these combined communities as though they had always formed a single people. Inventing chiefs, in short, led on to inventing tribes.

A good deal of modern tribalism was born in this way; and we need to understand how it came about, and what flowed from it. Let us take three cases from Tanganyika during the 1930s.

Inventing tribes

When the colony was made, officials found a number of communities living along the north side of Lake Tanganyika. These were related to each other in language and custom, but each governed itself through its own elders. At first, officials tried to combine these communities under invented paramounts, so that they could give orders to one man instead of several; but the communities disliked this invention, and refused to accept it. At last, in 1933, the British were able to set up a council of chiefs or elders for these peoples (and two others, the Kukuwe and Selya living nearby); and from then onwards they were all said to form a single people. This was called the Nyakyusa tribe, unknown before.

Much further north, south of Lake Nyanza, there lived another set of related but separate communities. Here, for Usumbwa, Kwimba, Buzinza and others, the British were able to appoint paramount chiefs. Then they set about combining these paramountcies into bigger groupings. All of these were then said to form a single people, forming another new 'tribe': the Sukuma tribe, likewise unknown before.

Eastward towards the Indian Ocean, on the slopes of Mount Kilimanjaro, the British found a number of related Chagga communities, each governing itself by means of its own chief. These communities had begun growing coffee under German rule (before, that is, 1918); and in 1925 they had formed the Kilimanjaro Native Planters' Association to organise the sale of their coffee. This led their chiefs, in time, to form a council of chiefs to defend their traditional authority; and in 1934 this council began to discuss the need to have a paramount chief. The idea of a united Chagga tribe was born.

The process, as we see, became a two-way one. The European rulers wanted to reduce many communities to a few 'tribes' so as to control them more easily. But Africans saw that this forming of modern tribes could also have advantages for them. As the British historian John Iliffe has pointed out, 'Europeans believed Africans belonged to tribes; Africans built tribes to belong to.' In this way they could combine in defence of common interests. Their spokesmen, speaking now on behalf of many people instead of few, could win more power to argue with colonial officials.

This idea of forming modern tribes made progress in the 1940s. In 1942, for example, the communities that were gathered by the British into the Nyakyusa tribe took a step of their own. They formed the Nyakyusa Union 'to preserve the good customs and habits of the tribe' – even though the Nyakyusa tribe had never existed in the past.

Other tribal unions quickly followed. In 1945, to give another example, the communities gathered under paramount chiefs south of Lake Nyanza formed the Sukuma Union: even though the word 'Sukuma', in the past, had meant no more than 'north' in the language of their Nyamwezi neighbours.

From unions to parties

Various pressures encouraged this modern tribalism. As towns expanded in the 1940s, people who had come from the rural areas found themselves jumbled together without friends and neighbours whom they knew. They looked for countrymen who spoke the same language, or came from the same district. They began to form tribal associations for their common interest, sometimes called 'welfare leagues', 'tribal unions', or 'progressive unions'. Nigeria alone had many such, as did other colonies.

These tribal unions and associations were not directly concerned with politics, or not at first. They were concerned with helping their members: with solidarity, education, and the coming-together for dances, drumming, and social occasions. As such, colonial governments tolerated them, and even welcomed them. But sometimes they were led by young men of energy and vision; and these soon began to see the desirability, and even the urgent need, of taking an interest in politics.

When Harry Thuku and his friends in Nairobi city founded the Young Kikuyu Association in 1921, this was a tribal union to protest against bad wages and work conditions. But it was not long before Thuku and his friends began thinking about anti-colonial politics. In fact, their association became a ground-work for the later ideas of all-Kikuyu union, and then of all-Kenya union. In short, the tribal unions and associations helped towards the rise of modern nationalism.

This idea of modern nationalism was, in fact, already bringing new political parties into existence. As these appeared, their leaders looked for support to this or that tribal union. Thus Igbo communities in Eastern Nigeria possessed an Igbo Union, strong in the late 1940s, which developed links with the National Council of Nigeria and Cameroons (see p. 78). And in 1948, partly in competitive response to this, Yoruba communities in Western Nigeria gave support to a new Yoruba union called Egbe Omo Oduduwa (Society of the Descendants of Oduduwa, a great Yoruba spirit-ancestor). The principal founder of Egbe was Chief Obafemi Awolowo, who soon after formed a largely Yoruba political party called the Action Group. Here again, we see that tribal unions and new nationalist parties were part of the same complex political development.

A contradiction at work

Modern nationalism was a big advance on modern tribalism. Within each colony, it combined the force of many peoples in pressing for an end to colonial rule. Further, it pressed for freedom by using the political arguments of the Europeans in Europe: arguments which many Europeans found hard to answer. 'If you want,' said the nationalists to the Europeans, 'we Africans were tribes yesterday. But today we are nations. And you yourselves say that nations must be free.' So the new parties of the nationalists went far beyond the small demands of the tribal unions, and, as they grew stronger and more experienced, began to press for national parliaments and governments. In this gradual way was built the great engine of mass pressure which would eventually shift the colonial governments off the scene.

How was this engine put together, and made to move ahead? Those are the central questions we need to examine next. First though, let us just take note of another major contradiction which was now at work. Later on, this was going to give a lot of trouble.

On one hand, there was the colonial organising of many old communities into fewer new tribes. Each new tribe or grouping, as well as older states or communities which had existed long before, naturally tried to advance its own interests. Often, it had to do this in rivalry with other groupings. That was how colonial rule worked: it played off one grouping or 'tribe' against another. Colonised peoples often found themselves organised against each other, and therefore discouraged from jointly organising against colonial rule.

In Ruanda-Urundi, for example, the Belgians deepened the natural differences between the Tutsi and Hutu peoples by taking the Tutsi into a sort of 'colonial partnership' against the Hutu. This gave the Tutsi, or at least their leading men, a belief in a Tutsi 'natural superiority' over the Hutu. This belief was to have terrible consequences in post-colonial Burundi (formerly Urundi). Having inherited power from the departing Belgians, the Tutsi continued to rule their unhappy country by force and persecution. Countless thousands of Hutu peasants were going to be killed in ferocious massacres. Here, indeed, was to be another case where nationalism, after independence, has become the reverse of a liberating force.

Most colonial powers raised security troops from certain 'preferred' peoples and sent them to keep order among different peoples elsewhere. Migrant workers in the South African mines were organised by the mine-owners into competing groups, setting Zulu against Basuto, and so on. This method of organising peoples against each other was another form of 'divide and rule'.

On the other side, more and more Africans began to see that escape from colonial rule called for another forward step. This was that the groupings or 'tribes' of each colony should join to form a nation, because only united action could set them free. Yet a new nation made up of competing tribes, each with its own spokesmen and political organisation, would not have unity. It would have disunity. This contradiction between modern tribe and modern nation was going to be one of the hardest of the legacies left to Africa by the colonial period and by Africa's own pre-colonial past.

NEW MEN, NEW ORGANISATIONS

The ideas of nationalism had taken shape, among the educated few, long before the 1930s. The story of the African National Congress of South Africa, of the National Congress of British West Africa, and of North African parties such as the Destour in Tunisia, has shown us this.

These were minority movements, restricted mostly to the 'lawyer-merchant class', timid in their protests, opposed to any call for mass support. Their idea was that the colonial rulers should accept them as collaborators, so that, in the end, they would take the place of the colonial rulers. Mostly, the British ignored them, or, now and then, allotted them some purely nominal importance in the form of a seat on a colonial advisory council. The French and Portuguese ignored them altogether. The Belgians permitted no 'lawyer-merchant' groups to exist. At this stage, nationalism may be called the trend of minority protests.

But now came the beginnings of another change. All through the 1930s, various developments led to this: the miseries of the Great Depression, Italy's invasion of Ethiopia, and then the experiences of the Second World War. A new trend appeared. Leaders and organisations began to turn away from the 'polite politics' of the educated few, and seek, instead, for 'mass politics' among the uneducated many. Weak as yet, this new trend marked another turning-point in African political development during the colonial period.

This emergence of new men and new organisations with bigger ideas about the future occurred in several colonies, notably Nigeria. Herbert Macaulay, sometimes called 'the father of Nigerian nationalism', had formed the first modern party in Nigeria as early as 1923; this was the Nigerian National Democratic Party (NNDP). But it was very much a Lagos party of the educated few, and the British were able to ignore it.

Early in the 1930s, younger men began to call for action. As so often on such occasions, a purely local issue gave them a start. There was discontent with Nigeria's only advanced secondary school, Yaba Higher College in Lagos. Critics said that it was not giving students an education capable of preparing them for leadership in many fields of life. Worse, it was said, the British authorities were stopping any such development. Partly out of this dispute, there came the demand for a new political organisation. In 1933 the Nigerian Youth Movement (NYM) was founded. It quickly developed the vision of a new and united Nigeria: of a Nigerian nation which would take its future into its own hands.

The NYM was the first nationalist movement in West Africa to call for a wide support, and find it. NYM leaders moved out of local Lagos politics; they campaigned in other regions of the country. They went on to win the support of non-Yoruba leaders such as Nnamdi Azikiwe and Ernest Ikoli. They worked out a programme for the eventual emergence of an independent Nigerian nation. Five years after its formation, in 1938, the NYM made history with a document called the Nigerian Youth Charter.

For the first time in any British colony (or in any African colony except for Madagascar, Cameroun, and Algeria in the French system), this Charter called for complete self-government, and it did so in clear words. Its key passage stated:

> The goal of our activities is a complete taking-over of the Government into the hands of the indigenous people of our country. We are striving towards a position of equal partnership with other member-states of the British Commonwealth of Nations, and enjoying complete independence in the local management of our affairs.

In 1938, this was a revolutionary demand. The colonial authorities ignored it, but thoughtful British observers began to see that something new was on the scene, and that the British in West Africa might soon have to give way. A new confidence was born among African leaders. A new militancy appeared. Mass action was now in the wings of the political stage, and about to appear on it.

As things turned out, that happened first in the Gold Coast. Here, too, new men and new parties were formed. One of these was the Gold Coast Youth Conference (GCYC), founded in 1930 by the lawyer J.B. Danquah (1895–1965). This was a rather conservative organisation, mostly of the educated few, but was ahead of the men of the 1920s. In 1934 it was partly responsible for sending an important delegation to London, asking for constitutional changes to the advantage of Gold Coast communities.

Much more radical was the West African Youth League (WAYL), founded in 1935 by the Sierra Leonean I.T.A. Wallace-Johnson (1895–1965), a forceful leader who gave a big push to mass politics and Pan-

Africanism. He distrusted the old school of 'respectables', and believed that progress called for 'new ideas and new vision; new determination and will.' This was close to the ideas of the Nigerian Youth Movement; and the no less forceful Nigerian, Nnamdi Azikiwe (born in 1904), was in fact active both in the NYM and the WAYL. After making a big impact in the Gold Coast, Wallace-Johnson went to London and then moved his chief scene of action to Sierra Leone, where, in 1939, he fell foul of the British authorities, who duly imprisoned him for a time.

But the decisive action in the Gold Coast came in 1937, and from an unexpected source. This was the great 'cocoa hold-up' by cocoa-growing farmers. The reasons for it were simple. Nine European companies bought all the cocoa produced for export by Gold Coast farmers. They had long agreed between themselves not to compete with one another, but to form a 'cocoa pool'. Through this 'pool' they all bought at the same price. Naturally, they pushed this price as low as they could. Finally they pushed it so low that the cocoa-farmers would take it no longer, and stopped all supplies. The British imperial government was forced to appoint a commission of inquiry; eventually this led to buying arrangements which were less exploitative. Though not a directly political movement, the hold-up brought confidence to those who were pushing for political change. The value of mass action was proved.

Elsewhere, the same trend was at work. In Tunisia, impatient with the polite talk of the old Destour, young intellectuals led by Habib Bourghiba (born in 1903) broke away in 1934 and formed the New-Destour, once again with ideas close to those of the NYM and WAYL. In Algeria the *Etoile Nord-Africaine* went from strength to strength under Messali Hadj. When it was banned by the French in 1937, a new party took its place, the *Parti du Peuple Algérien* (PPA). Morocco followed later, with the emergence at the end of 1943 of the *Istiqlal* (Independence) party of Moroccan nationalism.

In Kenya, too, the trend towards national political union saw the development of the Kikuyu Central Association (KCA), as well as effective strike action by newly formed trade unions in Mombasa. All these were banned or repressed at the outbreak of war in 1939, but they led the way to the emergence of Kenyan nationalism after 1945.

Defend Ethiopia!

The shock in the middle 1930s of fascist Italy's aggression (see p. 59) spurred the new men and their parties to fresh efforts. 'To a great extent', the Ghanaian historian S.K.B. Asante has told us, 'the Ethiopian question played a part in awakening a new generation of West African nationalists.'

It helped to create 'a new awareness of Europe's growing strangle-hold on Africa'; and this 'sowed the seeds of nationalism' more widely than before.

As a strategy for self-defence and for winning anti-colonial change, nationalism was developing in many parts of Africa. But the effect of Ethiopia's suffering was clearest in British West Africa, which had more liberty and more African newspapers. Many protests were organised. Especially active were the Nigerian Azikiwe and the Nigeria-based Pan-Africanist, Duse Mohamed Ali (1867–1944). In the Gold Coast, Wallace-Johnson launched an Ethiopia Defence Committee. Expelled in 1937, he went to London and, together with Caribbean activists C.L.R. James and George Padmore, organised an International African Service Bureau (IASB) with useful results.

A sense of outrage was widespread. The students of Fourah Bay College called for a day of mourning. Masses of ordinary people attended protest meetings. Even behind the 'walls of silence' of the Portuguese colonies, the news brought anger to people who, there, could not openly speak their minds.

The movement to support Ethiopia encouraged the nationalists; it also gave a new impulse to the ideas of Pan-Africanism. The NYM Charter, for example, was partly a reaction to the Italian fascist invasion. Chief H.O. Davies of the NYM was among those who now felt, as he said later, that 'we were against not only the Italians, but the whole system of imperialism and colonialism'. Reaching Kwame Nkrumah in London, news of the invasion found the future Ghana leader 'praying that the day might come when I could play my part in bringing about the downfall of such a system'.

At home and overseas: new rallying points

Many currents of African thought and action flowed into this rising tide of nationalism. Events and influences overseas reinforced them; and we have noted some of these. Another derived from the influence of young men and women who had gone overseas for the education they could not get at home. They were not many: even in 1932, there were in France only twenty-one students from tropical Africa, and not many more in Britain. There was none at all in Belgium, and the merest handful in Italy and Portugal.

Few though they were, those in Britain and France made themselves heard. In Britain, this was partly through the West African Students' Union (WASU), formed in London in 1925 by the Nigerian Ladipo Solanke (1884–1958) with the help of the Sierra Leonean Bankole-Bright and the moral support of the Gold Coast leader, Casely Hayford. WASU was under colonial supervision, and could not act directly. But its London hostel proved a useful meeting-place for discussions about the future. Later, Africans in Britain found a more effective means of action through the IASB (see p. 77).

Africans in the French colonies found protest in this period both difficult and dangerous. Some of them, such as the notable Dahomey (Benin) thinker Louis Hunkanrin (1887–1964), suffered much colonial persecution and were obliged to go into hiding or to accept exile. Hunkanrin himself was nonetheless able to attend the Pan-African Congress held during 1921 in London, Brussels and Paris. Others went to Paris and stayed there, finding the political atmosphere less oppressive than at home. Prominent among those who were politically active in Paris during the 1920s were another Dahomeyan called Touvalou Huénou (1887–1925), and the Senegalese Lamine Senghor (1889–1927), who should not be confused with the later Senegalese president of the same name, mentioned below. A third was the Algerian leader Messali Hadj. Other men followed them during the 1930s, notably the Soudanese (Malian) Tiémoko Garan Kouyaté (*c.*1900–1942), and the Senegalese Leopold Sedar Senghor (1906–).

These men, and others like them, found friends and allies among European liberals, socialists, and communists; some turned to journalism and wrote vivid articles in Paris-based African newspapers such as the *Cri des Nègres*. They acquired experience of European political ideas, and, through the communists, learned about the meaning and history of the Russian revolution of 1917. Among pro-African organisations active in the 1920s and 1930s were the leftwing *Union Inter-Coloniale* and the *League Against Imperialism*. These were support organisations which helped African activists, when overseas, to win useful contacts and political experience. A few individuals went to the USA for higher education. Among these were Nnamdi Azikiwe and other young Nigerians, the Ghanaian Kwame Nkrumah, the Malawian Kamuzu Banda. All were to play a leading part in their own nationalist movements in the years that followed the Second World War.

At home, as all this developed, the anti-colonial aspects of the Second World War came in to add their influence. In Nigeria, 1944 saw the launching of the first of the big nationalist parties of later years, the National Council of Nigeria and the Cameroons (NCNC), with Macaulay as president and Azikiwe as general secretary. The older nationalism had asked only for small advances, but this new one asked for much more. Azikiwe sketched its demands during 1944 in his Lagos-published *Political Blueprint of Nigeria*, writing that:

> we who live in this blessed country of Nigeria know that until we are in
> control of political power, we would continue to be the footstool of imperialist

nations . . . We are fed up with being governed as a crown colony . . . We are nauseated by the existence of an untrammeled bureaucracy which is a challenge to our manhood . . .

There were other such moves elsewhere. Once Somalia was liberated in 1941 from Italian colonial rulers, its political spokesmen began to organise; and for a time the British military government in Somalia allowed them to do this. In 1943 they formed the Somali Youth League (SYL). A year earlier, in the Sudan, the National Unionist Party (*Ashiqqa*) had emerged under Ismail al-Azhari; and in 1944 Sudanese students in Cairo founded the Sudan Movement of National Liberation (SMNL). As a communist organisation, the SMNL was made illegal; but it led to the later formation of the Sudan Communist Party, among the first of its kind to be formed in Africa after the launching of the South African Communist Party in 1921.

These are only a few examples; new men and new parties were widely at work, even while they often differed among themselves on issues of analysis and strategy. Everywhere there was talk of a fresh start after the war was over. 'After the war, what?' asked a headline in the Tanganyika African newspaper *Kwetu* (*Our Place*), in May 1942, and its editor, Erica Fiah, followed with another question:

> Will the African native be allowed a better place and a little more voice and responsibility in the administration of his country, or will he continue to remain a clerk, last on the list, as he has always been?

Three years later, in 1945, a Gold Coast soldier in India wrote home to the nationalist thinker and writer Kobina Sekyi, 'We have made up our minds,' he told Sekyi, 'to help build the country, free from all oppression, and in our oath to the Lord, we shall never miss you [forget you] in all our plans to build our motherland . . .' Though far away in India, he wrote that 'we are discovering the truths of Wallace-Johnson's writings: and I would to God that He gives us more Wallace-Johnsons when we come back home . . .'

And so it was to be. By 1945 the whole scene was set for dramatic changes.

CHAPTER EIGHT
Colonialism in Crisis

Peace opened in 1945 on a world very different from that of 1939: different in the balance of world power, different in the condition of the colonies. The colonised peoples now had a chance of making progress.

Big anti-colonial struggles, and then struggles for independence, soon began by peaceful means wherever peaceful means proved possible; otherwise, they began by violence. In the next part of this book we shall follow these always difficult and sometimes heroic struggles against the empire-owning countries and their friends. But first we need to look at the condition of the colonial systems as they emerged from the strains and changes of the Second World War.

As we saw in Chapter 6, while Britain and France were much weakened by the war, the USA at once became a 'super-power'. For the USA had both won the war and become much richer because of the war. Its reserves of money were now enormous; its powers seemed to be without limit. But although the USA was the ally of Britain and France, America's leaders had little wish to help the British and the French to keep their colonies. On the contrary, leading Americans believed that the old pre-war empires should be dispensed with. Instead, the colonised peoples should have political independence, while, at the same time, becoming part of a new international world system under indirect American leadership or influence and in line with America's national interests.

Not yet strong, but soon to become another 'super-power', there was also the USSR. Though from an ideological standpoint contrary to that of the USA, the USSR was also against the old pre-war empires. Yet its influence in Africa, exercised through a few African communists or through other African revolutionaries, was still very weak. (Later, through trade agreements, financial aid, and diplomatic relations, Soviet influence became a little stronger. But this could not begin to happen till the 1960s.) The USSR also wished that Africa should change in line with the national interests of the USSR.

All these developments pushed Britain and France on to the defensive. The same happened to the small colonial powers: Belgium, Portugal, Spain; while Italy lost its colonies altogether in the Second World War, just as Germany had lost its colonies in the First.

Although the colonial grip on Africa was, in fact, beginning to loosen, there was still one country where independent minority government was more firmly in control. Racist South Africa, as we shall see later, became stronger as a result of the war.

THE COLONIAL SYSTEM UNDERMINED

Weakened though they were, the colonial powers in 1945 still thought they had enough strength to keep their colonies for a long time ahead, and, outside West Africa, for the rest of the twentieth century or longer still. In West Africa, however, British colonial specialists had already begun to think that the consequences of the war, even while Britain and her allies were going to win it (as became clear after 1942), might well impose a need for constitutional advances in favour of African self-government.

Although African nationalism before about 1947 was still a practically unknown political force, the more liberally minded or mentally alert thinkers in London began to see that concessions to demands for African self-government might become unavoidable, at least in the non-settler colonies. There were those who argued that some measure of political power should be contemplated for chiefs and notables. There were others who thought that continued British control 'at the centre' should be made to go together with the development of local and municipal government 'at the periphery'. Above all there were those, increasingly influential as it would prove, who believed that colonial rule should now find ways in Africa of promoting a 'responsible middle class' to which political responsibility, soon or late, could be 'safely' transferred.

Here was one of the programmatic origins of what was later on to be labelled 'neo-colonialism': the handing over of power to African groups and persons who could be relied upon to safeguard the interests, at least the economic interests, of the former empire-owners. Dominant 'middle-class' interests in Europe, in other words, were to be defended and reinforced, in any prospective decolonising process, by the promotion of subordinate 'middle-class' interests in Africa.

We shall see how far this was to come about, and why it was to come about. Meanwhile it should be held in mind that these early thoughts about 'decolonisation' – the word itself had yet to be invented – foresaw an extremely *slow* programme of change. For the white-settler colonies, moreover, this programme likewise expected that decisive political power would pass to white minorities, not to black majorities. Even when it had at last become clear that power would have to be passed to black majorities in the settler colonies, the timetable remained cautious. As late as 1959, when all the old assumptions about continued colonial rule had passed away, the British government and its East African colonial governors considered that independence under black majority rule could not come to Tanganyika before 1970 (it actually came in 1962), while Uganda and Kenya, they forecast, would have to wait until about 1975 (Uganda became independent in 1961, Kenya in 1963).

Emerging from the disasters of national defeat in the war, the political leaders of France were at first ready for large constitutional advances in their African colonies, but then had second thoughts. In the end these second thoughts were reversed, in favour of African progress, only by African political pressures, as well as by the fact that major British concessions had already begun to take effect in neighbouring British colonies: in the Gold Coast during 1951, as we shall see, and soon elsewhere in West Africa.

Generally, then, as the war receded into recent history, the British and after them the French were beginning to get ready to meet some African demands. But their idea was to give way by small steps that would long delay the coming of independence (see also Chapter 9). Outside West Africa and most of the trusteeship territories under UN supervision, none of the colonial powers was ready to give way to any African demand. In the settler colonies, the white minorities now thought they held the eventual as well as the immediate future in their hands.

The rise of African nationalism was going to change all this. Meanwhile another pressure was also at work in the background. This was the real condition of the colonised peoples when peace came. For reasons we have discussed, it was a condition of poverty and social upheaval; by 1945, as was gradually recognised even by convinced imperialists, this meant that all the colonial systems were deep in trouble.

Half a century had passed since the chief colonial invasions. About a quarter of a century had gone by since the last big campaigns of 'pacification'; and the colonial systems had since become firmly planted within their colonial frontiers. As with great historical processes, all this produced results that were often contradictory for the distant as well as the immediate future of the peoples caught up in them.

Let us take, for example, the field of public health. The richer colonial powers – Britain, France, Belgium – campaigned to some extent against tropical fevers and diseases, whether by inoculating people or by other means. Colonial hospitals and clinics helped to reduce the number of children who died at birth or soon after. From about this time, or late in the 1940s, the size of most African populations was found to be growing less slowly than before.

This new wealth in people could be a big gain for the continent. But it could be a gain only on condition that these bigger populations could be fed, and could find jobs, housing, and other necessities. Above all, more people meant that there had to be more food. And this was where the chief trouble came. For the colonial systems now revealed that they were generally unable to increase the growth of food-production in line with the growth of population.

Why was this? The biggest part of the answer is that the colonial systems all wanted to produce more crops for export. They had succeeded rather well in doing this; but the more they succeeded, the less land and labour were left for producing food. In Algeria, to offer one example among many, the French took more and more fertile land for producing wine to send across the Mediterranean to France. But the land they took was land on which Algerians, before, had grown an abundance of food for themselves. So the Algerians had less food, just at the time when their numbers were growing bigger. It has been calculated that the amount of food in cereals, available to an average Algerian person in 1945, was little more than half the amount available in 1900.

Many peoples who grew crops for export began to suffer from a shortage of home-grown food: in the cocoa-rich Gold Coast, in Nigeria, in many of the settler colonies. Here and there they gained from better public health. But everywhere they lost by having less to eat, or by having to pay higher prices for food in shorter supply. And the loss began to be bigger than the gain. In Nigeria, said a report of 1947 to the British parliament, 'over 20 million people are living on an agricultural subsistence of a very low order, and malnutrition [hunger] and disease are widespread.' In other colonies, notably the Belgian Congo, official reports pointed to the same deepening poverty.

Yet the colonial powers, though they knew these facts, still believed that the colonies must help Europe to feed itself. Big efforts were made, after 1945, to export still more than before. Tanganyika, for example, had suffered a famine in its central region during the Second World War; many had died of hunger. Yet the biggest project now undertaken by the British authorities was an ambitious scheme to clear bush to grow groundnuts for export, not to grow food for local consumption. It proved a disastrous failure, and cost the British a loss of £35,870,000. But it was not the only scheme of that kind. Another, the Yundum egg scheme in The Gambia, failed at a cost of £900,000.

Such projects for producing food or other crops for export to Europe continued to be called 'colonial development and welfare'. But for whom was the development, and for whom the welfare?

Other results of the colonial systems enlarged a crisis that was now plain to see.

Effects of migrant labour

The steady increase of migrant labour in many colonies was one of these results. Especially in central and southern Africa, and to a lesser extent in French West Africa, bad consequences were already obvious in the 1930s. From Nyasaland (Malawi), for example, large numbers of men were working for long periods in Southern Rhodesia (Zimbabwe) and South Africa. A Nyasaland government inquiry sounded a note of alarm as early as 1935:

> The whole fabric of the old order of society is undermined when 30 per cent to 60 per cent of the able-bodied men are absent at one time. It is easy to criticise that old order, but it worked: the community was stable; and there was give and take [within the community]. Emigration destroys the old order, but offers nothing to take its place. The family-community is threatened with complete dissolution.

The warning went unheeded. By 1946 there were more than 200,000 migrant workers employed in mines and plantations in Southern Rhodesia; of these, 62 per cent came from Nyasaland and Northern Rhodesia. One out of every three African workers in Southern Rhodesia was from outside the country; but their families, for the most part, were still at home in their villages in Nyasaland and Northern Rhodesia. An even larger number of migrant workers from several colonies in central and southern Africa were employed in South Africa.

With their men away on work contracts lasting for a year at a time, or longer, villages decayed. Wherever forced labour was still much used, the decay was greater still. In 1945, a Belgian Catholic missionary, Father van Wing, wrote that village people in Ruanda-Urundi during the Second World War 'were treated without mercy. One term of forced labour followed another.' It was the same in the Belgian Congo, but the end of the war did not end that treatment. Back in 1928 a government commission had urged that women, old people, and children in the Belgian Congo should no longer be forced to build and maintain roads. Yet, as late as 1947 we find the same commission still having to urge the very same thing, commenting:

There can be no doubt that it is the forced labour services on roads which are the most unpopular, either because they mean long journeys to work, or else because they mean painful toil, often even for mothers of young children and for pregnant women.

After 1945, more and more village people left for the towns in the hope of finding a better life. Even children left, often on their own. As another Belgian missionary wrote from the Belgian Congo:

> At the beginning of October 1952, I was making my usual tour to register children for the regional primary schools. At Makalelu Tseke, a school which serves about 25 villages, I had called for 147 boys who were now old enough to begin their first year, I was much surprised to find that of these 147 boys, 34 had gone to Léopoldville [now Kinshasa, the country's capital]; yet not one of them was old enough to have to pay [and so try to escape] tax.

Already the colonial towns of Africa had begun to grow as village people left to escape an increasing poverty. Now these towns grew much faster. Several as much as doubled in size during the Second World War. Dar es Salaam, the capital of Tanganyika, was one of them; Léopoldville (Kinshasa), the capital of the Belgian Congo, was another; there were many more (see map 6).

The towns expand

Was this a gain? Living in town was a kind of modernisation, a way of getting into the 'modern' world. Villages were backward, often boring. Towns, by contrast, could be thought to have bright lights, piped water, better wages, even some buses and cars. Yet these expanding towns had few or none of those things. The colonial rulers did not want this flight from the countryside. They wanted families to stay in villages, and men to be available for migrant labour. They did little or nothing to provide houses and services for the multitudes who came.

So the new arrivals had to live in shacks and huts they built for themselves from flattened-out cans, canvas, or whatever they could find. Seldom was there piped water; often there was no electric light. Worse still, there were too few jobs. A few lucky newcomers might be able to buy a second-hand truck; most could not afford a bicycle. Even those who found jobs got little money. In the settler colonies, for example, the rule in towns was to pay wages to each worker as though he was unmarried. If he was married, it was held, then his family in the rural area could provide for itself.

Getting worried about these bad conditions in the towns, the British government in London appointed a royal commission, in 1953, to find out the facts in British East Africa. Its members took a lot of evidence;

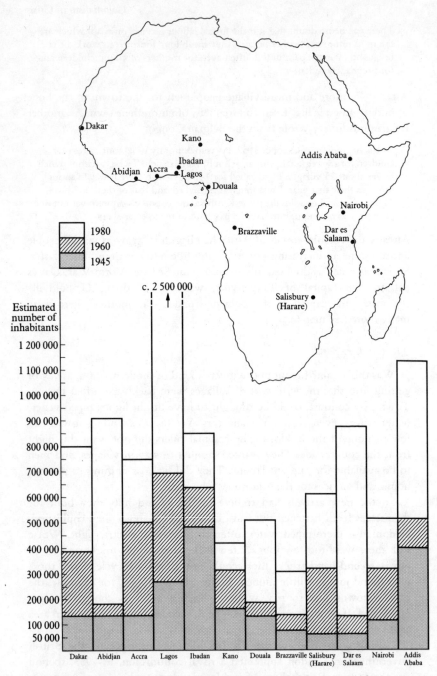

Map 6 Urban growth in Africa, 1945–80: a sample of 12 important cities

and the more evidence they took, the more worried they became. Here is what they found in the city of Nairobi, capital of Kenya, and reported in 1955:

> The wages of the majority of African workers are too low to enable them to obtain accommodation [housing] which is adequate to any standard. The high cost of housing relative to wages is, in itself a cause of overcrowding, because housing is shared to lighten the cost. This, with the high cost of food in towns, makes family life impossible for the majority.

Just pause for a moment to think about the last seven words of that quotation. Wages were so low in the capital city of Kenya, after half a century of colonial rule, that family life had become impossible for the majority of Africans living there. Could that royal commission have spoken more clearly about the crisis of the colonial system? Better wages were sometimes paid elsewhere; but also worse wages. Tens of thousands of migrant workers worked every year in the rich gold mines of South Africa. These mines made large profits, but largely because of cheap labour. In 1910, when the Union of South Africa was formed, mining wages for Africans were low. Forty years later, those wages were lower still in real terms: in terms, that is, of what they could buy. Not until the 1970s was there to be any improvement in the wages paid to black – as distinct from white – mineworkers in South Africa, and even then only because of successful black action to win improvement.

Of course there were pockets of some prosperity. Cocoa-farmers in the Gold Coast and Nigeria now got rather better prices than before. Chagga farmers in northern Tanganyika did well with coffee. Mouride producers of groundnuts in Senegal could make good money. But most rural people had no share in these gains. Here and there, workers in new industries were able to unite in trade unions, and improve their wages. Yet these, too, were a minority of industrial workers.

All this was part of the social crisis of the colonial systems. It formed the challenging but difficult ground on which the new nationalists had to take their stand. Utterly inadequate educational systems were another part of this social crisis.

Colonial schools: new source of anti-colonial criticism

An Africa without modern schools and teaching could never make progress; everyone agreed about that. But the provision of this kind of education ran into three big obstacles. One problem was that money for schools and teaching was always in short supply. In every colony, most children had no chance of going to school because there were no schools to go to. By 1945, even in the less backward colonies, the proportion of children who could go to school was smaller than one in every ten. The ability to read and write was still a rare skill. In the more backward colonies – those of Portugal after 1945 – the proportion of Africans who had been able to learn this skill was smaller than one in every hundred.

A second obstacle was the poverty of parents. Few could afford school fees, books, clothes, or journey-money if getting to school required a bus journey. Even if they sent their children to school, those sons and daughters might seldom stay for more than one year, or perhaps for two: they were wanted for work at home. The situation in Northern Rhodesia (Zambia) was typical of most colonies. In this copper-rich colony in 1942, there were said to be fewer than 90,000 school-students (for a total African population, then, of about 2 million people). Yet only 3,000 of these were in the fifth year, and only 35 were in 'early secondary' classes. Of the few children who went to school, most stayed too short a time to be able to learn much of use.

A third obstacle was the nature of colonial education. When young people managed to get to school, and stay at school, what could they learn? The elements of a little literacy and religion were the main subjects taught; in the first year or so, they were usually the only subjects taught. Later years included some history and geography, and perhaps one or two other subjects. But all these subjects were taught from a racist standpoint: tending to show that whatever came from Europe was good or useful, and that whatever came from Africa was either the reverse or not worth studying. In history, for example, British colonial schools taught about British kings and heroes, French colonial schools taught about French kings and heroes, and the smaller empires did the same. The general assumption behind such teaching was that Africans lacked the capacity to solve their own problems, and Europeans must show them how.

By 1945, however, a lot of people began to see that there was something wrong with this lesson. The economic depression of the 1930s and the Second World War had taught a different lesson: that Europeans had not been able to solve even their own problems, let alone the problems of Africa. And from this different lesson there came a new mood of questioning, of criticism. It was the point at which, after 1945, schools which were intended to teach students to accept and even to admire the colonial systems began to turn into schools where students became increasingly critical of those systems.

It was natural that African teachers should often take the lead in this growing trend of independent thought. Much as in the black American community at an earlier period – and black American leadership was now increasingly influential among literate Africans – thoughtful teachers began to question and reject the obedient orthodoxies of official textbooks and attitudes. They sought instead for ways of recalling and then of teaching the values of Africa's own life and history. From that kind of search it was only a step to the promotion of interest in the wider issues of anti-colonial politics; and here was a chief reason for the emergence of the Nigerian Youth Movement (see p. 75) and of Wallace-Johnson's West African Youth League (see pp. 75–76).

The same trend took shape elsewhere. In Kenya, an independent schools movement had been formed as early as 1929. It wanted to get away from the racist lessons of colonial schools, and promote, instead, a respect for African dignity and history. Strong among the Kikuyu of central Kenya, where colonial racism was also strong because of the white settlers who lived there, this Kikuyu Independent Schools Association (KISA) helped to win wide support, later on, for the politics of nationalism and for the Kenya African National Union (KANU).

FROM ELITIST PARTIES TO MASS MOVEMENTS

Much that happened in the fifteen years from the start of the Depression to the end of the Second World War – from 1930 to 1945 – helped to widen black peoples' understanding of the power-systems of the modern world. We can say that these years, gradually, produced a change in mental scale.

Many people now lived outside the small world of village or lonely farm. Often they lived in a harder world of towns, low wages, the search for jobs. But it was also a bigger world of new things and new ideas. And so people had to learn how best to live and work in this bigger world. That meant, with much else, thinking about politics.

With this change of scale, the narrow nationalism of earlier years had to change as well. Less and less, after 1945, were anti-colonial politics discussed only in the private houses of lawyers, clergymen, doctors or chiefs. More and more, political talk moved out to the verandah. Then this outward development of discussion moved further. Anti-colonial politics stepped off the verandah and went into the street, into many streets, and into the rural areas.

Here was a second change of scale, reflecting the first. It marked an end of the small world of élitist politics and parties – of politics and parties for the educated or otherwise privileged few – and a beginning of a much bigger world of mass politics and parties for large numbers of people.

Leaders could now look for a much wider audience; more and more, they found it. Some had thought of doing this in the 1930s, and a few, like Azikiwe and Wallace-Johnson, had really done it. Now the search for wide support became general wherever the colonial rulers would allow it. Only the British and French rulers allowed it, if cautiously, but they had most of the colonies. People in their colonies could give a lead for people in other colonies, like those of Belgium and Portugal, where all political action stayed forbidden.

The new mass parties, at this stage, were of several kinds. Very few of them had any tight organisation or list of members; nearly all were movements rather than organised parties. Some of these movements called for the united action of all the people in a colony; these were movements or parties of national union. Others looked for their main support only from a single people in their colony; these were ethnic or regional movements and parties, sometimes called tribal parties.

Others had a strong religious loyalty. Such, for instance, was the Somali Youth League. This was a national party which was also an ethnic party, because nearly all the people of Somalia are Somalis. It was also a party with a strong religious loyalty to Islam, a unifying force in this case because nearly all Somalis are Muslims.

Yet all these parties operated in much the same ways. Talented or privileged men took the lead and appealed for mass support. Often persecuted, such parties had to have a loose form of organisation. Besides this, most people were not yet familiar with modern ways of political action. They needed time to learn. It was largely through this process of learning modern politics that the great engine of mass pressure was set in motion.

Growth of workers' action: trade unions

Wage-workers in colonial towns began to organise themselves into trade unions, so as to improve their wages and conditions of work, even before the Second World War: in Tunis, for example, as early as the 1920s; in Kenya's great seaport of Mombasa during the 1930s; and in towns in other colonies. But all the pre-war trade unions or workers' associations met with colonial repression; they could make little headway.

During the Second World War – and here was another of its anti-colonial consequences – the British decided that they would allow trade unions in colonies where trade unions had been previously forbidden; and post-war French governments, emerging after 1945, did the same. The smaller colonial systems continued to forbid Africans to form trade unions. So did the racist South Africans. A big strike by African mineworkers in the South African gold-mines, in 1946, was ruthlessly put down by armed police with great violence.

But new trade unions could appear in the British and French colonies.

They could also act with success. A very successful railway workers' strike in French West Africa, during 1946, sustained a new power and new discipline. A trade union federation for Tunisia was formed by Ferhat Hached in 1945, but there things went differently. Passing to strike action in 1947, Tunisian trade unionists lost 32 killed and some 200 wounded at the hands of the colonial police or army; Hached himself was later killed by racist political murder.

Different, again, was the situation in Northern Rhodesia (Zambia). Strong strike action there by African workers in mines and railways in 1945 led to the formation, three years after, of a powerful African mineworkers' union, and of other unions. Those are only three examples, among many, of a new workers' ability to act together. The same occurred in Kenya, Tanganyika (Tanzania), Sierra Leone and elsewhere.

Struggling against colonial wages and conditions of work, the new trade unions could not stand aside from modern nationalism. They became part of it. In Northern Rhodesia, for example, the new African mineworkers' union gave solid support to the politics of national independence. Some of the most forceful leaders of the new unions – Siaka Stevens in Sierra Leone, Sékou Touré in Guinea, Tom Mboya in Kenya, to mention only three – became political leaders. Here was more evidence of the growth of mass support for the new parties of nationalism and, at least indirectly, for the black independence at which these parties aimed.

SUMMARY
Agencies of Modernising Change, 1930–1945

Two kinds of agency or influence for modernising change were at work in these years. One kind consisted of positive agencies which encouraged people to change their ideas and hopes in response to them. The other kind consisted of negative agencies: people changed in reaction against them.

Among the positive agencies we have discussed were:

1 A new Pan-African patriotism inspired by protest against the fascist Italian invasion of Ethiopia.
2 Development of associations, co-operatives, and social groups producing crops for export, and their efforts to improve prices (for example, the Gold Coast cocoa hold-up).
3 The wartime promise of the Atlantic Charter.
4 Encouragement from successes of Asian nationalism.
5 The anti-colonial ideas of ex-servicemen.
6 The weakening, because of the war, of the chief colonial powers; and the post-war influence of the USA.
7 Changes of scale in the thought and action of uneducated as well as educated persons.
8 New readiness of political leaders to look for mass support.
9 Formation and militancy of new trade unions.

Among the negative agencies were:

1 Hardships of the Great Depression of the 1930s.
2 Other hardships imposed during the Second World War.
3 Flight to the towns: low wages, bad housing, jobs hard to find.
4 Colonial repression of nationalist and trade union protest.

PART THREE

The Nationalists Win Through

PART THREE considers questions arising from the growth and success of African nationalist movements, in freeing their countries from colonial rule, during the years after the Second World War. Among these questions are:

Chapter Nine   The Conditions of Decolonisation
- How did British colonial policy begin to change after the Second World War?
- In which kind of colonies did peaceful pressures fail to win progress?
- In which ways did 'world factors' influence the conditions of decolonisation?
- Liberia and Ethiopia were not directly involved in the process of decolonisation. Why was this? What happened there?

Chapter Ten   Raising National Flags: North-East Africa
- What was agreed by the Anglo-Egyptian Treaties of 1922 and 1936?
- What happened in Egypt in 1952, and with what consequences?
- How did Sudan become independent?
- What happened to the Somalis, and the Eritreans?

Chapter Eleven   Libya and the Maghrib
- What led to the Islamic Republic of Libya?
- Which influences led to the independence of Tunisia, of Morocco?
- Why was the struggle for independence especially harsh in Algeria?
- How did the Algerians win?

Chapter Twelve   South of the Sahara: French Colonies
- What was the Brazzaville Declaration? The French Union? The RDA? The 'enabling Act' of 1956?
- How did Sékou Touré oppose de Gaulle?
- What was the French plan for indirect control?
- Who was Um Nyobé? What was the UPC?
- What events led up to Madagascan independence?

Chapter Thirteen   British West Africa
- What were Britain's 'small steps' in Nigeria?
- How did Nigerian regionalism take shape? With what results?
- What was the UGCC? The CPP? How did they differ?
- What did Ghana's independence mean for the rest of colonial Africa?
- How did Sierra Leone and The Gambia win independence?

Chapter Fourteen   East and Central Africa: British Settler Colonies
- What was the most important difference between Britain's colonies in West Africa and in East and Central Africa?
- What was 'closer union'?
- How did TANU develop? Why was TANU successful?
- What happened in Zanzibar before and after independence?
- What stood in the way of Ugandan national unity?
- Which were Kenya's chief problems? What was KAU?
- What led to the Kenya Emergency? What happened during and after it?
- What was the Central African Federation, and why was it dissolved?

- What did the Malawi Congress Party achieve for Malawi? UNIP for Zambia?
- Why was the Rhodesia Front formed? What did it do?
- How did Zimbabwe's war of liberation develop, and end?

Chapter Fifteen   In Other Empires: Belgian, Portuguese, Spanish
- Who was Patrice Lumumba? Why was he important?
- What was the legacy of colonial disunity in Ruanda and Burundi?
- When were PAIGC, MPLA, FRELIMO formed? Why did they have to launch wars of liberation, and with what results?

Chapter Sixteen   The 1980s and 1990s: Unfinished Business
- Was the *apartheid* regime in South Africa now moving towards accepting democracy for the non-white South Africans, whether Black, Coloured or Asian? What were the plans of that regime?
- What exactly does *apartheid* mean in practice?
- What were or are SASO, Black Consciousness, the Soweto rising, the ANC, the UDF? What did, or do, they stand for?
- Why did the South African armed forces invade Angola, and how were they defeated?
- Where is Namibia, and what movements there have worked for Namibian independence?

CHAPTER NINE

The Conditions of Decolonisation

The actual end of European empires in Africa, when it came, proved to be a complex and varying process. Each country added its own chapter to this story of decolonisation, an ugly but useful term which now came into use. Often these chapters were fruitful; almost as often they were also painful. All of them are important in the history of modern Africa, and they are reviewed in detail in this Part Three.

But first it will be useful to stand back from the detail, and to summarise or re-state the main trends and themes in this decisive process by which Africans, advancing out of the constraints imposed by foreign rule, began to shape their independent future.

Why did Britain, and then France, begin to consider withdrawing from some colonies? Why did they continue to refuse to withdraw from other colonies? Why did the lesser colonial powers, notably Portugal, delay or stubbornly refuse? What different methods did Africans have to use in order to win their independence? Why were there built-in limits to the amount of independence that could be won? Lastly, how have world factors reduced the progress that could be made, and what are these world factors?

A number of answers to these basic questions are given in the chapters on decolonisation that follow here. Other answers, concerning problems after independence, are considered in Part Four.

THE IMPERIALIST POWERS TAKE STOCK

We saw in Chapter 8 that the principal colonial powers were weakened by the Second World War. Britain could win against the Axis powers –

nazi Germany, fascist Italy, imperialist Japan – only at very great cost in national wealth. France had been entirely defeated; she limped from the war in ruin. Belgium had also been defeated. Italy was on the losing side, finally, and forfeited all her colonies. And although the USA was a most powerful force amongst the victorious Allies, and came out of the war with increased wealth, it had no interest in helping to maintain the empires of its business rivals.

Yet none of these external changes could alone have led to decolonisation without the pressure set in motion by the colonised peoples themselves. For although the colonial systems were deep in their own social and economic crisis, the resulting pressure was decisively strengthened by the rising tide of African nationalism which now made ever stronger demands for progressive change. So the colonial powers could hope to go on dominating Africa in the old way only with a big increase in European officials, police, armies and investment. Not only would this cost them money which they did not wish to spend, and resources which they did not wish to invest: but it also carried no guarantee of continued success.

So it became wise to think about how to dominate Africa in a new way. Looking at this difficult problem after 1945, the British had already begun to see that they might do well to retreat before the oncoming tide of nationalism: at least in West Africa, as well as in some other colonies where there were few or no British settlers. If they gave way in the political field, cautiously, slowly, they could hope to safeguard their interests in the economic field.

These economic interests were also undergoing an important change. More and more, after 1945, they became the new interests of major companies or corporations which began to operate in many different countries and in different colonial systems. This had happened to some extent in earlier years, but then the companies had been much smaller and more limited in their influence. Now the biggest corporations, the oil corporations among them, had grown into veritable giants, and their operations were practically worldwide. This new mode and scale of operation represented a further development of the world capitalist system. Recognising this change, people began to call them 'multi-national' companies, because they operated in many national territories, or else 'trans-national' companies, because they operated across many frontiers.

These big corporations – notably the largest, which were American – naturally wanted to operate in every country, or in every colony, where they could make good profits. But the old colonial empires, each guarding or at least trying to guard its own monopoly in its own colonies, got in the way of the new 'multi-nationals'. So the interests of the new corporations began to diverge from the interests of the old colonial monopolies. It began to be understood that the interests of the 'multi-nationals' lay in weakening or even destroying the old monopolies. This added a new pressure, even if indirectly and behind the scenes, towards getting rid of the political controls which safeguarded the old monopolies, and, to that extent, towards strengthening the position of African nationalists who were demanding political independence.

What was happening with this development of multi-national or 'trans-national' capitalism, in short, was that dominant business interests now saw that political control of a direct kind, colonial control, was no longer useful to, but could often be an obstruction to, the continued extraction of wealth from Africa. Weak African economies could continue to be milked by strong non-African economies without any of the costly and often hated apparatus of colonial government. It would therefore be better for the multi-national corporations if these weak African economies were endowed with their own political sovereignty: provided, of course, that these economies were securely tied into the multi-national network. The big US corporations saw this first, and led the way.

Out of this kind of calculation, as we shall see, came the great paradox of the whole anti-colonial process: political independence on one hand, but renewed and reinforced economic dependence on the other.

In West Africa, at least by 1950, the British and later on the French began to make ready to withdraw their colonial government and its political controls, naturally intending to do this in such a way as to safeguard their long-term economic interests. It was obvious, of course, that this could succeed only if newly independent countries remained within the general power of the Western or capitalist system. This, in turn, meant making political concessions of a kind that could avoid or prevent any far-reaching or revolutionary changes. It meant trying to ensure that there were built-in limits to the amount of independence that Africans could win and use. From the British and French standpoint, in short, the great need was to modernise the relationship between themselves and their colonies, and to bring that relationship into line with the requirements of the new multi-national capitalism.

This was to be part of the meaning of neo-colonialism, or new colonialism, after independence came (see also Chapter 18). It was a notably intelligent policy from the European or American standpoint, but it did not take shape all at once. The policy of creating neo-colonialism was developed gradually, and sometimes in a contradictory way, as often happens in history. Whatever one may think of its consequences for Africa, this policy has to be seen as an attempt by the principal powers to deal with their colonial crisis while, at the same time, protecting the substance of their interests – a substance, of course, that was economic much more than political. As time went on, the policy became clearer and was more consciously pursued. That this policy was going to lead into a profound economic crisis for the whole of Africa – a crisis which became visible only late in the 1970s – was of course neither understood nor intended.

Little by little, as these ideas of neo-colonialism developed, the chief powers were helped by finding African leaders who felt that they had no real alternative but to go along with these ideas. They were men who sincerely believed that Africa could progress to full independence only by successive stages in agreement with the colonial rulers, although, as well, there were others who merely looked to their own careers. They rejected a struggle for any far-reaching or revolutionary change in the relationship between their countries and Europe or America on the grounds that any such struggle was wrong, or was in any case bound to fail. There were some revolutionary thinkers, very few in number and at that time with very little influence, who thought differently. They believed that political independence on the lines of neo-colonialism would lead to a new surrender to the interests of big outside powers. It may be worth recalling what one of them wrote in 1964. The leader of the liberation movement in Portuguese Guiné (now Guinea-Bissau) and Cape Verde, Amilcar Cabral (1924–73), questioned whether the fundamental aim of the imperialist countries, in agreeing to African independence, was not to prevent:

> the enlargement of the socialist camp, liberate the reactionary forces in our countries stifled by colonialism, and enable these forces to ally themselves with the international bourgeoisie [middle class].

Only a handful of nationalists saw matters in this way, and even they did not question the nationalist strategy of pushing for political independence as a first step to further development later on. In any case it took some years for the new policy of the principal colonial powers to develop to a point where it could be widely understood. Gradually, as this development went on, the old kind of direct colonial dependence was replaced by a new kind of dependence, indirect and chiefly economic.

Could this new dependence be in any case avoided, or at least reduced? If there were strong African leaders who were nonetheless willing to become junior partners in the new multi-national economic system, were they not right and sensible? Could they, realistically, have acted in some other way, and have tried to build a new and different 'international economic order'? Was there, in those years, any real or useful alternative? These are questions for discussion. We shall return to them in Part Four.

THE DUTY OF THE NATIONALISTS

Meanwhile, during the 1950s or later, the nationalists had a prime and urgent duty to their peoples. They had to take the first steps towards liberation. These steps were to get rid of the direct and political controls of the colonial systems, throw off the racism and oppression associated with those systems, and free their countries from foreign rule. After that, and with this useful amount of freedom, a further struggle against indirect control, a struggle for a large measure of economic independence, could then begin, or could at least become possible.

The British, in these circumstances, began to move towards political concessions in West Africa. With somewhat different results, they were followed by the French; later, by the Belgians; later again, by the Spanish.

Only the Portuguese refused all concessions to the black peoples whom they ruled. Portugal's rulers were convinced that they would lose everything in Africa if they gave up their direct control. This was partly because Portugal was itself too weak and economically backward to try for a neo-colonial relationship, and partly because Portugal was ruled by a fascist-type dictatorship, which believed that Portugal's colonies were the 'glory' of Portuguese civilisation. Desperately, Portugal hung on to the last possible moment (see Chapter 15) and had to be thrown out by force.

Peaceful pressures or counter-violence?

Africa's nationalists had therefore to face a wide variety of situations. In British West Africa (see Chapter 13), they were usually able to make progress by peaceful pressures. The same was largely true in many of the French colonies (see Chapter 12), and sometimes elsewhere as well.

Yet peaceful pressures never worked in colonies of large European settlement. There the nationalists could make progress only by opposing the violence of the colonial systems with the use of their own counter-violence.

These differing conditions of decolonisation, as we shall find in Part Four, greatly affected the individual countries after independence was finally won. In a number of ex-colonies it proved possible, and sometimes easy, for the former colonial power to impose neo-colonial limits on independence, and, at least in the early years, to decide or direct the policies of the newly independent governments. Some of these governments, as for example in the Central African Republic, became little more than instruments of continued foreign rule.

But wherever colonised peoples were obliged to use their own counter-violence against the violence of the colonial systems, the later imposition of neo-colonial limits became much more difficult to achieve. These peoples could win their wars of independence only by destroying the colonial systems within their countries. In doing so, they greatly weakened the neo-colonial threat. That was a compensation they could set against the sufferings of colonial warfare.

INHERITED PROBLEMS

Africa's struggles for anti-colonial liberation produced, in any case, great and irreversible changes. They signalled the continent's entry into the modern world. They brought memorable victories, even if they also brought setbacks and defeats.

The setbacks and defeats have been caused, for the most part, by inherited problems that could not be avoided. Part Four will discuss these problems. They were partly the legacy of the colonial systems, and partly the legacy of Africa's own history. They were partly the problems of great world factors: for example, the nature of the international economic system and its inequalities between rich countries and poor countries; the development of the multi-national corporations and their huge economic power to extract wealth; and the growing conflict between 'West' and 'East' (that is, between the capitalist world-bloc and the communist world-bloc). All these factors affected the amount of independence that could be won, and they should be kept in mind.

TWO PARTIAL EXCEPTIONS: LIBERIA, ETHIOPIA

In the history of decolonisation there were two partial African exceptions: two countries which were not colonies, but which nonetheless failed to win a real independence. It will be convenient to say a little about them here.

Liberia: a false independence

Founded in 1822 by 12,000 free American black people who emigrated then and a little later to the unknown shores of West Africa, the republic of Liberia has understandably enjoyed a special place in the feelings of black Americans. But the feelings have often been contradictory ones.

At the outset, a majority of free American blacks opposed the plan to send American blacks 'back to Africa'. They insisted that 'America is more our country than it is the whites'. It was built by the sweat of our labour.' Against this a minority was ready to accept the plan, replying that: 'We love our country of America and its liberties if we could share them. But our freedom is partial, and we have no hope that it will ever be otherwise.' And so the 'black star republic' was launched.

Its early life was indeed a hard one. The settlers endured with great difficulty on land at Cape Mesurado where they founded Monrovia, their pioneer home. Not many African-Americans came to join the early ones. And whereas the anti-slaving warships of the British Navy freed some 40,000 African captives from slaving ships heading across the Atlantic, and released all these in Sierra Leone, Liberia's sister settlement, the American navy brought to Monrovia no more than 2,000 captives released from slave-ships (or 're-captives' as these rescued persons were curiously called).

From early years, in consequence, the Americo-Liberians were many fewer than the Creoles of Sierra Leone who were the descendants of 're-captives'. This meant that they were further removed from an understanding of the African peoples among whom they had settled, and whom they increasingly despised.

Determined to be Liberia's ruling group, the Americo-Liberians were obliged to accept a large dependence on their friends and backers in the USA. Only in 1841 could they elect one of their own number, named Joseph Roberts, as their first-time governor of Liberia. Only in 1847 could the Americo-Liberians declare their country to be an independent republic under a flag and constitution of its own. By this time Liberia had begun to develop a useful trading economy. But European partition of the rest of West Africa proved hostile to Liberia's further development of trade with African neighbours. Liberia's dependence on the USA became greater.

This dependence was again reinforced in 1926 by Liberian concessions, for big-scale rubber plantations, to the American Firestone Corporation. Some effort was made by Liberia's greatest political figure and long-time president, William Tubman (1895–1971), to broaden Liberia's economic links with the industrial world. This 'open-door' policy had its successes, but the basic source of trouble remained intact. This trouble lay in the continued ambition of the Americo-Liberian group to keep all power and privilege in their own hands at the cost of the majority of Liberians.

Tubman tried to deal with this rooted trouble by a policy of 'unification' that gave votes and parliamentary seats to the inhabitants of the 'tribal interior' who provided most of Liberia's taxes and labour. In 1947 an amendment to the 1847 constitution gave votes to all adults, women as well as men, provided that they paid taxes and possessed some property.

Other laws that were supposed to enlarge the country's political life followed in 1956 and 1963. But there was little real change. The inferior position of the 'tribal interior' was scarcely improved. The Americo-Liberian group continued to rule with an iron hand.

Tubman died in 1971 and was followed by President William Tolbert. Again, little changed. The regime became increasingly unpopular with all except the ruling group. Finally, in April 1980, the long-expected eruption took place. Master-Sergeant Samuel Doe, and 16 other army men, broke into the executive mansion and killed President Tolbert and 25 other Americo-Liberians who were in the building. For a while it was thought in spite of this violent beginning that the rooted trouble might now be removed, and steps taken towards a democracy for all the inhabitants of Liberia. 'The balloon of Americo-Liberian power', in the words of Professor Gus Liebenow (*Liberia: The Quest for Democracy*, Indiana, 1987, p. 186) had certainly 'burst in one loud bang'. Much was hoped of Master-Sergeant Doe.

But the trouble had gone very deep. The power-and-wealth gap between the Americo-Liberians and the 'ethnic' majority had steadily widened by promoting economic growth in Liberia without promoting economic development in Liberia. What did this mean? In 1966, answering that question, four US economists undertook an inquiry sponsored by the Liberian government and the US Agency for International Development, an arm of the US government. These economists found that 'enormous growth in primary commodities produced by foreign concessions for export has been unaccompanied either by structural changes to induce complementary growth, or by institutional change to diffuse gains in real income among all sectors of the population' (R. W. Clower *et al.*, *Growth without Development*, Evanston, 1966, e.g. p. iv).

More taxes were being paid, and a bigger wages bill handed out, so the Liberian economy was 'growing'. But this growth 'has merely raised imports', rather than leading to any consistent development of Liberia. And in this 'growing economy', it was above all the Americo-Liberians who continued to have the benefit.

Militarist failure

This situation clearly had to demand much more than a 'changing of the guard' at the top. It was the 'system in place', here as elsewhere in post-colonial Africa, that had seized this people by the throat. Consider these points by a leading West African commentator, Nii Bentsi-Enchill (*West Africa*, 13 April 1981): 'Liberia is in trouble, but no more and no less than other "under-developed" countries. Before (the 1980 coup by Doe), it was convenient to blame the Americo-Liberian élite for the fact that 3.9 per cent of the (whole Liberian) population received some 60.4 per cent of the national income, while 73.7 per cent of the people only had 24.6 per cent . . . (but) it cannot be too long before it becomes clear that the real problem is not who is in power: what matters is the system of production, distribution and consumption in force.'

Not only was this Liberian system grossly unfair to most of the people: it was also a system in which a vast quantity of Liberia's productive wealth, year by year, simply went abroad to foreign interests. 'At the time of the (1980) coup', Bentsi-Enchill found, 'about 90 per cent of the market value of goods and services in the country was said to be controlled by external forces . . . From iron ore, Liberia's major export commodity in volume and value, the World Bank had estimated in 1973 that out of every dollar earned, only 16 cents stayed in the country.'

Would Doe and his group, having grabbed power in 1980, develop the will and patriotic wisdom to tackle and solve the problems of this legacy of misgovernment and dependence? There soon appeared good reason to fear that they would not. Doe strengthened his personal hold on all effective power. Attempts to oppose or even remove him failed. In 1986 the Master-Sergeant proclaimed himself to be the country's new president of a new and 'second republic' presented, again in Liebenow's words, as 'a milestone in the history of Liberia's long quest for democracy'. But 'instead of this being the day of celebration and rejoicing that had been anticipated during the more than 5½ years of transition from military to civilian rule, it was a sombre day indeed. The honored guests . . . and even many of those who had voted for Doe and the NDPL (Doe's party) realised that the election of the preceding October had not been a fair one. The challenges to the legitimacy of the second republic had been immediate once the election "results" had been announced . . . and they became bloody and filled with acrimony in the ensuing two months. . . .'

By now there was much to suggest that here was one more proof of militarist failure, one more example of the depressing mediocrity, or worse, of so many of Africa's leaders during the 1980s. Nor was this all the bad news. The 1990s were going to open, in Liberia, on a scene of violence run out of control. Years would pass, after the end of Doe's fruitless reign, before Liberians could await the next day without fear of death or disaster.

With no clear authority left inside Liberia, neighbours began to fish in these troubled waters. At the head of various bands of rebels, self-proclaimed saviours marched across a scene of deepening violence and atrocity, culminating in September 1990 with the capture, torture and murder of Doe himself. Watching all this with dismay and indignation, the prime regional organisation of West Africa, which is the Economic Community of West African States (ECOWAS), saw that no good could now be done without the use of a peace-making force. Even before Doe's murder by one of the rival bands of rebels, six ECOWAS states (Ghana, Nigeria, Sierra Leone, The Gambia, Togo and Guinea) sent 2,500 of their troops in August 1990; and this force, ECOMOG (Economic Community of West African States Monitoring Group), rapidly asserted its authority. But keeping this peace soon proved difficult. Civil society and a rule of law were hard to restore once they had been shattered. It remained that ECOMOG, if only partially successful in quelling the tumult, marked an important new stage. Instead of turning to the outside world to settle a problem, Africa on this occasion had turned to itself, and not in vain.

Much the same lesson, though in very different circumstances, was meanwhile unfolding in Ethiopia on the far eastern side of the continent: if the outside world proved incapable of helping Africa, Africa could still help itself.

Ethiopia: federalism betrayed

As we saw earlier in Chapter 6, the ancient kingdom and empire of Ethiopia regained its independence in 1941 during the Second World War (see p. 60). But this was independence within the structures of government and rules of land-ownership which had existed before Italy's invasion of 1935. After the war, Emperor Haile Selassie extended this system of minority rule, essentially an aristocratic system under the emperor's personal government, and failed to introduce any reforms which could meet popular demands for equality and justice. Partly provoked by severe famine in some Ethiopian provinces, a revolution began in 1974. Poor farmers took the land of the nobles. Haile Selassie was dethroned. A new ruling council, known as the *derg* (committee), declared that Ethiopia was to become a socialist state. A profound process of social revolution promised to introduce new and democratic systems of education, health, trade and government. Each of Ethiopia's large ethnic minorities was promised federal equality and justice.

But the promise was not kept. In 1976 command of the *derg* was taken by one of its members, Colonel Mengistu Haile Mariam, who proceeded to develop into a military dictator. Turning away from the USA, which had been the principal patron of the imperial regime of Haile Selassie, Mengistu applied to the USSR for economic, military and political support, and received it in all three fields of action. By the early 1980s this highly autocratic regime had gone some way towards introducing an

Ethiopian version of the Soviet communist system: that same system, in short, which secretary-general Mikhail Gorbachev was about to strive to reform and change on the grounds that it had failed to defend the interests of the people of the USSR. But if the Stalinist system could not succeed in the USSR, what hope could it have in Ethiopia?

Working on these lines, Mengistu failed to confront his greatest problem. This was the growing dissidence and outright resistance of large ethnic minorities which had been enclosed, often against their will, within the Ethiopian empire. Haile Selassie had based his power on the Amhara minority; Mengistu continued to do the same. Resenting this Amhara domination, other minorities went to war against it. Accepting this challenge rather than trying to deflect it by measures of political decentralisation, Mengistu proceeded to throw enormous amounts of money, and many lives, into reckless wars of repression against insurgent nationalities far more numerous, in sum, than the Amhara. While poverty widened and famine spread, Ethiopia's military expenditure continued to rise. In 1976, when Mengistu took over command, that expenditure stood at about $103.4 millions. In 1979 it stood at $526 millions.

Backing this fruitless militarism, the USSR supplied large quantities of ground and air armaments. Time and again the military forces of the *derg* were thrown into major offensives against Eritreans, Somalis, Tigrayans, Afars, Oromos and others. All these failed, and by 1988 an increasingly demoralised Ethiopian army, under its hated Amharic dictatorship, had to suffer crushing defeats on the battlefield, notably at the hands of the Eritrean People's Liberation Front (EPLF). Operating on an intensely patriotic programme aimed at democratic liberties, the EPLF now began to reap the benefit of its policies of tolerance and reconciliation. Masters of the field inside Eritrea, the Eritreans were now supported in their aims by the rise of a companion people's movement in Tigray, northern Ethiopia. Soon, a coalition of Ethiopian anti-imperialist forces proved stronger than the faltering troops of the dictatorship. Advancing on Addis Ababa, the old imperial capital of Ethiopia, this coalition (known as the Ethiopian People's Revolutionary Democratic Front, EPRDF) was in strong alliance with the EPLF. It secured control of the large provinces of Gondar and Gojjam, during February 1991, and swept on towards the Ethiopian capital. The dictator Mengistu fled in May 1991 (eventually finding an exile's refuge in Zimbabwe). The EPRDF set about ending all hostilities.

This was bound to prove a hard task. It could not succeed quickly. But the EPRDF in Ethiopia, like the EPLF in Eritrea, believed that it held the key to success. This key was to make good the betrayal of the promise of federalism made in 1974, the promise betrayed by the Mengistu dictatorship. A first step was to win freedom for democratic rights for all Ethiopians. The second was to create conditions in which this freedom could be defended. (Further events in Eritrea on p. 155.)

To that end, awaiting the return of normal peacetime, the EPRDF introduced a 'transitional charter' of political reform. Article 1 in this charter of July 1991 pledged the right of all Ethiopians 'to engage in unrestricted political activity'. Article 2 pledged 'the right of nations, nationalities, and peoples to self-determination' within a democratised Ethiopia. Each should be free 'to administer its own affairs within its own defined territory, and participate effectively in the central government on the basis of freedom and of fair and proper representation'. There would be difficulties after so many years of confusion and repression. But the perspective could now be a hopeful one.

CHAPTER TEN

Raising National Flags: North-East Africa

This chapter, and the six chapters which follow it, give the record of how the nationalists won through to independence and, in so doing, opened a new era in the history of the continent.

Partly because the liberation of some of the northern countries came a little earlier in time, and partly for simple convenience in following a complex story, we begin in the north and move, in later chapters, step by step to the south.

EGYPT: FROM THE *WAFD* TO NASSER

Egypt in 1922 ceased to be a British colony in name, but not in fact. In that year Egypt became what has since been called a 'neo-colony' (or 'new-colony'): that is, Egyptians could now govern themselves, but under the control of an outside power which, in this case, was Britain. The British government recognised Egyptian independence in a treaty of 1922, subject to these four conditions:

1 British armed forces continued to guard imperial lines-of-communication through Egypt, between the Mediterranean Sea and the Red Sea, especially by way of the Suez Canal.
2 Britain continued to be responsible for defending Egypt against outside attack.
3 Britain supervised the 'protection' of foreign interests inside Egypt.
4 Egypt continued to accept British control of the 'Anglo-Egyptian condominium' (joint government) of the Sudan.

Egyptian nationalists had to accept this partial independence. Their main party, the *Wafd* (formed in 1918 by Zaghlul Pasha), was still weak, being essentially the projection of a modernising middle class still to reach political maturity. It was also disliked by Egypt's King Fuad; he rightly saw it as a rival which, sooner or later, would demand concessions of royal power and privilege. Meanwhile popular discontent widened with the Great Depression. This plunged Egypt into a sharp economic crisis. There was growing civil strife; and then came Italy's invasion of Ethiopia (1935). All this made Britain fear for her own position in the region. Attempts were made to improve Britain's relations with the Egyptian leaders. These led to the Anglo-Egyptian Treaty of 1936 between the British imperial government and the *Wafd* government under Zaghlul's successor, Nahas Pasha (1876–1965).

The new treaty of 1936 made some concessions to Egyptian national-ism. But it altered nothing of substance: only on the third and least important of the four conditions of 1922, the protection of foreign interests, did Britain give way. Within three years there followed the Second World War. Britain used Egypt as a military base from which to fight against Italian and then German attempts to occupy the country and thus destroy British power in the region. In turn the Nazi–Fascist invaders failed, and were thrown out of North Africa in 1943.

Egypt's own government did not declare war against the Italians and Germans. But the *Wafd* nationalists went over to a pro-British position because they believed that occupation by the fascist Italians and nazi Germans would be worse than continued occupation by the British. That simplified things. In 1942 a long-standing rivalry came to a head between King Faruk (born 1920, and king of Egypt after his father's death in 1936) with his courtiers on one side, and the *Wafd* on the other. The British settled it by forcing King Faruk to accept another *Wafd* government.

As elsewhere, the tide of Egyptian nationalism began to run more strongly after the Second World War. There was an additional reason here. This was the foundation of the State of Israel (see p. 67) despite Egyptian and other Arab attempts to prevent it, as well as Israel's steady expansion from its small initial base. Relations with Britain, which was held responsible for handing over most of Arab Palestine to Israel, grew steadily worse. Some Egyptian guerrilla fighting against continued British occupation of the Suez Canal Zone broke out in 1952. This was unsuccess-ful; and Egyptian nationalism seemed to be at a standstill. But now came a new development.

In that same year, 1952, a group of young army officers led by Lt.-Col. Gamal Abdel Nasser (1918–70) seized control of Cairo and then of the whole country. There was no bloodshed, and the action was widely popular, because the old nationalists, including the moderates of the *Wafd*, seemed unable to win a true independence. The young officers formed a new government under General Muhamed Naguib, and this government, on 10 February, 1953, declared Egypt a republic. The deposed King Faruk went quietly into exile.

Naguib was found too conservative by the young officers' movement and was ousted in 1954, when the dynamic and popular Nasser became president. In July 1954 the British agreed to evacuate their forces within twenty months. They kept this agreement, but by this time the USA and its western European partners had become strongly hostile to the Nasser regime. They saw it as a radical threat to Western influence. But Nasser tried to lessen this hostility by asking for American and British financial aid to build a high dam across the Nile at Aswan, so as to improve the use of the Nile waters for irrigation. At first the USA and Britain agreed, but in July 1956 the USA changed its mind, and Britain did the same. They would not help to build the dam (which was then built with Soviet aid). Nasser replied to this refusal by turning the foreign-owned Suez Canal Company into Egyptian national property. Its profits, he said, could help to finance the building of the dam.

This reasonable response to Western hostility confirmed the then British prime minister, Anthony Eden, although few of his expert advisers, in a determination to get rid of Nasser by any possible means. As so often in those years of 'Cold War', radical nationalism such as Nasser's was easily presented as some kind of surrogate communism posing a threat to Western supremacy. There was little or no truth in this. Yet the British and French leaders were content with superficial views which nourished their own prejudices. They gave way to an always latent racism. They were further egged on by an Israeli leadership eager to cripple the new-found national pride of Nasser's Egypt.

Invasion by British, French and Israeli forces was planned in secret, and put rapidly in motion. In November 1956 Israeli troops invaded the Canal Zone by secret agreement with Britain and France, and were supported by the landing of British and French troops. This inexcusable invasion was aimed chiefly at destroying the Nasser regime so that it could be replaced by a regime convenient to Western and Israel's interests. But the aim was not realised. The aggression met with world-wide condemnation, as well as strong opposition in Britain itself. When the USA likewise condemned it, the Israeli, British and French invaders quickly withdrew.

Egypt suffered casualties and loss of property, but emerged as a truly independent state for the first time in modern history.

SUDAN, SOMALIA, DJIBOUTI, ERITREA

Britain had long wielded all the real power in the Anglo-Egyptian Sudan, largely because of that country's strategic control over the upper waters of the Nile. In changing times, the old nationalists in Egypt had usually argued that Britain in due course should place Sudan under Egyptian control. But the new Egyptian nationalists accepted the idea of Sudanese independence. After the Naguib-Nasser revolution in Egypt of 1952, Britain accordingly said that she was ready to leave Sudan. On 11 February 1953, Britain signed an agreement with Egypt which said that Sudan should have independence within three years. President Nasser confirmed this agreement after taking power in 1954. On 1 January 1956, British and Egyptian troops left Sudan. A new Sudanese government declared the country an independent republic.

This easy decolonisation, without a shot fired on either side, nonetheless proved unstable. A deep conflict had long divided the Muslim and Arabic-speaking peoples of the centre and north from the largely Christian and non-Arabic-speaking peoples of the south; and long British control, separating the north and centre from the south, had helped to worsen rather than ease this conflict. There was also rivalry for power between the nationalist leaders of the centre and north, organised in the Ashiqqa and Umma parties. Each of these conflicts was going to give seemingly endless strife, and once again was to question, as we shall see, the capacity of nationalism to make any real peace and progress.

Eastward toward the Indian Ocean, the Somali people had been divided by the colonial partition, against their will, into four colonies. These were Italian Somalia, British Somaliland, French Djibouti – a very small colony consisting of Somali (Issa) and Danakil (Afar) peoples – and Ethiopian Ogaden. The last, although almost entirely Somali in population, had been enclosed within the Ethiopian empire, as part of the colonial 'share-out', in the 1890s. Ethiopia was given by Britain renewed control of it after Italy's defeat in 1941. In addition, Somalis also lived in the Northern Frontier District of colonial Kenya, and claimed this district from Britain (and then, after 1963 when Kenya became independent, from Kenya).

After 1943, the newly-founded Somali Youth League (SYL) campaigned for the independence and union of all five territories noted above. For a long time, they had no success. But the defeated Italians were restored in 1950 to control of Somalia, their former colony, only for a ten-year UN trusteeship. In 1960, they left Somalia. At the same time, the British withdrew from Somaliland, and that territory was at once united with Somalia. The two territories were merged to form the independent republic of that name.

113

This brought most Somalis together. But Ethiopia retained Ogaden, and France retained Djibouti, while the Northern Frontier District of Kenya remained as part of that country. Somali guerrilla fighting against Kenyan control broke out in 1963, and continued until a settlement of 1967 confirmed the district as part of Kenya. Much more serious Somali fighting against Ethiopian control began in Ogaden in 1976, but failed again. Djibouti won its political independence from France in June 1977, and stayed separate. (For later developments in Somalia, see pp. 204–206).

Italy's Red Sea colony of Eritrea passed under British military government in 1941, when Italy was ousted from the whole region of the Horn. In 1945 the United Nations agreed to put Eritrea under its own supervision, but that British military government should continue there until the country's future could be decided.

Eritrean nationalism was still weak at that time, while the Ethiopian emperor, Haile Selassie, put in an eager claim to the former Italian colony. His claim being partly accepted by the UN, the British withdrew in 1952, when Eritrea became a federated state within the Ethiopian empire. This arrangement was meant to give Eritrea a wide measure of internal self-government while foreign policy, defence, and financial control passed into Ethiopian hands. It satisfied a small number of Eritreans of that time. Most of them were merchants, lawyers or chiefs, who thought that their interests would be better served as a federal region of the Ethiopian empire than within an independent Eritrea.

But the arrangement failed to satisfy Haile Selassie and his court. They wished to have full control of Eritrea within the Ethiopian empire. In 1962, Haile Selassie managed to corrupt or otherwise suborn the Eritrean state assembly into renouncing the country's autonomous status, and accepting the Ambaric supremacy of the Ethiopian empire-state. In defiance of UN promises, Eritrea was absorbed into this Ethiopian empire as a mere province with no powers of its own. Trouble followed at once. Eritrean nationalism had grown much stronger and more effective by now. Challenging this Ethiopian annexation, young Eritrean nationalists began a guerrilla war for independence. Many years of bitter fighting followed, and not until the end of the 1980s did Ethiopian aggression appear certain to fail.

Following severely fought battles in 1985–88, and against bigger Ethiopian invading forces recklessly armed by the USSR, the army of the Eritrean People's Liberation Front (EPLF) now had the upper hand and controlled the greater part of Eritrea. All remaining resistance by the armies of the Mengistu dictatorship then collapsed. Eritrea had won its 30-year armed struggle for independence. However, the EPLF did not at once proclaim Eritrea to be an independent state. It announced that a referendum of all Eritreans would be held in two years' time, in 1993, and independence would then be declared if that is what Eritreans wanted. This delay, it was explained, would enable normal peacetime political activities to unfold after the long years of warfare, and Eritreans could in the meantime decide what political parties they then wished to form and join. Meanwhile they made a start, although in conditions of acute poverty and much hunger, to rebuild their shattered country.

Early in 1993 the promised referendum under international supervision gave more than 98 per cent of voters in favour of Eritrean independence, which was declared by a provisional Eritrean national government in May 1993. The newly empowered national government at once set about the tasks of organising a democratic political system.

While all these events were taking place, dramatic changes had been on the way in British West Africa. In 1951 the Gold Coast won internal self-government as a prelude to full independence as Ghana. Soon after, the same advance was made in the southern regions of Nigeria, and later in its northern region. But we shall find it more convenient if, next, we turn to North Africa where, apart from Egypt, three countries were already independent by 1956.

CHAPTER ELEVEN
Libya and the Maghrib

Libya became independent quite quickly after the Second World War. This was because the big powers could not agree on which of them should take the UN trusteeship of this former Italian colony. In 1951 the territories of Cyrenaica and Tripolitania were removed from British and American military government, and, with Fezzan, united as the kingdom of Libya under King Idris al-Sanusi.

But this independence was only partial, with British and American military and political control behind the scenes. Younger nationalists soon called for more independence, and more modern methods of government. Yet the king's power held firm till September 1969. He was then overthrown by young army officers; and a new Islamic republic was declared under Colonel Muammar Gadafi. This new government set about bringing the three provinces of Cyrenaica, Tripolitania and Fezzan into a closer unity. It also set about exploiting large oil deposits found by foreign investors in the 1950s.

Later again, the Gadafi regime would become involved in a destructive war in neighbouring Chad. The Libyans laid claim to part of northern Chad; and the power-hungry Gadafi himself, increasingly a source of aid to terrorist factions in various countries, would incur the justified enmity of many governments in Africa, Europe and America. But the country's wealth in oil could absorb the regime's adventures and its lavish spending on armaments, while, at the same time, financing new infrastructures of social and economic purpose. Western attempts to undermine this regime, and even eliminate its leader, as with a US bombing raid on the Libyan capital by way of Britain in 1986, met with failure.

Further to the west, in the Maghrib (Tunisia, Algeria, Morocco), the struggle for independence had to be both long and violent. For these were all settler colonies; in 1945, there were about 250,000 Europeans settled in

Tunisia, more than a million in Algeria, and about 300,000 in Morocco. These settler communities were minorities, but large ones and violently racist. They were determined to stay on top. And while France ruled Morocco and Tunisia as protectorates which might at some distant time become free to rule themselves, Algeria was ruled as part of the motherland. Its fertile northern regions, between the Sahara Desert and the Mediterranean Sea, were administered as departments of France itself. In a period of African political resurgence, all this ensured great trouble for the future.

TUNISIA AND MOROCCO

Formed in 1934 under Habib Bourghiba, the New-Destour (see p. 76) could make little progress in the late 1930s, and was soon suppressed by the French colonial authorities. In 1938 Bourghiba himself was imprisoned in France, and released only in 1942 by the nazi-German occupying forces, in France, because they wanted him to work for them. Bourghiba refused; after the war was over, he was able to return to Tunisia. At that point the national demands of the New-Destour, till then a rather weak party of the educated few, were beginning to be strengthened by mass support.

To this stronger pressure of Tunisian nationalism, the French answered with renewed violence. Finally, in 1952, they banned the New-Destour once more, and again imprisoned Bourghiba, as well as using their army against Tunisia's new trade unions. But already the cause of nationalism was winning wide support, and gaining fresh ground throughout the country. It became clear that many rural people, as well as poor people in the towns, believed now that national independence was going to be the only way for them to live better. They had to care very much about living better, even if, perhaps, they cared very little about the theory of nationalism and had little confidence in the middle-class leaders of nationalism.

They showed that they were ready to fight for their chance of living better. They began guerrilla war against the French forces. Their fighting bands were small and few; but they were strong enough, by 1952, to have made the French bring in 70,000 troops against them.

Fighting to regain control, the French saw that they would be wise to reach an agreement with the leading nationalists. For now they had another fear in mind. This was that the young men in the guerrilla bands would cut the political ground from under the feet of Bourghiba and other moderate leaders of the New-Destour. If that should happen, France might be unable to reach an agreement that would leave the French with any control behind the scenes. In March 1954 they let Bourghiba out of prison, and began to manoeuvre for the kind of agreement they wanted.

But another event pushed them further. It happened far away in Vietnam. There, a big French army had long been fighting to regain French colonial control of the Vietnamese, a control which they had lost to Japan during the Second World War. Now the Vietnamese proved too strong; in May 1954, they defeated the French in a decisive battle at Dien Bien-phu.

Sorely hit by this disaster, and therefore compelled to think again about the extent of their colonial commitments, a French government led by the liberal Pierre Mendès France decided to make peace in Tunisia. In August they allowed the New-Destour under Bourghiba's leadership to become legal and active, and agreed to Tunisian independence. With this promise, the guerrilla bands laid down their arms. In April 1955, the Tunisians were able to form their own government. In March 1956, Bourghiba led the country to independence, This was a victory for the educated men who led the New-Destour. But it was a victory, too, for the mass pressures without which the French would not have given in.

Much the same kind of 'double thrust' produced a comparable victory in Morocco. Here, too, economic depression had widened support for anti-colonial, and therefore nationalist, demands. These demands were much strengthened in 1934 and after by French political manoeuvres, which were seen as an attempt to split Muslim Moroccan loyalties. The goal of independence came nearer.

While the Great Depression brought new hunger and unemployment, better-off Moroccan merchants and professional men found themselves pushed aside by French settlers and businessmen. By the end of the 1930s the Moroccan anti-colonial movement, though still to assume any organised form outside the religious boundaries of Islam in Morocco, was clearly ready to be born. Then came the opening of the World War with the crushing defeat of France in 1940; and, in 1942, the landing in North Africa of powerful British and American armies. This brought an eclipse of the pro-Vichy (pro-Nazi) French administration in Morocco, and then the final destruction of the German forces of invasion.

All this ripened the cause of Moroccan nationalism. In December 1943, a strong group of professional men and merchants founded a party called *Istiqlal* (Independence). This marked two steps forward. First, as its name said, *Istiqlal* did not demand better colonial government; it demanded an end to colonial government. Nobody in Morocco had done that since the days of Abd al-Krim. Secondly, the *Istiqlal* leaders looked around for mass support. They appealed to the people to come in with them, just as the New-Destour was doing (if then illegally) in Tunisia.

Here, too, the French answered with new repression. In 1953 they even went so far as to depose the traditional Muslim ruler of Morocco, King Muhamed V, and put a 'puppet king' called Ben Arafa on his throne. This gave fresh fuel to the nationalist cause. Mass demonstrations of protest shook Moroccan towns where new trade unions were now in the lead. Many died in clashes with French troops. Then in 1955, in the moment when one guerrilla war had shown its power in Tunisia, and a second (as we shall see) was exploding in Algeria, a third guerrilla war began in Morocco. Acting on the old inspiration of Abd al-Krim, thirty years earlier, a people's army of guerrilla bands became active in the hills.

Faced with this, the French found themselves with no useful friends in Morocco. They had counted on the anti-nationalist support of several Berber chiefs, notably al-Glaoui of Marrakesh. But these men proved to be broken reeds; their following withered away. Giving in, the French restored King Muhamed to his throne and opened negotiations with *Istiqlal.* Morocco became independent on 2 March 1956, just eighteen days before Tunisia.

ALGERIA: THE HARSHEST STRUGGLE

Like the British in South Africa and Rhodesia, the French in Algeria had always acted as though the whole country was for them as settlers. Having taken control of Algeria by conquest against prolonged Algerian resistance, they had no hesitation in acting as conquerors. 'Wherever (in Algeria) good water and land are found,' their Marshal Bugeaud advised the French Parliament as early as 1840, 'settlers must be installed without questioning whose land it may be'; and the settlers, it was taken for granted, would be French or other Europeans.

The advice was eagerly accepted. By 1890 some 1,600,000 hectares (3,520,000 acres) of Algeria's most fertile land had been taken into European ownership by expelling the Algerian owners of this land. The process of expropriation continued until the Second World War. By 1940 settlers possessed some 2,700,000 hectares (5,940,000 acres). This was about one-third of all land in Algeria that was profitable for cultivation. In 1940 this one-third was owned by about two per cent of the Algerian population; and almost all these owners were immigrant Europeans.

That was not all. An important fraction of this expropriated land, some 378,000 hectares by 1953, had been withdrawn from cereal production and put under vines in order to produce wine for export. Algerian food resources were accordingly curtailed. By the middle 1950s it could be calculated that Algerian cereal production was back to the level of the 1880s, while the Algerian population, since then, had just about tripled in size. So Algerians fed far worse than before. And this growing food shortage, one should note in passing, was another structural consequence of the colonial systems: insisting on using land and labour for export crops, these systems presided over dwindling food production.

On top of all this, the system in Algeria was severely repressive. Settlers and colonial power alike remained deaf to Algerian demands for some movement towards equality of rights and treatment. Stiffly racist, they allowed Algerians to use their chief language, Arabic, only in religious schools. All privileges went to the settlers; all power of government stayed with them, or with Paris and its governor-general in Algiers.

Against that situation, the leaders of Algerian nationalism such as Messali Hadj had campaigned in vain. They achieved nothing in the ten years after 1945: nothing, that is, except a stronger colonial repression. Believing that no progress could be made by peaceful means, a younger generation of nationalists now decided to adopt violent means. After some failures, they formed a secret Front of National Liberation (in French: FLN), and launched a war of independence from the Algerian Aurès mountains during November 1954.

To begin with, they had only some 300 Italian rifles bought from war dumps in Libya, and their rising spread slowly. But it was well led by men, such as Ahmed Ben Bella, who had fought against the nazi-fascists in units of the Allied armies during 1934–45. Gradually, the revolt found mass support in every region. Once the revolt had won this mass support, volunteers flocked to it.

All through 1955–56 the fighting rose in ferocity and power: but, largely, to Algerian advantage. With some 15,000 fighters in the field, the army of the FLN held its own against a French army of some 200,000 men that was divided into some 530 garrisons and fortified camps. Meanwhile the FLN began to work out its political plans for independence.

But late in 1956 the fighting went against the Algerians. Partly, this was because the French brought in many more troops from France, and French generals began to adopt more effective anti-guerrilla tactics. Partly, it was because some of the Algerian leaders, in order to escape capture by the French, were obliged to take refuge in Tunisia during September 1956.

After that withdrawal, a gap widened between the Algerian political leaders and armed forces outside Algeria, mostly in Tunisia, and the fighting units and their political supporters inside Algeria. Seeing this gap, the French set about breaking all contact between the 'outside' and the 'inside', thinking that in this way they would be able to destroy popular support for the liberation war. They built electrified fences up and down the Algerian side of the frontier with Tunisia, laid more than a million land-mines along the fencing, and placed strong forces to prevent men and supplies from getting into Algeria from outside. At the same time, learning new military lessons of anti-guerrilla warfare, the French generals stopped trying to control every small district with fixed garrisons. They combined their very strong forces into 'hunt-and-destroy' units, backed up by helicopters and mobile support units. These had much success.

By 1960 the French had about 700,000 troops in Algeria, an enormous army, and had driven the army of the FLN nearly to defeat. But now the French had to swallow another hard lesson. They found that in this kind of warfare a win on the battlefield cannot be decisive, unless it goes together with a win in politics. This second success would have to mean that the FLN lost mass support. It did not happen. Great pro-FLN demonstrations in the cities proved, even now, that the FLN still held the loyalty of the people.

Meanwhile, across the Mediterranean, great disputes about the war were tearing France apart. Taking power in 1958, General Charles de Gaulle became president. He decided that he must negotiate an end to a war that France was not going to be able to win. He still thought that he could do this in such a way as to keep French control. In June 1959 he offered a ceasefire to the FLN, but with no promise of independence. The FLN rejected the offer.

The war continued, but now the settlers in Algeria were convinced that de Gaulle meant to desert their cause. They organised a settlers' rebellion against France, rather in the same way as the Rhodesian settlers were going to rebel against Britain six years later: but the circumstances were different and, unlike the Rhodesian settlers, they failed. On the contrary, their terrorist actions inside France, where they murdered opponents and blew up buildings, hastened President de Gaulle's willingness to make peace. He reopened negotiations with the FLN, accepting the Algerian claim to independence.

A cease-fire followed in March 1962, and Algeria became independent in July 1962. More than a million Algerians had died. Much of the country was a smoking ruin. Yet in that July, before the French left, the FLN won what may well be seen as its biggest victory. The whole population was asked to vote for what they wanted. Among the Algerians exactly 16,478 votes were cast against independence: but 5,993,754 votes were cast in favour.

CHAPTER TWELVE
South of the Sahara: French Colonies

Even before Sudan, Morocco, and Tunisia had become independent, significant advances in the same direction were being made by nationalists in the Gold Coast and Nigeria. Kenya was shaken by the rising of the 'Land and Freedom' armies. And the tide of popular pressure was gathering strength elsewhere: time and again, the British and the French were obliged to shorten the timetables with which they envisaged serious concessions to African demands. In this chapter we continue with the record of decolonisation in the French empire.

The peoples of French colonies south of the Sahara had the same problems as those to the north of it. They had to face the French policy of regarding all French colonies as part of a 'greater France': that is, the policy called 'assimilation' (see p. 38). Secondly, there were aggressive settler minorities in Ivory Coast, Senegal, Cameroun and Madagascar.

African populations in these colonies were much smaller than those of the British empire south of the Sahara, but they were still large. They numbered some 16 million people in the eight colonies of French West Africa – Mauritania, Senegal, Sudan (now Mali), Guinea, Upper Volta, Ivory Coast, Dahomey, Niger; and some 4 million in the four colonies of French Equatorial Africa – Gabon, Middle Congo, Oubangui-Shari (now Central Africa), and Chad. Two old mandates of the League of Nations, and since 1946 UN trusteeship territories, were also under French colonial rule: Cameroun, with a population of some 4 million, and Togo with about one million. Lastly, there was the great island of Madagascar, with more than 4 million in 1945, and a scatter of small Indian Ocean islands. Altogether, this added up to at least 30 million people.

What future did these people now want? What did France mean to offer them? Was there to be a struggle for independence, and, if so, how was it going to be settled? For some years after 1945, the answers were far from clear.

CHANGE AND REACTION

The Brazzaville Declaration

While the war lasted, France neither gave nor for the most part could give any sign of being willing for change. Up to 1942 its governors and generals in French West Africa all stayed loyal to the racist ideas of the wartime Vichy government in southern France, a puppet of the German nazi conquerors. They increased the use of forced labour; they filled their prisons with any who protested. In French Equatorial Africa, however, it was a little different. Leading French governors and others, there, decided to go against the Vichy government and support the 'Free French' movement of General Charles de Gaulle, who backed the Allies. There was talk of a 'new deal' for the colonies after the war.

But there was little more than talk. In February 1944, with de Gaulle's approval, a conference of 'Free French' colonial governors met at Brazzaville and discussed the future. Their Declaration of Brazzaville spoke of the need for new policies of respect for African rights and dignity. But it also spoke against any real concessions. Its key passage said:

> the colonising work of France makes it impossible to accept any idea of autonomy for the colonies, or any possibility of development outside the French empire. Even at a distant date, there will be no self-government in the colonies.

There might be new words about 'union and friendship'; yet that, it seemed, was all. In fact those governors, like de Gaulle himself, misread the real situation they were in. They misunderstood the dominant political forces that were now taking shape: in other words, they counted without the wider effects of the Second World War.

Africans in the French parliament: RDA and other parties

When France regained its own independence, after its liberation by British and American armies in 1944, the people of France also needed a 'new deal'. All their old conservative and middle-of-the-road parties – those that had made the empire – had gone down in defeat. Many were badly stained by collaboration with the nazi occupiers of their country.

Liberal and left-wing parties came to power, and some of them were anti-colonial. They shaped a new constitution for France and its empire.

Rather like the Brazzaville Declaration, this constitution seemed at first to make little change. The colonies remained colonies in fact; in name only, they were changed to become members of a sort of commonwealth called the French Union (*Union Française*). But the new constitution went further in one important respect.

Thanks to liberal leadership in Paris, the eventual constitution (agreed by national referendum in October 1946) provided for many colonial Africans to vote in elections for the French National Assembly. These were able to elect about 20 Africans to that assembly; while other Africans were elected to a less important but still useful platform of opinion in Paris – the Assembly of the French Union.

These African members of the French parliament came from several new parties. Some of these parties were colonial offshoots of French ones; but some were not, and the biggest among those was entirely African. This was the *Rassemblement Démocratique Africain* (RDA), or African Democratic Rally, formed in 1946 at Bamako (then capital of French Soudan, now of Mali) by go-ahead leaders of African opinion in many of the twelve colonies of French West and Equatorial Africa. Among these men were Félix Houphouët-Boigny of Ivory Coast, Mamadu Konaté of French Soudan (Mali), and Gabriel d'Arboussier of Senegal. Others who now took a lead were Léopold Sedar Senghor of Senegal, Sékou Touré of Guinea, and Barthelèmy Boganda of Oubangui-Shari (Central African Republic).

These men did not press for the separate national independence of each of their countries. They had to work inside the framework of French ideas about assimilation and 'greater France'. So they pressed for progress in winning rights for Africans, and in abolishing the worst of the colonial laws. They made some progress. A law of 1946, especially the work of the Senegalese Lamine Guèye, successfully abolished forced labour in French colonies, and, at least in name, greatly extended the rights of French citizenship. The future for 'French Africans' south of the Sahara began to look brighter.

Colonial backlash

These moves towards equality between French and Africans in the colonies were opposed by French settlers and businessmen who feared a loss of privilege and profit. And now, after 1947, these businessmen and settlers were reinforced by a swing back, in French politics, to conservative ideas and parties. Right-wing French ministers and business interests began a campaign to cancel out the gains won by Africans.

The first target of this colonialist fight-back was the strongest of the new territorial parties, the Democratic Party of Ivory Coast (in French: PDCI) led by Houphouët-Boigny. As Nkrumah's Convention People's Party in the Gold Coast, next-door, was about to do, the PDCI had won wide popular support. In 1949 the French government in Paris sent out a new governor, Laurent Péchoux, with orders to destroy the PDCI. He failed, but his repression was severe.

Laurent Péchoux had plenty of administrative force to carry out the orders he had received from the government in Paris. But in an atmosphere different from that of the 1930s he felt it desirable, as did other repressive colonial governors at this time, to justify repression by alleging that he faced some kind of communist-inspired plot. His staff accordingly informed their British colleagues in next-door Gold Coast (Ghana) that the RDA in Ivory Coast meant to transform the colony into a 'communist Ivory Coast in a communist Union Française'. This was pure invention, even while it was true that some of the RDA leaders had some parliamentary ties with the French communist party, then of course a member of the French governing coalition. Once again, accusations of 'communism' served as a cover for real plots to prevent progress.

As it was, several dozen African members of the PDCI lost their lives, hundreds went to prison. Elsewhere, too, there came the same administrative violence. It seemed for a while that settler and business interests had won the day. But this was not the case.

For trends now in play proved too strong for colonialist revival. The rights won by Africans – in their new political parties and trade unions, in the launching of their own newspapers, in other cultural and social fields – were defended; they remained in force. Now, too, 'French Africans' saw that other Africans were winning fresh advances, notably in the Gold Coast and Nigeria. Carefully playing the game of the French Union, their leaders took fresh courage. Those of the RDA pressed for the formation of two self-governing federations, one composed of the eight territories of French West Africa, and the other of the four territories of French Equatorial Africa. They wanted each federation to have its own central government, forming two big states inside the French Union. They argued that two big states would afterwards be able to win a real control over their future.

But the French were against this for the same reason as the Africans were for it: they believed that twelve small states would be much easier to control or influence than two big ones. So the French moved towards the idea of self-government for twelve weak states. This idea was then accepted by Houphouët-Boigny, who became a junior minister in the French government of 1952 and, with this, the decolonising project moved to a new phase.

In 1956, moving further towards this division of the two colonial 'federations' (West and Equatorial) into twelve self-governing states, the French parliament passed an important measure, the *loi cadre* or 'enabling Act'. This took power away from the two chief colonial governments (in Dakar and Brazzaville), and gave this power to the twelve territorial governments. The power thus transferred was, as yet, only for local affairs; the chief colonial governments in Dakar and Brazzaville still had control over finance, foreign policy, police and army. Yet this partial transfer of power proved decisive; it was going to shape the future.

In fact, a French plan for indirect control had now taken over from old colonial ideas. It opened against a wide background of change. In that same year of the *loi cadre*, 1956, Morocco and Tunisia became independent. The Gold Coast was about to become Ghana; similar moves towards independence were far advanced in Nigeria. In Kenya the anti-Mau Mau Emergency ended, leaving Kenya's nationalists with a good hope of political progress. Then came the French internal crisis over Algeria, and de Gaulle's return to power in 1958. Did plans for indirect control in Africa now mean that the French could still save much for themselves south of the Sahara?

A LIMITED INDEPENDENCE

De Gaulle and Sékou Touré

De Gaulle saw at once that French direct control south of the Sahara was no longer possible, and that he would have to move fast if France were to be able to maintain an indirect control. He accepted the idea of self-government for the twelve territories: each, he said, was to become an associated state within a new sort of union, this time called the French Community (*Communauté Française*). Each would have large local powers; but France would remain the 'motherland' in command of finance, foreign policy and military affairs. Each would have its parliament, government, flag and national anthem; but each would follow France in all big decisions. The horse would certainly be African; but the rider, just as surely, would be French.

De Gaulle's plan succeeded. By this time the leaders of African opinion were divided about what best to do. A few were solidly against the plan, thinking it could not provide a genuine independence; and they were ready to oppose it. A few eagerly accepted the plan, for it gave local power into African hands, and some could benefit from that. Others disliked the plan, but felt that they and their parties were too weak to oppose it. All were beginning now to think as nationalists, outside the framework of assimilation. But many still believed they could be nationalists only as junior partners in a French Community dominated by France.

De Gaulle set about isolating and defeating the opponents of his plan. He offered a referendum to each of the twelve colonies. The people had to vote 'yes' or 'no'. If they voted 'yes', they accepted the plan; if 'no', they could have full national independence, but in that case France would at once stop all aid and support. Appealing for a 'yes' vote, de Gaulle himself toured the colonies. He was sure that each of the colonies would vote 'yes', because each depended on French aid and support. Of course the French could also depend on their control of the voting machinery; yet mostly it was a kind of blackmail, and it worked. All gave 'yes' majorities: except one.

That was Guinea. Under Sékou Touré's determined leadership, the Democratic Party of Guinea (in French: PDG) not only won wide popular support; it also succeeded in undermining the influence of French-appointed chiefs. Not even French control of the voting machinery could help de Gaulle here. To his dismay and anger, 95 per cent of the votes in Guinea went against his plan. He cut off all aid at once, but it made no difference to the decision. Guinea became independent under a PDG government.

Another colony almost did the same. The biggest local party in Niger, *Sawaba*, led by Djibo Bakary, also campaigned for a 'no' vote. They failed; but there seems little doubt that the true voting returns were falsified by administrative action. The published results showed that about 100,000 had voted 'no' while 370,000 voted 'yes'. But no less than 62 per cent of the voters were said to have abstained, a claimed abstention hard to believe.

With Guinea winning independence in 1958, the whole outlook was in any case dramatically changed. It became clear that the other eleven colonies would now wish to move in the same direction, and that it would be very hard to stop them. Yet if de Gaulle's plan for twelve associated states was in ruins, the underlying plan for French indirect control was not.

1960: a fresh start?

Apart from Guinea, already independent, all the French West and Equatorial colonies, as well as the trusteeships of Cameroun and Togo, became national republics in 1960. All, except Guinea, had to accept French indirect control. Only the relatively rich Ivory Coast, Gabon, and to some extent Senegal, proved able to pay this price and still make overall progress.

Each of these neo-colonial states (again, except for Guinea) had to enter into agreements with France which placed their finance, foreign policy, and even national defence under strong French supervision. Through the Bank of France, the old 'motherland' continued to manage their finances by means of the so-called 'colonial franc'. Through various business interests, Paris continued to dominate their economic policies. Through military treaties, French armed forces stayed on their national soil. Through a host of links and habits, France remained their 'heart of civilisation'.

The grand vision of two strong federations, groundwork for a Pan-African future, had faded away. The old colonial policy of 'divide and rule', though under a new guise, stepped back into place.

Togo and Cameroun

Though in name a trusteeship territory and not a colony, Togo was governed by France in the same way as the rest of French West Africa. Togo shared the same road to independence in 1960, when Sylvanus Olympio became its first president. Meanwhile, in 1956, a referendum in British Togo (the western sector of the former Germany colony) had returned a majority of votes in favour of its integration with Ghana; this duly occurred in 1957.

Cameroun was covered by another League of Nations mandate converted in 1946 to a UN trusteeship, but governed as a colony like all the other trusteeships: in this case, as a French colony. Yet this special status was not without its value to anti-colonial Africans. It enabled them to argue that France (in the case of Cameroun) should carry out its 'missionary trust' and agree to the country's independence. Of course, before the Second World War Camerounians could not argue like this, at least publicly, inside Cameroun. But Camerounians in Paris could do it. And we find them doing it as early as 1933 in the columns of the anti-colonial *Cris des Nègres*:

> Cameroun demands its independence, and an end to a mandate which has done the country no good.

With the new French constitution of 1946, demands for Camerounian independence were heard more strongly; but now they were heard inside Cameroun. Local settler and business interests quickly mobilised against these demands. As in Kenya on the other side of Africa, settler interests were strengthened by the Second World War. They meant to command the country's future. Again like the Kenya settlers, they had powerful support in the 'motherland'.

If the majority interests of Camerounian Africans were to succeed against the settlers, they clearly needed the support of a political party. And if this party were to do any good, it must just as clearly stand for national union against tribal disunion. This was going to be difficult, because there were many different peoples in Cameroun, and the French, like other colonial rulers, had promoted the formation of 'modern tribalism' (see Chapter 7).

In 1948 a group of young nationalists, led by a trade union organiser called Reuben Um Nyobé, decided to tackle this difficult task. They formed the Union of the Populations of Cameroun (UPC). Um Nyobé proved a far-seeing leader. The UPC was among the earliest parties of African nationalism to show that the enemy to be fought was not only direct colonialism, but also its indirect form of neo-colonialism.

The UPC became a main target of the French colonial fight-back, just like the PDCI in the Ivory Coast. Harried by the colonial authorities, leaders and rank-and-file members of the UPC had to face much repression. Finally, in 1954, Governor Pré was sent out to destroy the UPC, as Péchoux had tried to destroy the PDCI in the Ivory Coast some years before. Pré banned all UPC meetings, set his police to harass Um Nyobé and others, and then declared the UPC illegal. But Um Nyobé and others managed to escape arrest.

Peaceful political action having got nowhere, the UPC responded with guerrilla action. Based in southern forests protected by UPC fighters, their liberation movement defied the French and began to build an independent life. But tribal disunity defeated them. While the people of two large areas supported UPC, the rest stayed inactive or sided with the French. In 1958 Um Nyobé was killed by a military patrol. Two years later, his successor Félix Moumié was murdered by rightwing extremists in Europe. Gradually, the UPC was destroyed.

The French, meanwhile, found other Camerounian parties ready to accept French plans. Chief among these anti-UPC parties was the Movement for Union of Cameroun (MUC) led by Ahmadou Ahidjo. Together with smaller parties, MUC won 60 out of 100 parliamentary seats in elections of 1960; and Ahidjo became president of a new Camerounian republic.

A peaceful Nigerian wisdom settled the future of Northern (or British) Cameroons, a UN trusteeship territory since 1946 (and before that governed under mandate of the League of Nations). The people of this northern region voted to stay inside Nigeria, and formed the Sardauna province in June 1961. The people of the southern region voted, during a

UN-supervised referendum of February 1961, to become part of the Cameroun republic.

Madagascar, Comoros

Fifteen thousand French soldiers, using 7,000 Algerian and Somali porters, had invaded the large island of Madagascar in 1894. Against much armed resistance, France had gradually installed a system of colonial rule. By the late 1930s, this system was essentially as follows:

1 All political power was held by French officials, who governed through Malagasy clerks, interpreters, police, and so on.
2 The economy of the island became a colonial economy: that is, more and more Malagasies worked to produce crops for export, under French control of prices and wages.
3 Education and social services were provided for a few Malagasies who accepted assimilation to French culture and loyalty to France.
4 By 1939 the Malagasy population was divided into a minority of about 8,000 assimilated persons, and a majority of more than 4 million 'natives' (*indigènes*) who were subject to colonial laws which imposed forced labour and other obligations.

As in other settler colonies, the Second World War appeared to strengthen local settler power in Madagascar. It brought other consequences that we have noted: a stiff repression went together with a deepening rural poverty, and Malagasy towns grew rapidly in size. But here, too, French defeat in 1940 shattered the prestige of the colonial system. A fresh hope of anti-colonial change appeared. This was spread further as some 10,000 Malagasy servicemen, returning home again, brought news of nationalist successes in Asia. Then came the changes made by the new French constitution of 1946.

Four men of Madagascar were elected to the French parliament in 1946. Two were settlers. But the other two were Malagasy nationalists. They represented a new party with mass support, the Democratic Movement for the Reconstruction of Madagascar (in French: MRDM). These two MRDM members of the French National Assembly, Ravoahangy and Raséta, were instructed by their electors to ask for Madagascan self-government as a step to independence. They put this demand in March 1946, but were refused, partly through the influence of some 60,000 French settlers, partly through the colonial fight-back mentioned above.

Events then moved fast. In September 1946 the French government instructed their colonial government in Madagascar to 'fight the MRDM by every means'. A new repression began. But this met widespread support for nationalism, and a big rebellion broke out against French rule. Starting in March 1947, this rebellion quickly won control of wide areas, but was smashed a year later by military force and by hunger resulting from a French blockade of rebel-held zones. Many thousands died: as many as 80,000 in French reports at the time, about 11,000 in later French estimates. By 1948, some 6,000 Madagascan patriots were in prison.

Only in 1956 did the French raise their 'state of siege', or direct military rule. Only in 1957 did they release the last of their Madagascan political prisoners. But the MRDM, together with its call for a strongly independent nationalism, was now destroyed. Here, too, the French plan succeeded. In the Gaullist referendum of 1958, about 77 per cent of voters were said to have voted 'yes' to the French Community; and Madagascar was given self-government within the Community in October 1958. Direct French control gave way to indirect control in 1960, when Madagascar became a republic.

The four inhabited islands of the Comoros became French property at various times, and were formed into a single colony in 1912. From then until 1946 they were governed from French Madagascar. During 1961 they were given some self-government. In a referendum of December 1974 the population of three islands voted overwhelmingly for independence; but that of Mayotte (Mahoré), the fourth and largest island, cast 64 per cent of its votes against independence. In July 1975, the three islands formed the independent state of the Comoros, while Mayotte, where French commercial interests were strong, decided by a large majority to remain under French control.

AN INTERESTING COMPARISON?

In later years a debate opened on the relative success of Britain and France in weathering the anti-colonial storms, and retaining power or at least influence in the new nation-states that were formerly their colonies. Who fared better out of the years of decolonisation? Which process, the French or the British, has been preferable for the African peoples concerned?

Or, in the end, was the result much the same?

To the new nationalist leaders and governments, there seemed at first to be a considerable difference between the methods pursued by the British and the French. Those in the former British colonies, or at least the former West African British colonies, seem generally to have felt convinced that they had won more freedom of choice and responsibility than their fellow-nationalists in the French colonies. There were solid reasons for their thinking this. Africans had more control of their finances and foreign policies. They were unhampered by military agreements which provided for the basing of British troops in their territories. Membership of the British Commonwealth organisation might have small practical value; but it carried a prestige that was more impressive, worldwide, than anything the French could offer.

Beyond these considerations, the states issuing from the British empire had more room for international manoeuvre than those issuing from the French empire: the former, for example, could more easily make effective business and political ties with the USA. There were Americans who could be heard commenting that in this affair of dismantling empires the British had been outsmarted by the French, and had 'given away' more than they need have done, or sensibly should have done.

This was possibly true in the short run. Was it likely to remain true? Africans in the former British colonies have tended to see the former French colonies as being no more than half-way to any genuine freedom of choice in attitude and policy; and no few Africans in the former French colonies have tended to agree with this judgment. By the 1980s, in any case, it was generally agreed that neither the French nor the British method of decolonisation had sheltered any of the former colonies from the generalised crisis of impoverishment which now overtook the whole continent. All were subject to the same legacies of wealth-extraction in favour of the industrialised countries, and all, in more or less degree, suffered from the same miseries of corrupt or dictatorial government. All were thrown together into the same search for routes of escape. Later chapters will resume discussion of these matters.

CHAPTER THIRTEEN

British West Africa

Decolonisation was less difficult in the four British West African colonies than in most other regions of the continent. Here there were no settler communities to get in the way of progressive change. Colonial advisers in Britain were already saying, even before 1945, that steps toward self-government for these four colonies would have to be taken. Governor Burns in the Gold Coast even appointed two Africans, in 1942, to be assistant district officers: a big step, as many thought then.

Yet it was still far from easy to push Britain into accepting African self-government, and then independence. For the British also had ideas about safeguarding British interests. These ideas were different from the French ideas inspected in the last chapter (see p. 126). The British had no policy of assimilation. They had no wish for the Africans in their colonies to become citizens of Britain. Nor did they think that their colonies should remain part of a 'greater Britain'.

But they did wish, very much, to keep a strong economic and strategic influence over these countries in the future. With that in mind, they aimed at less than the complete neo-colonial control achieved by the French in most of France's former African colonies. Their idea was that the four colonies should move towards eventual membership of the British Commonwealth of Nations. This was at that time a British-dominated 'club' of independent states, formed many years earlier with the old 'white Dominions' of Britain (Australia, Canada, New Zealand, South Africa), but enlarged, after the Second World War, to include independent India, Pakistan and Sri Lanka (Burma refused to join).

But the British wanted this movement to independence within the Commonwealth to be very slow, and by small steps. Many years must pass, the British thought, before there need be any real transfer of power. 'Let us go slowly', they said, 'and solve the problems of decolonisation as

133

we go along.' So they gave little or no thought to those problems: to the ways in which liberated Africans could best govern themselves, make their countries solvent, settle their own rivalries and disputes, and so on. On their side, the nationalists likewise gave little thought to the problems that would be posed by an independent and post-colonial future: their eyes were fixed on the immediate task of getting the British to pack up their bags and go.

This lack of forethought was probably unavoidable. But it had its price, and this price, as the early years of independence would show, could be a high one. As it turned out, the British were at first reluctant to withdraw their imperial power, although less violent than the French in their attempts to hang on and stay put. But then they got used to the idea of losing their empire: it could save them money and trouble, and might be the best thing for them after the strains of the Second World War. So the whole complex process of decolonisation went ahead without anyone bothering very much about what was going to come next.

DIFFERENT VIEWS AND PRIORITIES

The 'old nationalists' of the merchant-lawyer class in British West Africa had asked for 'colonial improvement'. But times were changed. New men and new parties were in the lead. Their demand was not for 'improvement', but for independence. Yet it remained that different kinds of people wanted different things; and this, indeed, was the case in every colony.

One important section of opinion, that of the educated few, was much larger than twenty years earlier. By 1945 or soon after, the Gold Coast had about 10,000 persons with some or much education, whether as lawyers, teachers, clergymen, or businessmen; while Nigeria, though with fewer, already had 114 lawyers, 38 medical doctors, 32 journalists, and 435 clergymen, as well as many businessmen.

All these persons, broadly, wanted political success. They looked forward to governing an independent country. A prominent Nigerian nationalist, Chief Obafemi Awolowo, spoke for them when he wrote, in 1947, that they were the persons who understood modern politics, and so 'it must be realised, now and for all time, that this articulate minority are destined to rule the country'.

Yet the great majority of people, whether in village or town, had less interest in winning power than in getting a better daily life. For them, nationalism was a way to become less poor; to send their children to school; to benefit from better roads, prices, public services. They looked to nationalism for social gains, while the educated few mostly had their eyes on political gains.

Later, as Part Four will show, this difference in expectations was to become a source of much conflict; and not only in West Africa. Meanwhile, the majority of people listened to the promises of the new leaders and movements; and these promises were large and many. They had to be large and many, for this was now a time of vivid hope after the years of colonial standstill or repression. People saw the winning of independence as the gateway to a better life. Whatever troubles might come later, they were not wrong about this. They went into the campaigns for independence with stout hearts and strong hopes.

NIGERIA: GIANT ON THE MOVE

The Nigerian giant moved, in fact, even before the Second World War was over. Founded in 1944 (see p. 78), the NCNC under Nnamdi Azikiwe took a lead in southern Nigeria. This the British had already divided into two regions, Eastern and Western. In 1950 a new party emerged in the Western Region; this was the Action Group (AG) under Obafemi Awolowo. The same year saw the formation, under Aminu Kano, of a modernising party in the vast Northern Region; the Northern Elements Progressive Union (NEPU).

But the Northern Region had been more or less cut off from the two southern Regions, by colonial rule, ever since 1922; and now its 'indirect rulers', the emirate chiefs, wished to conserve their powers against any constitutional 'outbreak of democracy' which might now be on the way. In 1951 they developed a far more influential party; this was the Northern People's Congress (NPC) under Sir Ahmadu Bello, the prestigious Sardauna of Sokoto. Other parties followed: notably, in 1955, the United Middle Belt Congress (UMBC), a merger between two earlier movements among the peoples of central Nigeria.

Already, as these parties showed, Nigerian politics were falling into a markedly regional pattern. Of course this must always have been hard to avoid in so big and diverse a country as Nigeria. But colonial rule had done nothing to lessen internal divisions. On the contrary, colonial rule had long isolated north from south, and strengthened regional distrust or rivalry. For all these reasons, the advance to nationalism, and to all-Nigerian unity, could never be an easy one. As things turned out, it became less easy as the leaders of this or that region came into competition for jobs and influence with the leaders of other regions.

Small steps: from Richards to Macpherson

Following their policy of going forward slowly, perfectly justifiable from their imperial standpoint, the British ventured on a first small step in 1946. Governor-General Richards brought in a new constitution which, for the first time, created an all-Nigeria legislative council. This was only an advisory council, and no more than two Nigerians were appointed to it. At the same time, however, Richards provided for three regional councils, one each for the Northern, Western and Eastern Provinces (later called Regions). Once again, this reinforced the regional pattern.

The Richards constitution met immediate criticism from leading nationalists. Here we may usefully recall some words of Chief H.O. Davies. He pointed out that the constitution said a lot about discussion, but nothing about participation. In it, said H.O. Davies, 'there is neither the intention nor the pretension to secure greater participation by the Africans in the management of their own affairs'.

Under such criticism, Britain's small steps to independence began to come less slowly. Due for revision only in 1955, the Richards constitution of 1946 failed to satisfy anyone. Another was introduced by Governor-General Macpherson in 1951. This gave way to demands for greater devolution of power to each region. These were strong demands because, by this time, Nigerian politics had largely become a three-way tussle between the NCNC (mainly Igbo), the AG (mainly Yoruba), and the NPC (mainly Hausa-Fulani). The Nigerian constitutional specialist Kalu Ezera has even gone so far as to say that 'from this time onwards [that is, from the end of the 1940s] tribal nationalism came to dominate the Nigerian political scene'.

The Macpherson constitution provided for an all-Nigerian federal government, seated in Lagos. But it also transformed the regional councils into regional parliaments. Each of these now elected its own regional government.

'Tribal nationalism': or one Nigerian nation?

Under strong nationalist pressure, the British agreed to faster steps. In 1954, only three years after its introduction, the Macpherson constitution was scrapped. Another new constitution, named this time after Lyttleton who was a British colonial minister, was brought in. This Lyttleton constitution did something to strengthen the powers of the federal parliament and government. But inter-regional rivalry was very sharp by now; and it was the regions that still dominated the situation.

In August 1957 the Western and Eastern Regions became self-governing states, while the vast Northern Region, adjusting less quickly to the pace of change, moved into self-government in March 1959. That cleared the way for the last act in the drama of colonial withdrawal. On 1 October 1960, Nigeria became independent as a federation of three self-governing states.

Was this to mean that Nigeria would be one nation, or merely a combination of separate nations? Historians, since then, have said that the greatest success of Nigeria's leaders was to keep this great country as one country, and to hold firmly to the creating of a single Nigerian nation against all the rivalries of the regional pattern. Yet the regional pattern of power and privilege for active nationalists – what Kalu Ezera called 'tribal nationalism' – still had great disruptive force behind it. This force was to be violently felt within the following ten years (see Chapter 18).

GOLD COAST UPHEAVALS: GHANA TAKES SHAPE

The Gold Coast also had regions. But the country is smaller than Nigeria, and its regional divisions were less evolved. Here, too, strong differences developed between the ideas and aims of the educated few, including powerful traditional rulers such as the Asantehene (king of Asante), and the founders of a mass nationalist movement which soon took the lead. The former were traditionalists and conservatives, and therefore wanted to safeguard their positions; the latter worked for the wider aims of a broad-based democracy which they, in their turn, should command.

But the educated few still pressed for anti-colonial change. Under veteran spokesmen such as J.B. Danquah (1895–1965), they formed in 1947 the United Gold Coast Convention (UGCC) as an instrument of political pressure. They meant to use the UGCC as a way of pushing the British into progress towards independence. But they meant to use it carefully, and without appealing for mass action to support them. It turned out differently.

Looking for a competent secretary for the UGCC, Danquah offered the job to Kwame Nkrumah (1909–1972), then in London after returning from several years of higher education in the USA. Nkrumah came home at once and took the job. But he took it with ideas that were markedly different from those of the UGCC leaders. He believed that mass action was required, and began to organise it. Young nationalists were actively on his side. They called for a country-wide campaign of pressure for change. Soon, Nkrumah was inviting mass action through strikes and boycotts of imported goods.

At this point, the UGCC leaders began to regret their choice of secretary. But mass action now came on the scene without being invited. A minor chief and trader of Sierra Leonean origin, Nii Bonne, organised a boycott of European goods in Accra, the capital, in January 1948. It proved a success, and colonial government agreed to reduce the prices of European goods. But on 28 February 1948, the day when prices were to come down and, as colonial government hoped, the boycott would end, there came another of history's accidents. It changed everything.

A group of ex-servicemen marched that day to the governor's castle, in a peaceful demonstration, to ask for a settlement of their grievances about pensions and jobs. Colonial police barred their way. A row developed, and stones were thrown. A British police officer shot and killed two ex-servicemen, also wounding four or five others.

Though planned by no-one, the effect was shattering. For years the British had thought of the Gold Coast as their 'model colony', always peaceful and patient. Now, suddenly, it exploded. Down the road from the castle, in the middle of Accra, angry crowds began looting and burning European shops. From Accra the rioting spread to other towns, and it went on for days. Army and police restored order in the end, but many people were dead by then, and much property was destroyed.

Taken by surprise, the British governor arrested the 'big six' leaders of the UGCC, including Danquah and Nkrumah, although none of them had the least responsibility for the riots. As usual in those days, the police wanted to believe that they had discovered a communist plot, even though the UGCC was known to be against any left-wing ideas, and above all against anything like communism. Their 'discovery' did the police no good. All six leaders had to be quickly released for lack of evidence. But five of them came out of detention determined to get rid of the sixth, who was Nkrumah. They blamed him for the bad name they were getting with the authorities. They were more than ready, now, to go slowly. But Nkrumah was not.

Nkrumah and the CPP: a breakthrough

Ousted from the UGCC, Nkrumah and his followers formed their own party, the Convention People's Party (CPP), in June 1949, and prepared to use mass support to win independence without delay. Their immediate aim was to call a general strike through the trade unions. This strike began on 8 January 1950, and many joined it. The governor at once replied to their peaceful action by violence which proved decisive, though in no way that this governor had expected.

Three days after the strike began, the governor declared a state of emergency. Arrests followed, and clashes. Two policemen were killed. Arrests continued. On 21 January the police took Nkrumah and his chief aide into prison.

But now, with the country in growing ferment, the British began to see that they would be wise to change their ground. Seven years before de Gaulle was going to do the same, they acted to regain control by seeking agreement with the nationalist leaders and above all with Nkrumah. Pushed on by mass pressure, they prepared for a new general election. This would lead to a constitution. And the new constitution would open the way for further steps toward self-government and independence.

In this general election of February 1951, CPP candidates won a clear majority of seats. Though still in prison, Nkrumah himself won almost all the votes in Accra Central. A newly-appointed Governor, Sir Charles Arden-Clarke, at once recognised, as he said later, that 'Nkrumah and his party had the mass of the people behind them.' He released Nkrumah and asked him to become the leader of an African government with useful internal powers. This amounted in some measure to self-government; while independence, Arden-Clarke promised, would come later. In the circumstances of those days, it was a breakthrough. Nkrumah accepted. His party and mass following gave their enthusiastic agreement.

Looking back, one sees that this was only a partial breakthrough. It was enough in the end to secure independence, but the CPP still had to struggle for another six years before the Gold Coast became independent Ghana. As in Nigeria, these were years when many of the problems of coming independence were hardened into conflict. Nkrumah and the CPP had to meet very sharp opposition from chiefs and their allies in the UGCC or successor-parties to the UGCC. They had to overcome the strong drive for a regional break-away in Asante, and they had to win the trust of the Muslim north.

Beyond these problems of political structure, there were others of an economic kind; and these were no less difficult to grasp and deal with. Many mistakes were made for which the new leaders had only themselves to blame; much nonsense was talked, and much vanity displayed. Yet these leaders faced great obstacles. Few of them were equipped to analyse economic matters, fewer still had any experience of economic realities. They were obliged to rely upon the advice and guidance of colonial officials who stayed on to work for the new government, as many also did elsewhere. These colonial officials, and others brought in from outside, might be good and honest men. They still remained men, for the most part, imbued with Euro-centric attitudes and misunderstandings. Yet big innovations were urgently required. Bold new thinking was necessary. Old habits of mind would have to be cast away. Few of these innovations proved forthcoming.

Given the obstacles, a surprising amount was achieved, even while much that was done during those six years became a matter for angry debate. Yet the greatest task was achieved with full success when, in 1957, the people of Ghana became the first colonial people south of the Sahara – the first people in what was then generally known as 'black Africa' – to win through to independence. Especially in their breakthrough of 1951, they gave a wide encouragement to nationalists in every part of the continent, even in the distant and very isolated colonies of Portugal. For their success taught a lesson highly valued in those times. No matter how tall and tough the colonial barriers to freedom might be, they could still be overthrown.

SIERRA LEONE AND THE GAMBIA

After 1950, in these lively though smaller colonies, the underlying pattern of events was much the same as in Nigeria and the Gold Coast. Sierra Leone also had its internal divisions: of these, the most important was a result of the slave-trade and colonial periods. It consisted in a division between the Creoles in and around Freetown, many of them the descendants of freed captives from other parts of West Africa, and the peoples of the interior, known in colonial times as 'the tribal interior'. In a much less sharp degree, this was the same structural problem as in Liberia (see pp. 103–104).

In 1951, a revised constitution gave local power to African ministers drawn from the majority party in parliament. This was the newly founded Sierra Leone People's Party (SLPP) under a medical doctor turned politician, Sir Milton Margai (1895–1964). He was from the 'tribal interior', but succeeded in making an agreement for joint action with the Creole leaders of Freetown. In 1960, the SLPP combined with other groups in a coalition called the United National Front; and this led Sierra Leone to independence in April 1961.

Here was another good breakthrough, linked also to the growth of an effective trade union movement led especially by Siaka Stevens (born in 1905 and national president 1971–85), who became the first secretary of the Sierra Leone Trades Union Congress as early as 1946. Like others of its kind, this independence solved the problem of getting rid of colonial rule, but left other problems to be tackled later. Among these other problems was the sharp difference, as in other countries, between the expectations of the educated few and the expectations of the mass of people.

Though The Gambia had a population of only some 300,000, its nationalists were determined not to be left behind. Their first parties naturally took shape among educated groups in the capital, Bathurst (now Banjul). These were The Gambia Democratic Party and The Gambia Muslim Congress, both formed in 1945, and the United Party (UP) formed in 1951. For the most part, their leaders were the younger generation of those who had worked in the Gambian section of the National Congress of British West Africa twenty years earlier (see pp. 35–36).

But the politics of nationalism could succeed in The Gambia, as elsewhere, only by calling on mass support. This, largely, had to come from the 'tribal interior'. It began to be organised in 1959, when Sir Dawda Jawara and others formed the People's Progressive Party (PPP). The PPP swept the polls in a general election of 1960, a victory which led the British, in 1962, to produce another new constitution. Under this, The Gambia won internal self-government in 1963. After combining in a coalition with the UP led by P.S. Nijie, Jawara and the PPP led The Gambia to independence in February 1965. In December 1981 a Confederation of Senegambia was proclaimed, between The Gambia and Senegal, by the two governments concerned; but this at once ran into opposition which rapidly annulled it.

CHAPTER FOURTEEN

East and Central Africa: British Settler Colonies

If Britain's withdrawal of colonial control from West Africa came with little violence and often with goodwill, the story in East and Central Africa was a harsh one. This was not because East and Central Africans asked for different and more difficult things, nor was it because they were essentially different kinds of people. Many contrasts of history, culture and ecology lay between these two great African populations in West and East; but these were not the contrasts that counted now. The bitter and often violent story of decolonisation in East and Central Africa came from one over-riding difference. In East Africa there were large white-settler minorities. In British West Africa there was none.

In order to see into those years, and make our way through their complexities, we can best divide these countries into two groups: first, those of British East Africa: Kenya, Tanganyika, Uganda, and Zanzibar. Secondly, those of British Central Africa: Northern Rhodesia (Zambia), Nyasaland (Malawi), and Southern Rhodesia (Zimbabwe). Each had to follow its own separate road, although in basic ways their history of anti-colonial struggle was much the same.

BACKGROUND TO CONFRONTATION

Except Uganda with its very few settlers, and Zanzibar with almost none, each of the British East and Central African colonies was the scene of an often sharp confrontation between settlers and Africans. On one side were the white-settler minorities, determined to 'stay on top' and take over control from colonial government. On the other side, after 1945, there was the African advance from colonial tribalism to modern nationalism.

And from that advance there came the formation of new parties or congresses of national union, aiming at independence under majority rule, which of course meant African rule.

We have looked at the nature of this political advance (see pp. 71–72). It occurred everywhere, and proved decisive. In Kenya, for example, 1945 saw the formation of a Kikuyu General Union and of a Luo Union, and again, in 1947, there was added a Bara African Union for the benefit of other 'modern tribes'. Yet the advance from those ideas of limited union, based on old traditions of history, to new ideas of national union, of nationalism, was already overtaking these tribal unions and welfare associations.

Thus 1944 saw the emergence of the Kenya African Union (KAU); and then, with a further advance to modern nationalism, 1960 brought the formation of the Kenya African National Union (KANU) and of the Kenya African Democratic Union (KADU). The same advance was made elsewhere. Then it was the big national parties, such as KANU in Kenya, which carried the day against the white settlers and colonial government alike.

Imperial policies

Confrontation between British settler minorities and African majorities was painful everywhere. But it was most violent in Kenya and Southern Rhodesia, where settlers were many. That was the same as in the French empire. Wherever French settler communities were large, above all in Algeria and Madagascar, the road to independence became soaked in blood. We shall find similar features in the Portuguese empire.

Yet settlers and Africans in these east and central colonies were not the only powers on the scene. There was also the power of colonial government directed from London. Which side of the confrontation, the settlers or the Africans, was backed by imperial policy?

In East and Central Africa, British imperial policy liked to say that it backed both sides: it claimed to 'hold the balance'. On the one hand, it was solemnly pledged to regard the interests of the majority – that is, of the Africans – as having first place whenever a conflict of interests arose. On the other hand, strong business and political interests, in Britain, still wanted the settlers to have first place. In practice, this meant that the settlers usually got what they wanted, later if not sooner. They got it more than ever in the aftermath of the Second World War.

Before looking at the detailed record, one other complication must be noted.

Asians in East Africa

Though few in Central Africa, Asians in East Africa were an important minority. Some had long settled in the coastal ports of the Swahili, and could look back through centuries to the peace and prosperity of the old Indian Ocean trade before the coming of Europeans. Mostly, these long-settled Asians were the East African descendants of Arabian peoples. But other Asians came from the Indian sub-continent during the colonial period, either because colonial government invited them to work in East Africa, or because they saw the chance of a better life and came of their own initiative.

Immigrants from Asia grew in numbers after the Second World War. In Kenya they increased from about 50,000 in 1939 to 170,000 in 1960; they also increased in Tanganyika (about 87,000 in 1960), and in Uganda (about 75,000 in 1960). They belonged to different Asian communities. In Kenya about two-thirds were Hindus; in Tanganyika, Hindus were rather less than half the total. Apart from a small Sikh and Jain community of about 32,000, mostly in Kenya, all the Asian Muslims belonged to one or other of three Shia brotherhoods: the Ismaili Khoja, Ithna'ashri, or Bohra.

Some of these immigrants were literate in English at a time when few Africans had been able to learn to read and write. As such, they were useful to colonial government in junior civil service jobs. Other Asians used their trading skills, developed in the less colonial and larger economies of the Indian sub-continent, to find a place for themselves between wholesale European commerce and the retail needs of African communities. They were welcomed by colonial government in this role of intermediary traders. They often played a valuable and even necessary part in these colonial trading systems.

Yet their positions and work brought them, steadily, into growing conflict with Africans. As civil servants, they were not supporters of African anti-colonial action. As intermediary traders, they were often the only traders. Africans came to resent their prices, retail monopolies, and command of village credit. Unhappily for these Asians, they and their leaders generally proved unable to adjust to the interests and needs of the overwhelming African majority in this new period of decolonisation. They were not alone in this failure, but it was still bound to bring the Asians into trouble.

'Closer union': settlers attempt to join forces

We need to consider one other background point. It arose in the 1930s.

Settler politicians began at that time to push for closer union between

Kenya and Tanganyika and also, if possible, with Uganda as well. In this way, they believed, they would be able to combine their minorities so as to strengthen their chance of governing the whole region.

The Kenya settlers, more numerous and brashly self-confident, took the lead. Their farmers in the so-called 'White Highlands' of Kikuyu country already numbered about 2,000 in 1934, owning just over 2 million hectares of good land. Soon, they argued in the 1930s, other settlers would start industries in Kenya. Then a white-ruled Kenya could dominate the whole East African region. It could become the central country, they hoped, of a new white-ruled Dominion of the British Commonwealth.

They failed to get this closer union, partly because imperial policy was pledged to give first place to African interests (even if, in practice, the pledge was seldom kept); and partly because the Great Depression made Britain unwilling to risk any big change. Yet the idea of white-dominated union was not forgotten; it was going to emerge again after the Second World War.

Settlers in the three Central African colonies also tried for closer union in the 1930s. They argued that if four territories in South Africa could be united under white rule, as these had been in 1910, then so could three territories in Central Africa. But here, too, the settlers failed until, in 1953. They succeeded with the Central African Federation (see pp. 150–151). In the end that also failed, but only through the rise of a still more successful African nationalism.

TANGANYIKA AND ZANZIBAR (TANZANIA): ADVANCE TO INDEPENDENCE

Confrontation here was less severe for two reasons. One was that the settlers numbered only some 20,000 in the 1950s, compared with three times as many in Kenya; besides, many were not of British origin, and had less support from political interests in Britain. Since the First World War, governors had been generally careful to protect African land and labour from white settlers in search of land to take and labour to exploit. Another but related reason, after the Second World War, was that Tanganyika became a UN trusteeship territory in 1946. As such, it could scarcely be allowed to fall under settler control, whether directly by settlers in Tanganyika or indirectly by settlers in Kenya.

Nationalism developed after 1945. Up to then, the country's many peoples and communities had often accepted the colonial division into 'modern tribes', and had taken no part in anything but purely local politics. Even so, the forerunner of an all-Tanganyika union, the Tanganyika African Association (TAA), had emerged as a discussion group among educated persons as early as 1929. Then, with all the new ideas and influences of the period of the Second World War and following years, there came the advance to forms of national union, to nationalism.

The men of the TAA moved with this new tide. They became more and more involved in all-Tanganyika affairs. In 1953, under the skilful chairmanship of Julius Nyerere, the TAA was reorganised as a political party, leading directly to the formation of the Tanganyika African National Union (TANU) in 1954.

Other currents of action strengthened TANU. Trade unions became more active. So did strong producers' co-operatives among peoples growing crops such as coffee and cotton. Soon, with the small settler community in political retreat, TANU candidates were winning big majorities in general elections; in many constituencies, they now faced no rival candidates. This national unity had its reward. In 1961 the country became independent, with British agreement, under a TANU government with country-wide support.

Two years later, in December 1963, the island of Zanzibar (together with the smaller island of Pemba) also became independent by a peaceful process; but, this time, under a government without wide support. This was a government dominated by the Sultan of Zanzibar and a minority of land-owners of Arab origin. These numbered some 50,000. But the rest of the population, consisting mostly of landless Shirazi (Swahili-speaking islanders) and recent immigrants from the mainland, totalled some 230,000.

Two months after independence, in January 1964, the Sultan's government was overthrown by local policemen, and power passed to non-Arab parties. Much violence followed; several thousand Arabs were said to have lost their lives. The new regime brought in a plan for social revolution, and received aid from East Germany and China. But Zanzibar's new leaders also wanted to keep close links with the mainland. They accepted a Tanganyika proposal for a loose kind of union. In April 1964, Tanganyika and Zanzibar joined to form the United Republic of Tanzania. But each country continued to have its own government.

Through all these events the TANU leaders, and especially Nyerere, supported the idea of an East African Federation as soon as the colonies were free. They joined with Kenya's and Uganda's leaders in forming organisations with that aim. Pan-Africanism remained for a while on the agenda (see pp. 254–256).

RIVALRIES IN UGANDA: INDEPENDENCE FOR WHOM?

Unity such as TANU was able to achieve among Tanganyika's many and diverse peoples proved impossible in Uganda. As in Tanganyika, there existed strong loyalties to ancient kingships and other pre-colonial authorities. But colonial rule in Uganda had greatly deepened these divisions, above all by taking the kingdom of Buganda into a 'junior partnership' with colonial government.

Buganda's leaders, including their king (*kabaka*), welcomed this opportunity of working with and for the British. It gave them privileges. They won better positions than the leaders of other old kingdoms, notably those of Buganda's traditional rival, Bunyoro. Generally, the Baganda had better chances than other Ugandan peoples of going to school, getting good jobs, and making money. This was resented by others less well placed.

There were, as well, strongly-felt religious differences. Many northern Ugandans were Muslims; but most of the educated nationalists, especially in the southern regions, were Christian. Yet some Christians were Protestant and others Catholic; and these two Christian communities in Uganda had long competed against each other. Not all these Christians had 'loved one another'.

Rivalries and resentments such as these worked against national union almost from the start. Led by competing groups of mostly educated men, two main parties during the 1950s began to struggle against each other for the powers that Britain was soon going to hand over. These parties were the Uganda National Congress (UNC), formed in 1952 with support from northerners and Protestant Christians; and the Democratic Party (DP), formed in 1956 with largely southern and Catholic Christian support.

This rivalry between the DP and UNC – and the UNC's successor party, Uganda People's Congress (UPC), formed in 1960 – was less about winning independence than about who was going to get the most benefits from independence. Instead of working together to build their new nation, they worked against each other. They built disunity instead of unity. This disunity was increased by the Baganda king (Kabaka Mutesa II) and his chiefs, who pressed hard for their own Baganda nationalism. In 1960 they even went so far as to claim that Buganda must become an independent state. The British rejected this; but Baganda separatism remained very much alive. (Bu- means the country, Ba- means its people.)

Against these sharpening conflicts, there was little to unite the mass of

Ugandans except economic grievances: especially, a widely-felt grievance against European and Asian control of the marketing and ginning (processing) of African-grown cotton. So the internal struggle for power went on.

With none of these rivalries resolved, Uganda finally became independent in October 1962. This was under a government formed by the UPC, led by Milton Obote, and a Baganda nationalist party called Kabaka Yekka (meaning: 'the King alone'), with the DP in opposition. But trouble soon followed. Not only was Kabaka Mutesa the president of this Ugandan republic, but his kingdom, Buganda, enjoyed a special and separate position within the republic. And the separatist ambitions of Buganda rapidly led to wider troubles.

Here we reach questions of general importance, and ones that are well worth thinking about.

We have seen that only the road of nation-building could offer an escape from colonial rule. But was it therefore necessary for African nationalists to build their new nations within the frontiers laid down by the colonial partition? Or, if those frontiers were accepted, would it have been better to build to a different pattern? Would Uganda have done better as half a dozen separate mini-states: as a separate Banyoro nation-state and a Baganda nation-state and so on?

Then, what kind of independence could these mini-states have expected? Or again, turning to a different question, would it have been better for Uganda to have become a federated state of the East African Federation which leaders like Julius Nyerere of Tanzania wished to form?

These difficult questions had to stay in the background during the struggles to remove colonial power and foreign rule. Winning independence within the frontiers and structures imposed or reinforced by the colonial powers, chiefly Britain and France, had to be the first and most essential task. Almost all the leading nationalists, and certainly all who had great influence, were in agreement about that. Many disagreed with each other on the tactics of how to win this independence, but nobody disagreed on the objective itself. And if there was little discussion about ideas and policies that should follow the winning of independence, this was because the everyday problems of winning it were more than enough to fill the thoughts of the men and women who led the parties of nationalism. The future, they felt, would have to look after itself. Not until the 1980s, as we shall see in final sections of this book, did the future of this nationalism, aimed at transforming colonial states into nation-states, come seriously into question. Political thinkers in Africa would then begin to question the credentials of this 'nation-statism' derived from the colonial partition. Meanwhile the scene was unavoidably dominated by immediate struggles.

KENYA: A HARD ROAD TO FREEDOM

African nationalism in Kenya proved powerfully successful in winning *uhuru* (freedom) against internal divisions, against settler domination, and against colonial government. But the road was hard.

Kenya was the home of many different communities who had long lived together and traded with each other, but had known no general unity. Some of these communities were large, such as the Kikuyu and Luo; others were small, some very small. There were many differences of culture between them. But the pressure of settler domination, together with strong African leadership, gave them a common ground to stand on; and, after the Second World War, they stood more firmly on it than before.

When the war was over, colonial government lifted its ban on African politics. An advance to modern nationalism began. At once, it ran into sharp settler opposition.

The settlers had won more power during the war. Their 'hard core', now composed of more than 3,000 farmers owning about 2.6 million hectares of Kenya's best land, had made big economic gains. Their spokesmen were strong in the colony's legislature; and colonial government in Kenya now listened to them more often than it listened to London. They were determined to win political as well as economic control, and to keep both. They decided that they must destroy the power of this new African nationalism.

Formed in 1946, the Kenya African Union's first president was the Harry Thuku of whom we have heard before (see p. 25). But a new and. more effective leadership was now required. This was found in Jomo Kenyatta (1891–1978), who came home in 1946 from a long stay in England and took over the KAU leadership in 1947. Touring the country and speaking to multitudes, Kenyatta showed the way to freedom from settler and colonial dictatorship. Other notable men, such as Oginga Odinga (born in 1911), did the same. They and their message of freedom became very popular, especially among all those people, very many by now, who suffered landlessness, unemployment, or starvation wages (see for example pp. 85–87).

Faced with the popularity of the KAU and its leaders, the settlers became more violent. Far from seeking an agreement with the KAU, or trying to reduce African grievances, they redoubled their demands for settler control of the country. By 1950, now numbering some 60,000, this settler community was in fact ready for collision, and even wanted collision, thinking that in this way they could destroy African political resistance. Giving way to settler pressure, colonial government did nothing to prevent a clash.

149

So collision came in 1952. Replying to sporadic acts of violence and pushed on by the settlers, colonial government declared a state of emergency, and arrested Kenyatta with other KAU leaders. In rising fear and anger, thousands of young men and women in Nairobi fled to the shelter of the Aberdare Mountains and Mount Kenya. There they formed the 'Land and Freedom' armies, as they called themselves, although the British insisted on calling them 'Mau Mau'. Their armed groups began to attack police stations, settler farms, and other targets.

Four years of bitter warfare followed. Heavily outnumbered by colonial forces, the Land and Freedom armies held out until 1956; in the end, the British had to send 100,000 troops and armed police against them. About 10,000 Africans were killed in this war or died as a result of it.

In one sense, this great and painful rebellion failed. Among all the peoples of Kenya, only a part of the Kikuyu and of their Embu and Meru neighbours took the side of the 'Land and Freedom' armies. More than three-quarters of the colonial forces sent against it were composed of African troops from other parts of Kenya; and these were reinforced by some 30,000 Kikuyu men organised as 'home guards' in local-defence militias.

But in another sense, more important for the future, the rebellion did not fail. Though smashed, it wrecked the foundations of settler power. Shocked by the fighting and its cost, opinion in Britain began to favour an advance to African majority rule. At last seeing the wisdom of agreeing to some progress, the industrial and business settlers began to turn against the 'hard core' farming settlers. Demands for independence grew stronger. A big national union was formed in 1960: Kenya African National Union (KANU); and a smaller one, Kenya African Democratic Union (KADU). In 1961, with Kenyatta now released from detention and their leader, KANU formed a coalition government with KADU. With the settlers politically discredited and divided, Kenyatta and his colleagues went on to win independence for Kenya in December 1963. Here was another case when nationalist unity had its reward.

CENTRAL AFRICA: A SETTLERS' FEDERATION

Similar kinds of change and drama occurred in the three Central African colonies of Britain. Here there was the same advance from ideas of tribal union to ideas of national union. There was the same resistance by white-settler communities; and in the end, in Rhodesia (Zimbabwe), there was a long war.

Before African nationalism could win, however, these colonies had to undergo ten years of settlers' federation. Here the leaders were the settlers of Southern Rhodesia, more than 200,000 by 1950 (with smaller numbers in Northern Rhodesia and Nyasaland). Britain had given them full control of Southern Rhodesia in 1923, after which Southern Rhodesia was a colony only in name. They proceeded to take the best land for themselves. They continued to make African farmers work for them by money-taxation or other means. They denied Africans any political rights. Their system was one of repressive racism, and much like the system in South Africa.

These settlers had long failed to win closer union with the settlers of the other two colonies (see pp. 144–145). They succeeded in 1953, when Britain agreed to a Central African Federation. This was to be a 'settlers' federation' aimed at keeping government in white hands. The Southern Rhodesian settlers were going to be in control, but the settler communities in Northern Rhodesia (Zambia) and Nyasaland (Malawi) agreed to this because they accurately saw federation as a dam to stem the advancing tide of black independence.

The Southern Rhodesian settlers had the upper hand from the start. Dominated by mining companies located in Southern Rhodesia and South Africa, the new system was able to 'milk' the Northern Rhodesian economy, rich in copper, of a large part of all its mining profits. These totalled, after tax, no less than £260 million in the ten years that the Federation lasted (1953–63). That was a much bigger sum than all the money spent in those years by the colonial government of Northern Rhodesia. Little of these profits were invested in Northern Rhodesia, but a large part of them went to help white-settler development in Southern Rhodesia and South Africa.

Yet the settlers still did not have the full control they wanted: the two northern colonies stayed under colonial governments. Those governments now had to take account of new and strong movements of African nationalism. In Northern Rhodesia these began in 1948, with the formation of the Northern Rhodesian African National Congress and then, in 1959, with the emergence of its stronger successor, the United National Independence Party (UNIP) led by Kenneth Kaunda. Organised nationalism began still earlier in Nyasaland (Malawi) with the formation, in 1944, of the Nyasaland African National Congress. This had determined leaders, and was further strengthened in 1958 with the return home, after many years abroad, of a forceful independence pioneer: a former medical doctor, Hastings Kamuzu Banda. These movements of national union now offered a determined challenge to settler control and colonial rule.

MALAWI AND ZAMBIA: BREAKING THE SETTLERS' POWER

Their challenge in these two countries was a peaceful one. Its central claim was that parliament and governments should be chosen by democratic elections. If all grown-up persons had the vote, the result would be majority rule: necessarily, African majority rule. The settlers would have their share of power, according to their voting numbers, but it would be a minority share because they were few.

Neither the settlers, nor at first the colonial governments, would listen to this claim. Collisions followed, though smaller than in Kenya. Both Kaunda and Banda were arrested, and many others. A state of emergency declared in Nyasaland in 1959 led to the death of 52 Africans, and many arrests. Two years later there were more collisions in Northern Rhodesia, when 27 Africans were killed in clashes and some 3,000 arrested.

But in 1961 colonial policy began to change, for in London there were leading politicians, such as Prime Minister Harold Macmillan, who now saw that Britain should move with the times. Under strong African pressure, Britain allowed a step-by-step advance towards democratic elections. In August 1961 a newly formed Malawi (Nyasaland) Congress Party, with Banda again firmly in the lead, won a large majority of seats in the local parliament. In January 1963 Malawi achieved internal self-government; and in July 1964 it became an independent state. Meanwhile, the same advances were made in Northern Rhodesia, where, in January 1964, UNIP with Kaunda in the lead also won a large majority of seats in the local parliament. Northern Rhodesia became the independent state of Zambia in the following October.

By the end of 1963, these advances had utterly destroyed the settlers' federation; and it had to be dissolved.

RHODESIA: THE SETTLERS' REPUBLIC

South of the Zambezi River, in Southern Rhodesia (known simply as Rhodesia after Northern Rhodesia became Zambia), the African majority and the settler minority had each been watching the tide of anti-colonial change as it swept south towards them. It encouraged the Africans. But it greatly worried settlers; they already had all power and privilege in Rhodesia, and were determined to keep both.

By 1960, these settlers were asking the British government in London to let them become independent in name as well as in fact; then, they believed, the tide of change would never be able to cross southward over the Zambezi. But the British government, already warned by the great rebellion in Kenya and fearing other bad collisions, refused to agree. It replied that Rhodesia could have full independence only when the settlers agreed to accept African majority rule at some time in the future.

Some of the less extreme settlers did agree to this. Their government accepted a new constitution, in 1961, which gave Africans a small share in parliament. This was very little; but it proved too much for most of the settlers. A new settler government came to power in 1963, formed by an extreme racist party called the Rhodesia Front, heavily and fatally influenced by the spectacle of successful whites-only power in South Africa.

This government again demanded full independence, and London still refused. Faced with that refusal, the most extreme settlers took the lead. Under a government led by Ian Smith, they rebelled against Britain in November 1965. They declared that Rhodesia was independent under their minority rule. This was called UDI: unilateral (one-sided) declaration of independence.

Though a painful blow to British prestige, this rebellion was met with little more than verbal protest from London, and then, hesitatingly, by partial economic sanctions against the Smith government. These British sanctions were adopted by the UN, but the 'bite' in their blockade had many missing teeth. Unlike the sanctions applied against fascist Italy in 1935, these sanctions included oil; but that was only in theory, as in practice oil supplies continued to get through to Rhodesia. Besides that, South Africa and Portugal (then in control of neighbouring Mozambique) refused to apply the sanctions. Both of these backed the settlers' rebellion, as did some big-business interests in Britain and elsewhere.

Another war for freedom

Ian Smith's government was able to carry on. It did so by hitting still harder at all African protest of any kind. At the same time, it multiplied laws to safeguard and enlarge settler power and privilege. For most Africans, Rhodesia became a police state.

The question for African nationalists was what to do next? Their organisations were badly hit by settler repression, and found it hard to find the answer. Here, too, colonial tribalism had its dividing influence, making it difficult to build a firm unity between the Shona majority and the Ndebele minority. Apart from that, some nationalists continued to think that peaceful protest was still the only way, however little it could promise. But by this time there were others who thought differently.

153

They believed that armed resistance was necessary, as earlier in Algeria and then in the Portuguese colonies (see pp. 158–160).

The earliest mass party, the African National Congress of Southern Rhodesia (formed 1957), had proved a failure, largely through lack of political experience. A more determined party, Zimbabwe African People's Union (ZAPU), had appeared in 1961. Two years later ZAPU split. A big section broke away and took the name of Zimbabwe African National Union (ZANU). It called for more effective action. Almost at once, the Smith government arrested as many of the leaders of both parties as it could find, while others, escaping, went into exile (mostly in Zambia, independent late in 1964).

Now there was no way left but armed resistance. Yet this was hard to carry out, with any success, until the mass of African people inside Rhodesia (Zimbabwe) were ready to support and take part in the struggle. Time was needed to win that support and participation. Zimbabwe guerrillas sent in from Zambia made their first armed attacks in 1966–67. But all failed, then and for some time after.

The decisive change came only in 1972. Zimbabwe guerrillas had by then gained experience in fighting alongside Frelimo guerrillas, in north-western Mozambique, against joint Portuguese and Rhodesian forces. And when Frelimo defeated the Portuguese in 1975, Zimbabwe guerrillas were able to use Mozambique, as well as Zambia, as a base for a bigger effort. Meanwhile, African opinion inside Rhodesia began to accept the need for war. Great numbers of fighting volunteers came forward.

Mostly ZANU men, the guerrillas won control of a big part of Rhodesia by 1978. The settlers faced defeat. They tried to win over African opinion by forming a joint government of their Rhodesia Front and an African party under Bishop Abel Muzorewa. But the trick, though with backing from Britain and the USA, proved a failure. ZANU, and ZAPU on a smaller scale, continued to fight.

Their victory came in 1980. With the settlers beaten, Britain agreed to a one-man one-vote election. ZANU swept the polls; it won most of the African seats in parliament, while ZAPU took the rest. This great majority formed a new government under Robert Mugabe, leader of ZANU, and Rhodesia at once became the independent republic of Zimbabwe.

The record of this regime of African nationalism, together with other records elsewhere, will be discussed in Part Four.

CHAPTER FIFTEEN

In Other Empires: Belgian, Portuguese, Spanish

A wide range of peoples were enclosed, by partition, in the vast colonies of Belgium and Portugal. To them, the movement of liberating ideas came later than elsewhere. There were various reasons for this.

BELGIAN REPRESSION: UNHAPPY OUTCOMES

The Belgians prevented the emergence of an educated few who could lead the way to an understanding of the modern world, and its ideas and possibilities, so very different from the world of traditional Africa. They refused to allow any of 'their Africans' to study overseas, or even attend secondary school, rightly believing that any such experience would lead to anti-colonial 'disobedience'. The Portuguese were less repressive in this way, but more repressive in other ways.

So it was exceptionally difficult for Africans in these colonies to make the advance from colonial tribalism to modern nationalism. When they began to make this advance, late in the 1950s, the road ahead proved exceptionally dangerous to follow.

From the Belgian Congo to Zaïre

In size of territory, the Belgian Congo was huge, several times larger than Nigeria or Kenya or Tanganyika. But its population, six times smaller than Nigeria's, was spread thinly through great forests and grasslands, and so had evolved into many communities and cultures.

These peoples were unable to combine in defence of their common interests. On the contrary, they were carefully divided from each other by colonial government. One 'tribe' was played off against another 'tribe'. Men from one region were recruited into the colonial army, the *Force Publique*, and sent to 'pacify' the people of other regions. There were many anti-colonial revolts in the 1920s and 1930s, and again during the 1940s. None gave rise to any wide resistance because each, in isolation, was defeated on its own.

But here, too, the Second World War worked its changes. With more forced labour, with a greater drive for export-crops, villages became poorer. From about 1942, there was the beginning of a 'flight to the towns'. As we have seen earlier, small colonial towns such as Léopoldville (Kinshasa) and Elizabethville (Lubumbashi), grew into large concentrations of village people looking for food and jobs.

The Belgians tried hard to stop this flight. But they were no more successful than other colonial rulers. Village people went on coming to the towns. Often they failed to find food or jobs. But among the things they did find were new ideas about how to combine together, and why combining could help them. Soon, tribal unions were many. And then, early in the 1950s, there came from British and French colonies the first ideas about nationalism, about national union.

At first, the Belgians put down all such ideas, and imprisoned anyone who tried to use those ideas for political action. But the times were changing in other colonies; and the Belgians, after 1955, gave a little gr und. They began to allow political parties. Most of these grew out of tribal unions or associations such as the Bakongo Alliance, ABAKO; and each within their vast colony had a narrowly regional influence and following.

Only two of the new parties, formed late in the 1950s, had any real loyalty to the idea of all-Congolese unity of action and aim. Of these two national parties or movements, by far the more important was the Congolese National Movement (in French: MNC), formed in 1959 under the leadership of Patrice Lumumba (1925–1961).

Pressures for anti-colonial change now grew fast. In 1959, after anti-colonial rioting in Léopoldville, the Belgians at last decided to try to catch up with those pressures. Up till then, they had believed that 'their Congo' would remain theirs for many more years, perhaps for another hundred years. Suddenly, they changed their strategy. In January 1960 they offered to give independence only six months later. However intended, this could only be a plan for confusion and disaster. The new parties had no political experience. Most were little more than tribal groups. The civil service had no Africans in senior posts. The *Force Publique* did not possess a single African officer.

Independence came in June 1960, with Lumumba as prime minister;

but so did confusion and disaster. Most of the Belgian civil servants went home at once. Soldiers of the *Force Publique* mutinied. Separatist tribal parties in Katanga (now renamed Shaba) and Kasai provinces lost no time in trying to form their own independent governments. Foreign business interests, especially in mineral-rich Katanga, saw that this separatism could safeguard their interests, and supported it.

As the only unifying political force in the country, Lumumba and his government (MNC with some smaller partners) appealed for United Nations' help against mutiny and separatism. This help came, together with UN military contingents provided by several African and other countries. It did in fact help to bring regional separatism to an end, but its outcome was a failure to support or protect Prime Minister Lumumba and his government. There were many troubles, but what made matters worse was that the affairs of the ex-Belgian Congo, now called Zaïre, became entangled with international politics.

Power was seized in September 1960, only three months after independence and in circumstances of great confusion, by a US-sponsored army officer called Joseph Mobutu. He was given strong Western support, especially American, on the grounds that he was 'pro-Western' while Lumumba, it was alleged, was hostile to Western interests. But the evidence shows that Lumumba merely wished to follow policies of non-alignment and, so far as possible, of independence.

Faced with Mobutu's military take-over, and fearing what might happen next, Lumumba sought the protection of the United Nations in Léopoldville (Kinshasa), and received it. But in December he left this protection and tried to make his way to Stanleyville (Kisangani) where he had strong support. He was seized by men under Mobutu's orders, and in January 1961 was flown as a prisoner to Elizabethville (Lubumbashi), at that time still the capital of the Katanga (Shaba) separatists led by Moise Tsombe. These separatists at once murdered Lumumba.

Many upsets followed, and civil war. MNC leaders formed a government in Stanleyville to oppose a new Léopoldville government formed after Lumumba's murder; and then, in 1964, two major rebellions broke out, led by Lumumbists such as Gaston Soumialot and Pierre Mulele, against Mobutu and his government in Léopoldville. These spread across large regions but rapidly failed, and were put down before the end of the year by General Mobutu's army with the aid of American and Belgian paratroops and various white mercenaries. Following upon this, Mobutu dissolved the Léopoldville government in 1965, and declared himself the country's sole ruler. After that he remained in personal control of the situation, while the country's economy fell ever more deeply into corruption and dependence on Western loans. Opposition protests failed to win any wide support. It was remarked, however, that the name of Lumumba and the patriotic cause for which he had stood were not forgotten. Fresh dissidence broke out from time to time. It was contained, but it continued.

Ruanda and Burundi

The fate of the Belgian trusteeship territory, for a long time, was not much less unhappy. In 1962, Ruanda-Urundi became the two independent states of Ruanda and Burundi, but once again with a legacy of sharp internal divisions.

Here the Belgians had ruled indirectly, largely through the chiefs of the Tutsi, a people who numbered about one-sixth of the population, while the rest of the population, the Hutu (with about one per cent of Twa, or 'pygmies'), provided most of the colonial labour and taxes. Parties formed in 1959 reflected these old and less old divisions. The approach to independence was a brief period of rapidly growing rivalries between Tutsi and Hutu.

Rivalries turned to violence. Soon after independence the Hutu majority in Ruanda won control at the expense of the Tutsi minority, but with much upheaval. In Burundi the Tutsi minority managed to stay in control, but at great cost: a Hutu rebellion, in 1972, was met with ferocious Tutsi repression. Thousands died. Even as late as the 1980s, by which time many refugees had fled into neighbouring countries, Burundi had still to overcome its legacy of conflict. (see also p. 246.)

WARS OF LIBERATION IN THE PORTUGUESE COLONIES

From an African point of view, Portuguese rule was much like that of Belgium. It was a particularly stiff dictatorship, with Africans divided into 'tribal' compartments. Not even the white-settler minorities were allowed to form political parties of their own. The colonial authorities ruled everything.

There were also some differences. Unlike the Belgians, the Portuguese rulers never changed their minds about refusing all African demands. They were privately sure that Portugal itself was too backward and too poor to support change. So Portugal must hold on to everything or else lose everything. While this belief was probably accurate, it unavoidably prepared the ground for violence on the scale of French-ruled Algeria.

The Portuguese, like the French, had a policy of assimilation. They were ready to allow a small number of Africans to become 'black Portuguese'. These could have some civil rights, though no political rights, but they were very few in number. By 1950, fewer than one in every hundred Africans of Angola and Mozambique, and fewer than one in every three hundred in Guiné (Guinea-Bissau), were classified as 'assimilated persons' (*assimilados*). All the rest were 'natives' (*indigenas*), subject to forced labour and other forms of racist persecution.

Most of these rare *assimilados* joined the Portuguese system and served it. But a handful turned to anti-colonial thought and action. Among them were several brave and brilliant individuals: notably Amilcar Cabral of Guiné and Cape Verde, Agostinho Neto of Angola, Edouardo Mondlane of Mozambique. They were joined by others from the Cape Verde Islands (where, at least in theory, all the inhabitants had been granted, in 1914, a nominal Portuguese citizenship). Notable among these Cape Verdean nationalists was Aristides Pereira (1924–).

These men made the advance into modern nationalism. Their way was hard, often going through bitter persecution. But they worked towards the forming of nationalist movements. These emerged in Guiné (Guinea-Bissau) in September 1956, with the underground formation in Bissau of the PAIGC (African Independence Party of Guiné and Cape Verde); in Angola in December 1956, with the formation of the MPLA (People's Liberation Movement of Angola); and in Mozambique in 1962, with the formation of FRELIMO (Mozambique Front of Liberation).

At first these underground movements hoped for peaceful change. They appealed to the Portuguese, asking for progress. They sent messages to the UN, asking for help. But the Portuguese replied with more violent repression, and the UN proved deaf or ineffective. Soon, the leaders of the liberation movements saw that this violence of the colonial system could be met effectively only by counter-violence. They prepared for armed struggle.

Three wars of liberation followed: from February 1961 in Angola, from January 1963 in Guiné, and from September 1964 in Mozambique. They lasted through many years of savage colonial efforts to destroy the guerrilla armies and their political movements. Like the French in Algeria, the Portuguese spared no weapon of mass destruction and no torment of repression. Yet the liberation movements won a complete victory in 1974–75. They liberated their own countries, Guinea-Bissau in 1974, Angola, Mozambique, Cape Verde and São Tomé in 1975. But in doing this they also made it possible for the Portuguese people to liberate themselves from their own dictatorship in Portugal; and Portugal became, once again, a parliamentary republic. This was a case, so far unique, where a liberating revolution in Africa led to a liberating revolution in Europe.

That was a long and heroic story. Here we should note two central points.

First, the underground liberation movements had to begin as 'nationalists without nations'. They had to organise and fight in ways that spread and deepened the advance to national union among peoples long divided by their own history, and then by colonial rule. They found that their liberation struggles were a great help in doing this. More and more people saw that there was no choice for them but unity or defeat; and defeat would be terrible disaster. Out of this growing unity – whether in Angola, Guiné, or Mozambique – there came the force to win these bitter wars.

Secondly, they had a different problem from most colonised peoples. For the Portuguese said: 'Either accept our system, or we shall destroy you.' So they could not take over, reform, or improve the Portuguese system: once they began to fight it, they had to destroy it or be destroyed. From top to bottom, if they wished to win, they had to make a revolution against the Portuguese system. They had to build an alternative system of their own.

And this they had to do even while the wars continued. For they liberated wide areas from Portuguese control; and the people of these areas, freed from the Portuguese system, needed a new system of their own. They needed to be led to govern themselves in new ways. Worked out first in liberated areas, these new ways of 'people's power' (*poder popular*) became a policy for independent republics. They formed a new and hopeful trend in African political action; and this, of course, was the liberating trend against which white South Africa and its friends duly went to war in 1975 and after, by invasions of Angola and Mozambique. Continuing until 1988, these South African invasions now became extremely damaging (see pp. 168 and 171).

THE LEGACY OF SPAIN

During the early years of the Second World War, the pro-nazi dictatorship of Franco in Spain hoped, if the Allies were defeated, to spread its power over Nigeria and the French equatorial colonies. But nazi defeat put an end to such dreams, and, here too, came the beginning of the end of colonial rule.

When France withdrew from Morocco in 1956, Spain had to do the same. Spain's colony in northern Morocco became part of the newly independent state. So it was the dream of the African liberator, Abd al-Krim, that came true: not the dream of Spain's dictator, General Franco.

In 1975 Spain also withdrew from its occupation of the Western Sahara. A conflict over the future of this territory followed between its inhabitants on one side, with Morocco and Mauritania on the other. A Sahrawi (Western Sahara) republic could eventually emerge (see p. 285).

Spain's other holdings were the island of Fernando Po (Bioko) off the Nigerian coast, and a small piece of the equatorial mainland, Rio Muni. In 1959 these were re-named as 'provinces of Spain'; their inhabitants were supposed to have become 'black Spaniards'. Newly formed nationalist parties then began to work for independence. They won some self-government in 1963. In 1968 the two territories became independent as the Republic of Equatorial Guinea. Sadly, it fell almost at once into the hands of a pitiless dictator, Francisco Macias Nguema.

This man exercised an absolute personal power from July 1972 until overthrown in August 1979, and did much damage. He was followed by a nephew, Obiang Mbasogo, who continued to rule by authoritarian means. Through all this, the country's economy barely improved. Its external debt trebled between 1980 and 1985, while the cost of servicing this debt went up by 800 per cent.

CHAPTER SIXTEEN

The 1980s: Unfinished Business

The long process of European imperial withdrawal from Africa had begun with the formation of the kingdom of Libya in 1951. Nearly thirty years later, with independence for Zimbabwe, the process was almost complete.

For meanwhile, in the far south, three other British colonies had won their independence. These were the so-called 'High Commission Territories' of Botswana (formerly Bechuanaland), Lesotho (Basutoland) and the kingdom of Swaziland. Their position was difficult, because each was heavily dependent on racist South Africa, and Lesotho, as the map shows, is right inside South Africa. Yet their leaders were determined not to be left behind. Botswana and Lesotho won their independence in 1966, and Swaziland in 1968.

Yet the far south still had unfinished business in this matter of decolonisation. Namibia remained unfree. Above all, there was racist South Africa.

SOUTH AFRICA: NEW RACIST AIMS

As we noted earlier, the Union of South Africa became an independent British Dominion in 1910; and, in 1961, a republic outside the Commonwealth. Through all that time the local whites kept and used all power and privilege, although blacks outnumbered them by four to one. Exploiting African land and labour, as well as Coloured and Asian labour, these whites were as arrogant as they were rich.

By the end of the Second World War, their racist system was no longer based on a purely colonial economy. It had largely ceased, that is, to draw its main wealth from exporting minerals or other raw materials,

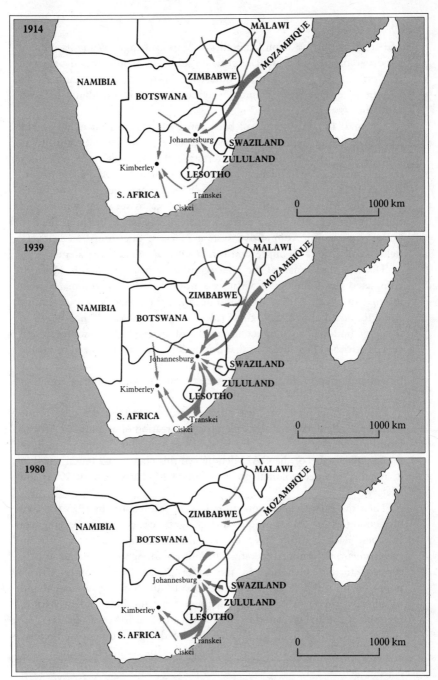

Map 7   Patterns of labour migration in southern Africa in 1914, 1939 and 1980

and from importing manufactured goods in exchange. While its mineral exports remained important, especially gold, this economy had begun to rely on its own manufacturing industries. Formerly, racist South Africa had been a dependent colonial economy; now it had built its own capitalist system.

Up to 1948 this system had been run by a government in which the English-speaking whites had most influence. They were racist in all matters that touched on their interests and privileges; otherwise they could sometimes be 'moderate' in the use of their system of discrimination. But in 1948 there came a sharp change. A general election brought to power the Afrikaner National Party of Afrikaans-speaking whites; and this party was in all ways a party of extreme racism. It began at once to build a much more oppressive system of racist discrimination in every field of daily life. This oppression was labelled *apartheid* ('separateness').

This was the climax of the long white dictatorship in South Africa. It completed the building of what was now, in effect, a colonial system internal to South Africa. At the same time, the system's new economic strength, noted above, gave these rulers a wider ambition. They began to think of building an indirect imperial system throughout southern and central Africa. Their idea was that South Africa would not need to invade newly independent African countries to the north. Instead, using economic power and military threats, South Africa would pressure all these countries into accepting its indirect control.

Publicly, this plan was first put forward in 1964 by the then prime minister, H. F. Verwoerd. He called for the creation of a Southern African Common Market under his government's domination. Replying, most of the member-states of the OAU denounced this plan. But a few listened to it, notably the neo-colonial government of Madagascar until 1972, and Malawi.

Then the tide of liberation surged again southward. In 1975 the two big countries of Mozambique and Angola ceased to be Portuguese colonies. Each became independent under a strongly patriotic African government, determined to refuse all indirect foreign control and to help towards further liberation in the south. Next, racist South Africa's puppet-state of Rhodesia, ruled since 1965 by the Smith government and its allies, vanished in 1980; instead, there came the independent African republic of Zimbabwe, another large setback to South Africa's plans.

Yet it would still be some years before the government in Pretoria could be brought to abandon its plans for sub-continental domination; and this stubborn persistence in subversion and aggression partly relied on encouragement from influential groups and even governments in the West. For a long time after 1975 the armed forces of the South African

Republic continued to invade, harass, and try to destroy their black neighbours to the north. The South African government used its white troops. It used black troops supplied by one or other puppet movement, such as UNITA in Angola and RENAMO (also called MNR) in Mozambique. Its troops and agents wrecked and ruined and killed by any means they could. But all these aggressions eventually failed. As Cuba went to the defence of Angola against the South Africans (see pp. 174–175), so now did Zimbabwe and Tanzania go to help Mozambique.

Meanwhile Pretoria continued to keep firm hold on its virtual colony of Namibia, defying world opinion, determined that Namibia should remain under racist South Africa's control.

THE STRUGGLE IN NAMIBIA

African leaders in Namibia began asking the UN for help, against Namibia's colonial status and its South African racist laws, soon after the Second World War. They asked in vain.

Then a generation of younger men, just as earlier in other colonies, began to form political movements pledged to work for independence. The earliest of these new movements was the South West African Union (SWANU), formed in 1959, chiefly among the Herero, Damara and Nama. Much bigger and more determined, the South West African People's Organisation (SWAPO) was formed in 1960, with growing support from the Ovambo people in the north of Namibia.

Finding that polite appeals for change made no difference, SWAPO passed to armed struggle in 1966. Its guerrillas attacked the South African occupying forces. Namibian nationalists won mass backing for this anti-colonial action, as well as for workers' strikes against low wages paid by foreign companies.

All these pressures received general support from the OAU and the UN; and in 1971 the International Court of Justice advised that South Africa's occupation of Namibia was illegal, and said that South Africa must withdraw. Ignoring this judgment, and turning its back once again on the great balance of world opinion, the South African government worked to divide Namibia into ten 'tribal homelands', and then devise a formula for giving this divided Namibia a nominal independence. The plan, in short, was to defeat modern nationalism by use of modern tribalism; and it might well have worked had the Namibian national movement, empowered by SWAPO (South-West African Peoples' Organisation), been less effective and less determined. All through the 1980s it seemed possible that dominant powers in the outside world, notably the USA and Britain, might 'come off the fence', and throw their weight behind the Namibian national movement. But only in 1988, after a major South African military defeat inside Angola, did independence for Namibia seem to become at all likely (see pp. 171–172).

By this time, however, it had became clear that South Africa's massively destructive invasion of the Angolan republic was not going to succeed. Strongly backed by its ally, Cuba, the Angolan army held firm. The *apartheid* invaders were obliged to withdraw. They lost their bid to include Angola within their sphere of domination. Now they met another albeit political defeat in Namibia. Cuba tied an agreement on ending hostilities to an agreement on Namibian independence. After many manoeuvres, this led to a general agreement on a United Nations plan for Namibian independence. Cuba withdrew its armed forces with which, since 1975, it had decisively helped to defend Angola against South African invasions. Arrangements for a pre-independence general election in Namibia went ahead with South African agreement, given albeit reluctantly. Some of the worst *apartheid* laws in Namibia were scrapped. The peaceful election of an independent Namibian government followed in November 1989.

Having thus become able to elect a constituent assembly with Sam Nujoma as first president, Namibia declared itself independent on 21 March 1990, and was welcomed into the community of nations. Many problems with South Africa remained, notably the future of the port of Walvis Bay, claimed by South Africa. But peaceful solutions were now at last possible. For the first time in nearly half a century, *apartheid* South Africa was on the defensive, and world opinion was powerfully against its policies and oppressions. How this came about forms an important chapter in Africa's modern history.

RESISTANCE IN SOUTH AFRICA

The developments of the Second World War, and its victory over nazifascist racism, had certainly brought new hopes of democratic progress to black people in South Africa, as they did elsewhere. But the ruling white minority, whether of English or Afrikaner origin, had no intention of consenting to any such progress. They were determined to maintain their dictatorship over black people so as to exploit black labour and land.

Black people responded with peaceful protest. In 1946, for example, African mineworkers in the Transvaal gold mines went on strike for an improvement in their very low wages. Armed police shot them back to work; thirteen miners were killed and many others wounded. In other protests African farmers gathered in demonstrations against discriminatory laws that hurt them. They too were crushed.

Then, life grew harder still. So far, governments formed by the English-origin minority had built up a system of anti-black discrimination which was harsh but still had some loopholes. Now the loopholes were stopped, and the system was made much harsher. A whites-only general election in 1948 gave power to a government formed by the extreme racist party of the Afrikaner minority, the Afrikaner National Party. Year by year after 1948, new forms of persecution of black people were invented, made legal by Acts of the whites-only parliament, and ruthlessly enforced by the police. This was done by additional 'pass laws' (which already insisted that all blacks must carry a series of residence, work or movement permits); by the forced removal of black families from 'whites-only areas'; by the banning of even the mildest political action or protest; and by much else. This much harsher form of racist dictatorship formed the system called *apartheid*.

Black organisations launched passive (non-violent) kinds of protest. In 1952, the African National Congress (ANC) and the South African Indian National Congress joined in a campaign of mass demonstrations against the pass laws. At once the government brought in new laws to punish non-violent protesters by lashing with whips or by imprisonment, or both.

Apartheid was said to mean that the two 'races', black and white, were to 'develop separately'. In truth it meant only that the whites continued to rule and exploit in any way they chose, while the blacks continued to be their servants. After the passive-protest campaign against pass laws, all black protest was declared automatically illegal. All black political action, no matter how moderate, was banned.

Even peaceful demonstrations were now met by shooting. In 1960, at the little town of Sharpeville, police fired into a crowd of black people demonstrating against the pass laws, led on this occasion by the Pan-African Congress (PAC, formed in 1959). Sixty-seven men, women and children were killed (several were found to have been shot in the back while running to escape); 186 others were wounded.

This massacre shocked the world, but to African leaders in South Africa it brought a new conviction: peaceful protest of this kind costs lives, but wins nothing. The most determined of them now turned to counter-violence. They began to organise sabotage, but to begin with were betrayed and tracked down. Some of their outstanding men, including the ANC leader Nelson Mandela, were imprisoned for life.

With this setback there came a pause in African political resistance within the *apartheid* state. For a while the racist rulers were triumphant, believing that their system of repression had killed further protest. The last years of the 1960s seemed to be a 'time of silence.' Inside South Africa the leaders of the anti-apartheid movement were in prison, banned from public life, or dead; outside South Africa, those who had managed to escape were thrust aside or ignored by official opinion. It looked like victory for *apartheid*. But the truth proved otherwise. Beneath the surface of everyday life, hidden from hostile eyes, new democratic forces were coming to life.

Mass strikes, Black Consciousness, pro-apartheid banditries

Workers in many industries took the next step and made their protest felt. In 1972–73 they came out on mass strikes against starvation wages; and this time they were too many for the police to shoot back to work. Thousands won higher wages. Repression ruled as before, but was now met by a new spirit of resistance.

This new spirit appeared also among black students in secondary schools and colleges of higher education. These colleges were founded by the government on a 'tribal' basis: one for Zulu students, another for Sotho students, and so on. Student leaders such as Steve Biko (soon afterwards murdered when in prison) saw the need to work for unity against this 'divide-and-rule' system of 'tribal' colleges. In 1969 they formed the South African Students' Organisation (SASO). Then, looking for a way of political action in spite of the repressive laws, they launched in 1970 a movement called Black Consciousness. The successful strikes of 1972–73 gave them fresh encouragement.

Black Consciousness was not a black racist answer to white racism. Its aim was to raise African self-confidence after the defeats of the 1960s. Like SASO, but more widely, it was a political way of working for unity against racist oppression.

Then, in 1975, African movements of anti-colonial liberation won out in the colonies of Portugal. First came the success of Amilcar Cabral's PAIGC in Guinea-Bissau, independent in September 1974; Mozambique, Cape Verde, São Tomé and finally Angola, followed in 1975. These impressive achievements altered the whole balance of power against racist South Africa. Reacting, South Africa sent its army into Angola, even before the declaration of Angolan independence, in order to prevent the emergence of an independent Angolan regime. But the invasion was thrown back in large part because of the arrival in Angola, in the wake of this South African aggression, of military forces from Cuba. Thanks to

Cuba, Angola was saved from becoming a client or subject state of South Africa. Badly mauled, the South African invaders of Angola had to withdraw in March 1976.

But the *apartheid* leaders in South Africa, and many whites there, still believed that they could get their way by fresh violence against the black populations; and they were further encouraged, for a while, by continued support from pro-*apartheid* trends in the USA and some other Western powers. After their failed invasion of 1975–76, the South African army and airforce repeatedly struck again at southern Angola, wrecking towns and killing civilians. But still they won no lasting military gain. Meanwhile, to Angola and Mozambique, more ruthless damage was caused by subversive groups and armed bands. Most of these were promoted by the South African Government, once again with Western connivance, notably the UNITA organisation in the case of Angola. Others, as the misery continued, derived from a consequent breakdown of law and order.

Widespread destruction of civilian lives and property followed in the wake of these UNITA subversions in Angola, and those of its 'sister-movement' called RENAMO in Mozambique. Each violent banditry was designed to 'destabilise' – a polite word meaning to upset and destroy – the legal and constitutional system of African self-government in these two former colonies. Between 1981 and 1988, for example, the banditry in Mozambique initially inspired and fuelled by *apartheid* South Africa wrecked several hundred public-health clinics and looted many others, although Mozambicans desperately needed all the medical help they could get.

About half of Mozambique's primary schools were forced to close by bandit attacks of one kind or another. Many teachers were slain. In 1989 the UN estimated that this politically-motivated banditry, or merely criminal banditry deriving from it, had caused the deaths of some 494,000 Mozambican children under five years old, and had driven about one million Mozambicans into exile as refugees. Perhaps as many as another million Mozambicans died as a result of banditries. Many of the social gains of the long anti-colonial struggle died with them. Even by the early 1990s it remained unclear how these miseries were to be brought to an end.

Soweto

Defeats for racism in neighbouring countries gave new hope to South Africa's black people, especially to the younger generations. Meanwhile the strike movement of 1972–73 had grown larger; in 1974, for example, there were 374 strikes by a total of 57,656 workers, and new gains were won. Yet bigger protests now burst upon the scene, at first in the million-strong township of Soweto, near Johannesburg in the Transvaal.

In April-May 1976 the school students of Soweto declared a boycott of their schools in protest against discriminatory education, organising it themselves. The police replied by shooting them in the streets. Many were killed or wounded, but the students held firm under their own young leaders; they would not go to school. This was not because they did not want to learn. It was because they did not want to have to learn their lessons in the language of their oppressors, the Afrikaner rulers. But a new government order had just declared that students would have to learn half their subjects in that language, known as Afrikaans.

That was the immediate reason for protest. Soon it was seen that the political ideas of Black Consciousness and of the banned ANC were also at work. Rapidly, too, the school strikes spread to other towns. They continued for months, a massive demonstration against *apartheid* oppression.

Many students escaped abroad rather than give in. They went secretly over the frontiers. They joined the ANC there. They trained for guerrilla action against the racist system. After 1976, they began returning secretly across the frontiers. Back in South Africa they launched actions of sabotage, attacks on police stations, railway lines, oil refineries – in other words, on instruments of state repression or targets that contributed to the system's economy. Their ANC-launched guerrilla organisation was called Umkonto we Sizwe, Spear of the Nation.

At the same time the strike movement had won other gains besides better wages. Black factory workers, striving for unity, had succeeded for the first time in forming groupings of independent trade unions. The largest of these groupings, the Federation of South African Trade Unions (FOSATU), had won 200,000 worker members by 1981, while the racist government, forced back once again, conceded that unions formed by black workers could be officially registered as 'non-racial' unions, open to members of all the 'races'.

BESIEGED BUT STILL DANGEROUS

All through the 1980s, and prospectively since, the drama of South Africa continued to move from one tortured scene to the next, but increasingly with the likelihood of eventual success shifting to the side of the anti-racists. Frustrated in their plan to become the 'great power' of southern and central Africa, the Afrikaner National party and its government turned to new ways of riveting their domination on the non-white peoples within their republic. Although the black communities (whether African, Coloured, or Indian) now outnumbered the whites by some 22 millions to 5 millions, they were not to be given any equality of rights and powers. But some gestures in that direction, it was now seen by the ruling whites, might have to be made.

Against strong opposition from extremists within the Afrikaner (Boer) community, President P.W. Botha introduced a new South African constitution, late in 1984, providing for three legislative chambers instead of one. But it remained that the 'races' were still represented *separately*. The white chamber retained all decisive power over national affairs. The Indian and Coloured chambers, in any case voted into being by much less than a fifth of the eligible Indian and Coloured electorate, could be little more than talking shops. And there was still no representation of the African majority: there was no chamber of any kind for blacks.

Even before this largely cosmetic change, another *apartheid* policy had relabelled the old 'native reserves' as 'Bantu homelands'. These were, in fact, labour reservoirs for the scheduled 'white areas'. Desperately poor and overcrowded, their soils long since hopelessly eroded, these 'Homelands' were given some powers of local self-government, and presented in official propaganda as being 'independent states.' Nothing had really changed. The outside world refused to recognise any such faked independence.

Meanwhile the movement of democratic protest and organisation had begun to recover from the crushing setbacks of the 1960s. Strong evidence of this, in the political field, came in the emergence during August 1983 of a broad coalition of many anti-*apartheid* groups and bodies. With the approval and backing of the African National Congress, banned and driven underground but still effective, this coalition took the name of the United Democratic Front: potentially, this UDF was clearly the prototype of an all-South African democratic party, and, as such, almost at once became the target of government persecution. Moving from one new act of oppression to the next, the government declared a state of emergency in 1985, and set on its police to shoot down all who might stand in its way. This state of emergency lasted for 229 days; 757 people lost their lives, and more than 8,000 were thrown into prison. It settled nothing else. Black protest continued.

'No easy walk to freedom'

This internal resistance to *apartheid* was increasingly supported by events in neighbouring countries. In 1988, as we have seen, the South African invaders of Angola suffered a painful defeat at the hands of Angolan and

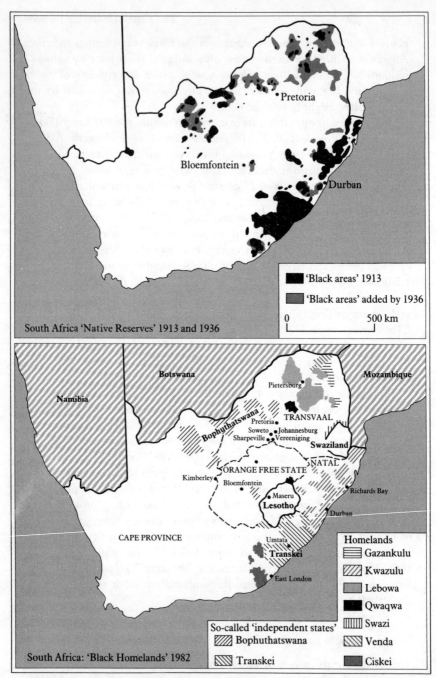

South Africa 'Native Reserves' 1913 and 1936

'Black areas' 1913

'Black areas' added by 1936

0   500 km

Botswana

Namibia

Mozambique

Pietersburg

Bophuthatswana

TRANSVAAL

Pretoria

Soweto • Johannesburg

Sharpeville • Vereeniging

Swaziland

NATAL

ORANGE FREE STATE

Kimberley

Bloemfontein

Richards Bay

Maseru

Lesotho

Durban

CAPE PROVINCE

Umtata

Transkei

East London

Homelands

Gazankulu

Kwazulu

Lebowa

Qwaqwa

Swazi

Venda

Ciskei

So-called 'independent states'

Bophuthatswana

Transkei

South Africa: 'Black Homelands' 1982

Map 8 South Africa: 'Native Reserves' in 1913 and 1936/'Black Homelands' in 1982. As the maps show, only the labels changed

Cuban defending forces. This defeat occurred near the town of Cuito Canevale, in south-eastern Angola. It drove the South Africans into a retreat so humiliating that another invasion did not follow. Various banditries continued in Mozambique, but here too the established government held firm. Namibia, again as we have seen, was advancing rapidly towards the expulsion of direct South African control, and in a large sense could no longer be counted upon as part of the *apartheid* sphere of action. History's doors were closing on the whole evil system.

These largely internal pressures were now reinforced against the system by other pressures from external sources. Powerful trends of political opinion in the West, and decisively in the USA, came round to the view that there could be no stable peace in South Africa, and therefore no security for investments and dividends, so long as *apartheid* extremism remained in control there. And since the *apartheid* system was clearly unable to reform itself, pressures for change must be applied from outside the country. This meant, above all, financial and other economic sanctions.

Pro-*apartheid* trends tried to prevent sanctions from being applied. They had only partial success. In the USA the Congress insisted, over-ruling a presidential veto, that strong sanctions be applied. During 1986 alone, responding to growing demands by public opinion, some fifty US corporations terminated their South African operations; financial sanctions, meanwhile, were beginning to prove still more effective. The South African government was faced by an acute difficulty in finding the means to meet payments on its foreign debt.

Other Western governments, with the partial exception of Margaret Thatcher's Conservative government in Britain, agreed that the outside world had a duty to limit the tragedies caused by *apartheid*. The last years of the 1980s opened with the *apartheid* regime under tightening siege although by no means yet defeated. The onset of really hopeful change came in 1989. External and internal pressures began to have their effect. The hard-line Afrikaner state president, P.W. Botha, was forced out of office by his colleagues, and was replaced by the more diplomatic F.W. de Klerk. At first nothing changed. A highly oppressive 'state of emergency', a trick for giving free reign to police and army, was retained and even extended. Yet the writing was on the wall. Something had to give. It gave with huge effect in February 1990. De Klerk announced the unbanning of all the major, and many of the minor, anti-*apartheid* movements, including the majority-backed African National Congress (ANC), the Pan-African Congress, the South African Communist Party, and 33 other organisations. This sudden unleashing of political freedoms was capped, a few weeks later, by the release from 27 years of political imprisonment of the ANC leader, Nelson Mandela.

A new era might now begin. This was confirmed in 1991 by the repeal of some of the system's worst racist laws. At the same time it became clear that many decades of acute racist oppression could not be easily swept away. The poisons had gone deep. Extremist trends within the ruling Afrikaner white community still had strong influence or even control over the police and army. Soon it was known, convincingly from information given by men from within the police and army, that these extremist trends within the white community were actively plotting to reverse or nullify every democratic gain that was being scored. It likewise became clear that De Klerk and his government were unable or unwilling to move against the extremists with any decisive effect.

These police and army extremists had meanwhile looked around for men or groups among Africans who could be bought and used for pro-*apartheid* purposes. In 1991 it was officially admitted that such men and groups had been found in various splinter 'movements', notably one called 'Nkata'. The Government had made secret payments to them as well as using police and army to cover their subversive violence. Many hundreds of people in African townships were to lose their lives in consequence of these subversions. Years earlier, in one of his brave speeches in defence of his people, Nelson Mandela had warned that there could be no easy walk to freedom. In this, too, he was proved right.

The Struggles for Independence

Success in escaping from direct colonial rule came from a number of developments. Among these were:

1 The rise of mass movements of nationalism, demanding progress towards independence in each colony.
2 The weakening of Britain and France, though for different reasons, by the Second World War.
3 The effects of war experience on African opinion.
4 The rise of the USA to super-Power status during and as a result of the Second World War. This new America was not interested in helping to maintain the European colonial systems of monopoly. It was ready to be the patron of or to favour African demands for an end of those systems.
5 Driven to retreat, Britain and then France became willing (in non-settler colonies) to withdraw their political controls and colonial governments. At the same time, they intended to safeguard their long-term economic and other interests. They developed a policy known as neo-colonialism, or 'indirect colonialism'. The French were especially active in promoting it.
6 African nationalists took advantage of this British and French political retreat. They pressed for political independence, believing that this advance could open the way to further advances later.
7 But in all colonies of major white settlement, a peaceful struggle for independence proved vain. The use by Africans of violence to counter the violence of the settler/colonial systems could not be avoided. Long guerrilla struggles ensued. They were painful, but all in the end succeeded.
8 In most colonies a variety of other forms of pressure were used by

African organisations. These included strikes and boycotts. Wherever the colonial system would allow it, African trade unions gathered strength in this period of struggle for independence.

By the early years of the 1990s, as a result of all these struggles of one kind or another, often at painful cost in life or happiness, almost the whole black continent had won free of direct or colonialist control. And the world gave due recognition to this big historical achievement.

So now in this book we move forward into the years after independence. Up to now we have followed in detail the progress of anti-colonialist liberation. Africans have taken possession of their own continent after nearly a century of dispossession. They have begun to be free to show themselves, and the world, what they can do with their regained freedoms. It is one of the grand chapters of human success in the modern world.

But the present remains the child of the past, and history can never be a simple tale of gain or loss. Direct forms of foreign or colonialist rule were removed; indirect forms still remained. These indirect forms of foreign control now proved hard to deal with. They drew their strength from outside interests and pressures, coming from the so-called 'developed world' of industrialism, as well as from shortages of African experience, and, of course, from the frailties and failings of human nature.

Africans since independence have won victories for progress. They have also had to suffer defeats. Real history, as distinct from sentimental history, is always like that. The costs of a century of colonialist dispossession have proved much more difficult to meet than the liberators had foreseen, while the outside world, often with troubles of its own, has proved far less helpful than had been expected. In this 'young' continent, most ancient in time yet now with half its population under the age of 15, the ardent hopes and plans of youth have had to wrestle ever harder with problems left over from the past.

What have been the worst of these problems? Why is Africa poorer than it used to be, hungrier, more beset with conflicts? The drama of liberated Africa is not a sad story: but surely it is a tough and contradictory story. Above all it is a very human story, matching courage with defeat, despair with stubborn optimism, and human good against human evil.

Part Four takes us into the living history of these years, and shows us, in all their complexity of themes and breadth of ideas, how these years brought Africa to the threshold of the 21st Century.

In what follows here it is important to remember that Africa and the World are not separate from each other. On the contrary, they belong to each other: whatever happens in Africa is influenced by whatever happens in the rest of the world, and of course the same is true in reverse. The mistakes and confusions and miseries of post-independence Africa – and these have been many – have to be seen as part of the world's wider problem: how to build communities of people who work together with each other for the common good? History so far has given us no agreed answers. Meanwhile, since the ending of empires in Africa, the record in this huge continent shows repeated effort by Africans, in spite of African failures and crimes, to use and enlarge their new freedoms whenever possible.

New Freedoms: Progress and Problems

PART FOUR is concerned with questions about the gains, and the problems, of African independence, largely in the years 1960–90. Some of these questions are:

Chapter Seventeen   History Begins Anew
● How did independence affect Africa's place in world affairs?
● What educational changes came after independence?
● What were literacy campaigns? Why were they necessary?
● In what ways did business expand?
● What are the chief gains of independence?

Chapter Eighteen   Questions about National Stability
● What was, or is, 'neo-colonialism'?
● Was political stability threatened by regionalism? By separatism? By tribalism? By élitism? If so, how?
● How and why did foreign interventions occur?
● What were the reasons for military government? Were all military governments of the same kind? If not, how did they differ?
● What party systems took shape after independence?
● What is 'people's power?'

Chapter Nineteen   Questions about Development
● What was the colonial economic legacy? What was or is its 'machinery of control'?
● Is the poverty of most Africans caused by themselves, or by the outside world?
● Why did food imports increase?
● What was Africa's debt crisis'?
● What were the basic requirements of national development?
● How did the strategy of private enterprise (capitalism) operate?
● What alternative strategies came on the scene?
● What were some of the basic problems of rural development?
● What were the advantages and disadvantages of foreign aid?

Chapter Twenty   Questions about Unity
● How did the ideas of pan-Africanism develop after independence?
● What were the Mali Federation and the Ghana-Guinea Union?
● What were the groupings called Casablanca, Monrovia, Brazzaville?
● What is the OAU? When was it founded, and by whom? What does its Charter declare?
● What was OCAM?
● How did the OAU deal with frontier disputes?
● What new steps towards regional co-operation began to appear, and when?

CHAPTER SEVENTEEN
History Begins Anew

In 1990 it was just on forty years since the first African colony emerged to independence from the colonial systems of Europe. That country was Libya, and the independence which it gained had to be at best a partial one. Many changes and upheavals lay unavoidably ahead; but this has had to be true, and remains true today, of every country in the black continent. Its peoples have had to cope with great political problems of adjustment, as well as harsh economic problems. These derive from the legacies of the past as well as from the conflicts of the present; and in a continent of such rich diversity of culture and experience, it cannot be surprising that human disasters have been added to natural disasters.

Yet none of these setbacks and sorrows has been able to lessen the sovereign value of anti-colonial liberation. The struggle for independence and the chance of progress have given Africans what the colonial systems denied them: the keys to their own future, and the freedom to use those keys. They have become able to study and understand their own continent. They have become able to take stock of their own capabilities and potentials, to search for their own solutions, to stand free and equal with all mankind.

So it is that the time of independence, few years or many, has been a time of experiment and renewal, sometimes positive and sometimes not: a time of development in small things as well as in big things; a time of self-discovery within the arena of the modern world. When independence came, reading and writing, cars and trucks and bicycles, even shoes and radios, were for the chosen few. Now they are part of the daily scene, like the industry and science that have made them possible.

Few Africans travelled far from home before independence came. Countless numbers now do so every week. They have become citizens of the world for the first time for several centuries. They

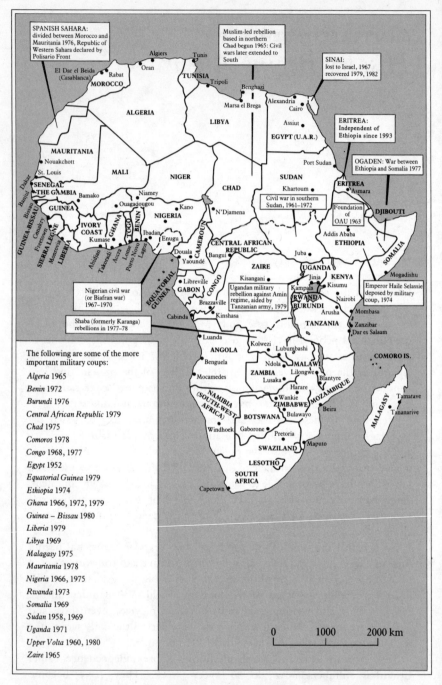

SPANISH SAHARA:
divided between Morocco and
Mauritania 1976, Republic of
Western Sahara declared by
Polisario Front

Muslim-led rebellion
based in northern
Chad begun 1965: Civil
wars later extended to
South

SINAI:
lost to Israel, 1967
recovered 1979, 1982

ERITREA:
Independent of
Ethiopia since 1993

OGADEN: War between
Ethiopia and Somalia 1977

Foundation
of
OAU 1963

Civil war in southern
Sudan, 1961–1972

Emperor Haile Selassie
deposed by military
coup, 1974

Ugandan military
rebellion against Amin
regime, aided by
Tanzanian army, 1979

Nigerian civil war
(or Biafran war)
1967–1970

Shaba (formerly Karanga)
rebellions in 1977–78

Algiers
Tunis
Oran
El Dar el Beida
(Casablanca)
Rabat
MOROCCO
TUNISIA
Tripoli
Benghazi
Marsa el Brega
Alexandria
Cairo
ALGERIA
LIBYA
Assiut
EGYPT (U.A.R.)
Port Sudan
MAURITANIA
Nouakchott
St. Louis
MALI
NIGER
SUDAN
ERITREA
Asmara
Dakar
SENEGAL
THE GAMBIA
Bamako
Khartoum
DJIBOUTI
Bissau
GUINEA-BISSAU
Conakry
GUINEA
Niamey
Ouagadougou
Kano
N'Djamena
CHAD
Banjul
Freetown
SIERRA LEONE
Monrovia
LIBERIA
IVORY
COAST
Kumase
Abidjan
Takoradi
GHANA
Accra
TOGO
BENIN
Ibadan
Lomé
Porto Novo
Lagos
NIGERIA
Enugu
Douala
Yaoundé
CAMEROUN
CENTRAL AFRICAN
REPUBLIC
Bangui
Juba
Addis Ababa
ETHIOPIA
SOMALIA
Mogadishu
EQUATORIAL
GUINEA
Libreville
GABON
CONGO
Brazzaville
ZAIRE
Kisangani
UGANDA
Jinja
Kampala
RWANDA
BURUNDI
KENYA
Kisumu
Nairobi
Arusha
Mombasa
Zanzibar
Dar es Salaam
TANZANIA
Cabinda
Kinshasa
Luanda
Kolwezi
Lubumbashi
Ndola
MALAWI
Lilongwe
Blantyre
COMORO IS.
ANGOLA
Benguela
Mocamedes
ZAMBIA
Lusaka
Harare
Wankie
ZIMBABWE
Bulawayo
Beira
MOZAMBIQUE
NAMIBIA
(SOUTH-WEST
AFRICA)
BOTSWANA
Windhoek
Gaborone
Pretoria
Maputo
SWAZILAND
LESOTHO
SOUTH
AFRICA
Capetown
MALAGASY
Tamatave
Tananarive

The following are some of the more
important military coups:

Algeria 1965

Benin 1972

Burundi 1976

Central African Republic 1979

Chad 1975

Comoros 1978

Congo 1968, 1977

Egypt 1952

Equatorial Guinea 1979

Ethiopia 1974

Ghana 1966, 1972, 1979

Guinea – Bissau 1980

Liberia 1979

Libya 1969

Malagasy 1975

Mauritania 1978

Nigeria 1966, 1975

Rwanda 1973

Somalia 1969

Sudan 1958, 1969

Uganda 1971

Upper Volta 1960, 1980

Zaire 1965

0   1000   2000 km

Map 9   Independent Africa, 1980. South Africa remains a white-ruled state.

have forged personal and professional contacts and friendships in every continent.

These years have therefore been the most momentous time of change in all of Africa's long history. And this time of change has moved at a startling speed. Africa's new generations already live in a world vastly different from that of their grandparents. In 1985, for example, every Nigerian born since independence was still under the age of 25; every Kenyan under 22; every Zambian under 21; every Angolan under 10. Never before have young Africans – and in the 1980s about half of Africa's whole population was under the age of 15 – possessed the privilege of living through so great and challenging a time of change.

In Part Four we shall look at the troubles and problems of these opening years of regained independence. But first we shall look at something more important. We shall look at the gains of independence. These gains were large, and they were many.

CITIZENS OF THE WORLD

When independence came, the men and women of those days could take none of the gains for granted. They had needed to struggle for these gains, often meeting violence or persecution; and now, with independence, they had to struggle hard to keep them. Rightly, they saw the gains of independence as victories for progress.

The racism of the colonial rulers had gripped them at every stage. All the colonial systems, as we have seen, had used the weapon of racism. They used it to keep Africans at the bottom of the ladder of development. They used it to teach Africans that the bottom of the ladder was their proper place. Consider again, for a moment, what this really meant.

In Zambia, before independence came, no African worker was allowed to drive a railway train; he could only shovel coal for the white-settler driver. In Kenya, for many years, no African farmer could share in the profits of growing coffee; that was a 'white man's crop'. No Ugandan could gin the cotton he had grown. In the Belgian Congo, no African could move from one place to another without permission from the police. In the Portuguese colonies, many farmers could not even decide which crops they would grow. Even in more advanced colonies, such as Nigeria, all banking and big business were long barred to African enterprise, or, if a few Africans could enter those fields in West Africa, their operations were severely restricted. Only a handful of Africans, no matter how talented, could hope for reasonable jobs in public service or academic work. Beyond all such handicaps, no Africans could determine the policies of governing their own countries. Even if they had managed to acquire the necessary education, which was possible only for a very few, the essential facts and figures were debarred to them.

This all-powerful weapon of colonial racism could be destroyed when independence came. Free of its oppression, Africans could begin to develop their talents and energies. A new confidence flowed from this freedom, a new self-respect, as well as openings for every kind of job or duty. There came the promise of a revolution in Africa's chances, a revolution in Africa's standing in the world.

Africans could begin to know their own continent. Before independence came, even the few Africans in secondary schools could know little about countries outside the colony they were in. 'French Africans' could learn something about 'French Africa', and more about France. But they could learn nothing about the rest of Africa. 'British West Africans' might learn about British history or geography, but little or nothing about the history or geography of their own countries.

Now the gates of knowledge were opened. Africans could learn about other continents and peoples. They could become citizens of the world as well as of their own countries. They could take their place in the councils of the world: in the assemblies and organisations of the United Nations as well as in world-wide meetings of the non-aligned movement and other such bodies.

A REVOLUTION IN EDUCATION

Knowledge is the way to understanding; and understanding is the way to power. The colonial systems blocked each of these ways. The systems were there to keep power for the colonial rulers.

Missionary schools and government schools existed before independence. But most of them were colonial schools; they taught colonial values. Basically, as we have seen, these were racist values (see Chapter 8). Such schools provided an inferior education for people who were said to be inferior; they were also not many. Even in the least backward colonies, by 1960, no more than ten children in every hundred could hope for a place in a primary school. In the most backward colonies only one in every hundred, or fewer still, could hope for such a place.

When independence came, a revolution in education was therefore needed. Independent governments had to provide many more schools and teachers. This need in quantity was all the more urgent because the size of

African populations was now growing fast. From the 1950s, Africa became a very youthful continent compared with Europe or North America. By 1975, for example, 442 Africans in every 1,000 were under 15: whereas the corresponding proportion for the industrialised countries was only 260 in every 1,000.

But quantity was not the only need. There was also need for a new quality in education. Consider three statements about the kind of education provided by the colonial systems. The first is by the Nigerian historian J.F. Ade Ajayi. He wrote that the colonial education of the black student had been controlled:

> not only through the prejudices of the white teacher and the white textbook author, but also sometimes by actual directives of the administrations in laws said to be designed for the best interests of the black man.

Discussing the same subject in 1967, the President of Tanzania Julius Nyerere wrote:

> [colonial education] was not designed to prepare young people for the service of their country. Instead, it was motivated by a desire to inculcate the values of the colonial society, and to train individuals for the service of the colonial state . . . This meant that colonial education induced attitudes of human inequality, and, in practice, underpinned the domination of the weak by the strong, especially in the economic field.

This meant, in practice, that colonial education for Africans was education for inferiority. In their franker moments, the colonial rulers said as much. Here is what the Patriarch of Lisbon, Cardinal Cerejeira, told 'Portuguese Africa' in a Christmas message of 1960:

> We need schools in Africa, but schools in which we show the native the way to the dignity of man and the glory of the nation (Portugal) which protects him. We want to teach the natives to write, to read, and to count, but not to make them learned men.

Improving the quality of education, after independence, proved more difficult than increasing the quantity. And wherever countries became independent under indirect foreign control, as usually by the French plan (see pp. 126–127), the quality scarcely improved. Madagascar was an example. It became independent under indirect French control in 1960, and won a real independence after 1972. Its new leaders then said that Madagascan education, up till then, had been totally inadequate:

> a system of teaching which is out-of-date and out-of-touch with real life and with the country's needs; it has done nothing but increase joblessness and under-employment.

Faced with these needs for improvement, both in quality and quantity, strongly independent governments acted with vigour and success. In quantity, at least, the expansion was general throughout the continent. In 44 African countries, between 1960 and 1972, the number of students attending school at the three levels – primary, secondary, higher – rose from 17.8 million to 37.6 million. In twelve years of effort, school attendances more than doubled.

Another part of the colonial legacy in education was the inferior position of girls, reflecting the inferior position of women. Many fewer girls got to school than boys. Some effort was begun to be made towards righting this. The proportion of African girls and young women who were getting education, between the ages of 6 and 19, became a little larger. In 1960 this proportion was 33.7 per cent of all students then at school; in 1972 it was 37.6 per cent of double the total of students. The proportion of girls and young women getting education in Africa was still lower than in Asia, and much lower than in Latin America. Yet it was also true that the actual number of girls and young women in education had more than doubled since 1960.

At the same time, new lessons and classes aimed at giving students a 'decolonised' education. Generally, syllabuses and textbooks were Africanised: that is, they were redesigned to meet the realities and needs of Africa, not of Europe. This was done, with much success, in two ways: first, in terms of what was taught; secondly, in providing different types of education after the primary level.

In terms of syllabus, for example, students now began to be taught the history of their own peoples, instead of the history of Europe's peoples. As never before, students could learn about the past development of their own countries and regions, instead of being taught that all development came from Europe. In terms of different types of education, new kinds of schools and colleges were opened with specially trained staffs: vocational schools for practical training, agricultural schools, medical schools, colleges of various kinds. New universities were founded to give African students a wider chance of standing level with highly educated persons overseas. More African scholars could take their place in countless meetings and conferences of learned people in other continents. In these ways, too, Africans became citizens of the world.

A pointer to the aims of independent Africa, in this great matter of education, was found in 1965, at a conference of African educational authorities in Addis Ababa, the capital of Ethiopia. Drawing up a charter for further development, they laid down the following conditions.

1 Primary education shall be universal, compulsory, and free.

2 Education at the secondary level shall be provided for 30 per cent of the children who complete primary school.

3 Higher education shall be provided, mostly in Africa itself, for 20 per cent of those who complete secondary education.

4 The improvement of the quality of African schools and universities shall be a constant aim.

If we summarise the gains that were made by the 1970s, we shall see that they were of great importance. There was huge expansion in quantity in all but the poorest countries; there was some expansion even in those. This often went together with a 'cultural revolution' in what was taught. Students in new schools could learn about the worth and dignity of African traditions and beliefs. They could open their minds to the science of the modern world. They could reinforce their understanding of the need for national unity in facing common problems.

Kenya, for example, had many different peoples formed by a long history, each with different traditions and beliefs. The new Kenya educational system did not deny those differences. But it aimed at providing all Kenya students with a common ground to stand on: all could learn the same lessons of national unity, all could feel gathered into the same nation. And so it was, often, in other countries too.

Along with these gains, there were others. In the less backward countries there were important advances in the field of social hygiene, and the provision of nurses, doctors, clinics, hospitals.

The best of the independent governments fully recognised that this expansion must continue. There were more schools and teachers by the 1970s; in the stronger countries, many more. But the size of populations was still outgrowing them. A race developed between growing numbers of young people and growing numbers of school places. Lack of resources, or bad government in the weaker countries, meant that the first would overtake the second.

African educational pioneers saw this problem. Between 1960 and 1972, for example, independent governments provided more than 16 million new primary school places. But the growth of population, during those same years, provided almost as many more children between six and eleven years of age; and this growth was still rising fast. Soon it was also seen that the target for secondary school places – 30 per cent, as the 1965 charter urged, of all children completing primary school – could not be reached by 1980. Only in higher education was the target reached and even passed. By 1972, for the whole continent, there were three African students in higher education for every two in 1965.

Apart from a shortfall in primary and secondary places, there were wide differences between countries. By the middle 1970s, for example,

Ghana had found primary school places for about 70 per cent of all Ghanaian children in the primary age-group. Yet neighbouring Upper Volta, much poorer and less independent, had found places for only 10 per cent. Then in some countries, perhaps in most, the standards of teaching and examination-passing fell away as rapid expansion continued. That could not be avoided, but more time and fresh effort were needed to put it right. Another result of very rapid expansion was that the number of 'drop-outs' in or after primary school became disturbingly high; and this number stayed high.

As elsewhere in the world, the conclusion was that progress and new problems went hand-in-hand. Great advances were made; and on a scale never even thinkable before. Just as surely, tough problems arose in line with this progress. Yet here, too, there was another difference from the colonial past. In the truly independent countries, and sometimes even in the nominally independent ones (chiefly of the former French empire), these problems could now be understood, discussed, and tackled.

Language and literacy: Swahili and Somali examples

Africa has more than 700 languages. Many are spoken by small communities. Some are spoken by numerous peoples, though often in different dialects: such is the case with the Yoruba language in Nigeria, and the various branches of Akan or Twi in Ghana. A few are spoken by several or many neighbouring peoples. Important among the last are Arabic in North Africa and Sudan; Swahili in East Africa; and Hausa in West Africa.

When independence came, a number of African peoples had long used a 'common language' between each other such as Arabic, Swahili, or Hausa, for purposes of trade and discussion. But because most countries had many languages, most new states had to continue using the European language of their former colonial rulers. Perhaps the future would change this situation. Meanwhile most students, at least after primary school (and often during primary school), had to learn their lessons in a European language. In some cases, however, there could be progress towards a different solution. That was so, for example, with Swahili and Somali.

Used for centuries along the eastern coast of Africa, Swahili is a large and flexible African language with an intake of Arabic forms and words. Its very name indicates this, for it derives from the Arabic word for coastland. Gradually, spreading inland, Swahili became the second language of many peoples in Kenya and Tanzania. When independence came, the new governments of those countries could almost at once decide to adopt Swahili as a national language. Progress could be made towards using Swahili as the language of instruction in schools.

Like Arabic in North Africa (and elsewhere in Muslim regions), Swahili has long possessed its own way of being written. Arabic writing dates from the earliest times of Islam. Swahili began to be written, several centuries ago, in a form of Arabic writing; afterwards, in the colonial period, it began to be written in the western (Latin) alphabet. So the use of Swahili as a national language raised no problem about how to write it.

Somali was an interestingly different case. The colonial rulers had mostly ignored the Somali language: the Italians had ruled in Italian, and the British had ruled in English. When Somalia became independent in 1960, there was no difficulty about deciding that Somali should be the national language, for nearly all the people of Somalia are Somalis. The difficulty came in knowing how to write Somali.

Learned Somali Muslims had tried to write their language in an Arabic script, but this proved inefficient because of the linguistic differences between Somali and Arabic. How else could they write it? At last, in 1972, Somalia's government and academics agreed to devise a way of writing Somali in the western (Latin) alphabet. They found this worked well. Somali became a national written language as well as a spoken one, and here again progress could be launched in using Somali as the language of instruction in schools. Up to about 1980, when disaster struck in Somalia, this new literacy was producing good results.

Yet writing a language is not much use unless many people can read it. The knowledge of how to read and write, *literacy*, was very rare in the colonial period; only the educated few possessed it. Independence brought the need, but also the possibility, of changing that. Many *literacy campaigns* were launched in Africa, often linked with the teaching of elementary arithmetic.

Given all the difficulties, the results of these campaigns were impressive. Between 1961 and 1970, the proportion of illiterate persons – people knowing neither how to read nor how to write – fell steadily throughout most of the continent. But of course the number of illiterates remained high. For the problem of literacy is not only how to teach people to read and write. It is also how to produce conditions in which people form the habit of reading and writing, and go on doing both.

By 1970 it seemed likely that only about 27 per cent of Africans had achieved a firm grasp of literacy; large territories such as Angola and Mozambique had still, at that time, to be liberated from colonial ignorance. After this, the growth of population began to outrun the literacy campaigns, and fresh efforts were needed.

Education: a summary

By the early 1980s the results of educational and literacy expansion were already much better than anything ever achieved before. Sometimes, as in Nigeria and Ghana, or in East and Central Africa, they were sensationally better. In Angola, to quote another example, fewer than 350,000 Africans were in colonial primary schools before independence in 1975. By 1980 about 1,500,000 Angolans were in primary schools with new syllabuses and new textbooks.

Summing up, the picture of educational advance looked like this. In 1960, when the tides of independence began to flow in most parts of the continent, the proportion of young Africans enrolled for study in primary schools south of the Sahara Desert stood at around 36 per cent of all young Africans of school-age. That figure is of course a crude average, probably too high, and the proportion in some colonies was a lot smaller than in others. But it gives us a rough base to work from. Using it, we can measure the gains of educational progress. For in 1981, some twenty years later, that same proportion stood at 78 per cent. The content of primary education available had meanwhile improved. Young Africans no longer had to learn the history of their former colonial masters; now they could learn the history of their own peoples. There was a comparable enlargement in secondary and higher education. Colonial Africa had almost no universities; independent Africa has many, as well as vocational colleges.

Have girls been given less of a chance than boys to profit from this educational progress? The answer is yes. Women in Africa have always suffered from male supremacist attitudes and customs; and they have continued to suffer from them since independence. But they have begun to suffer less. In 1960, for example, the same set of educational figures for sub-Saharan Africa – Africa south of the great desert – showed that only 24 per cent of school-age girls could go to school, but in 1981 this proportion stood at 64 per cent.

Here again the legacy of the past laid on a heavy handicap. In general, the colonial period had worsened the position of most women, whether in daily life or work. They were more exploited even than before. When husbands and brothers had to leave home on forced labour, or as migrants seeking the money to pay tax and to buy useful things such as farming tools, wives and sisters were left with more work than before: in gardens, in the fields, in the home. Through all the long social crisis of the Great Depression and the Second World War, women had to bear the heaviest burdens of poverty and oppression.

Gross inequalities between men and women have generally persisted.

But some progress has been made against them, and continues to be made. Not only have girls and young women found new educational opportunities: adult women have also joined in the drive for education, attending literacy classes and various forms of vocational training, while a wider range of jobs has become available for women in towns. Beyond this, too, women have begun to join together in self-defence so as to claim, and sometimes get, a better status in society. Several African countries, by the 1980s, had vigorous organisations for the advancement of women, staffed and run by women, forming their own programmes for the benefit of women. None of this had been remotely possible during colonial times.

NEW ARTISTS, NEW ARTS, JOURNALISM

Freedoms came, with independence, that were valuable across the whole field of culture. Growing from many seeds, a new harvest of the arts began to ripen.

The older arts of Africa, as everyone knows, had long been famous up and down the world, not least in the USA. There, and in some other countries, there are great museums which honour African sculpture in wood and metal, cloth-weaving, jewel-making, and much else that was done in the past. But many of those old arts died during the colonial period. Then the 'world outside Africa' said that Africa had no more makers of art.

But independence showed that the 'world outside Africa' was wrong about this. The old skills were now revived in new skills. Aside from drumming and dancing, which of course had never stopped, Africa's peoples began to reveal a new originality and inspiration. New kinds of sculpture won praise at home and overseas: work of high quality in wood or stone or metal, whether in Nigeria or Ghana, Zimbabwe or Zambia, Tanzania or Kenya, or elsewhere. New kinds of dramatic art came to the fore: with new theatre groups and plays, new dances and rhythms, new displays of mime and comedy. Once again the genius of Africa was free to move and speak.

Many 'popular arts' began to flourish: those of sign-writing, of painting scenes on transport-trucks, of decorating the walls of houses, of cloth-weaving in fresh designs and colours. All these sang a song of freedom: of the new freedom for artists to depict the way we live today in all its sorrows and its joys.

Other arts were added: arts of the modern world such as writing for publication in poetry and prose. As early as the 1960s, the novels and verse of new African writers began to make their mark in many countries. Gradually, as literacy grew in the 1970s, these written arts began to have an audience at home as well as overseas.

Another development added to this cultural revolution. This was the rapid growth of bigger and better means of public information: by national news agencies, many newspapers, broadcasting, book-publishing, cinema, television.

African journalism was far from new when independence came. Sierra Leone had its first African owner-editor as early as 1855, while the Gold Coast had another, Charles Bannerman, as early as 1857. During colonial times, British West Africa possessed an exciting range of lively African newspapers, sometimes edited by outstanding journalists such as Thomas Horatio Jackson of Nigeria. But there were few African newspapers anywhere else; in many colonies there was none at all.

After independence, this also began to change. In the more advanced countries, African newspapers enormously expanded their circulations; even the poorest country now had some kind of newspaper. Here too, of course, there were big contrasts. Writing of the 1960s, the Ghanaian scholar Jones-Quartey has noted that the English-speaking countries, in West Africa, were ahead of the French-speaking countries. Even by 1967, Nigeria was far in advance of others with 18 daily newspapers, 15 weeklies, and 22 periodicals, several with very big daily sales; as well as 17 radio-transmitters broadcasting in many languages to nearly 700,000 radio-receiving sets; and five television stations. Compared with that, the richest of the ex-French West African countries, Ivory Coast, was a long way behind.

Progress again brought its problems. All this vast expansion in the news media raised tough questions about censorship and government control. Critics tackled these questions. Summing up the publishing scene in West Africa (but the same was true in other regions), Jones-Quartey found much to criticise. He said that this was:

> all in all, and everywhere, a period of uneven struggle for the West African press, and one also of monumental misconceiving of role and responsibility on the part of fast-changing, mostly authoritarian governments.

Generally, press and publishing freedoms have met with growing restrictions as the newly formed nation-states fell increasingly under one or other form of undemocratic rule. This failure of democracy in the new nation-states was not especially African. It has occurred everywhere in the modern world, and above all wherever new nation-states have emerged from old Empires. What is interesting, in the African record, has been the struggle against that failure.

BUSINESS EXPANSION

With independence, Africa's peoples won the opportunity not only to govern themselves but also to speak for themselves, and, through their many arts and media, to display the strength and fertility of their cultures. There were comparable gains in other fields. African businessmen, at last, could move into many fields of enterprise and profit-making from which, during colonial times, they were debarred by foreign monopoly or racist bans.

How far they could do this depended on the degree of economic or other indirect control still kept by outside powers and business interests. In the weakest countries, African businessmen could often do little more, even now, than serve as junior agents of foreign businessmen. By the 1970s, however, there were strong countries where Africans had taken over a wide field of managerial and business enterprises. Here we should note some central points of change.

First, it was possible to take a measure of national control over money, credit, banking and investment across a wide area of business activity. It was possible to nationalise foreign banking and insurance interests, as well as promoting the interests of African banks and companies. As understanding of economic matters widened, it was possible to construct national plans for the development of national resources. All this meant that the stronger countries could begin to decolonise their economies: that is, chiefly, accumulate and use the power to build national economies constructed so as to serve the national interest.

In another field of progress, it was possible to introduce crash programmes for the rapid training of men and women who could take the place of European or other foreign technicians, managers, civil servants, and professional persons. Even the weakest of the newly-independent countries were able to make some progress in this Africanising of their managerial and professional jobs.

THE GAINS OF INDEPENDENCE: AN OVERVIEW

These were made in every field of national life. They were political, cultural, social and economic.

Political gains included the power to build national political systems capable of making national decisions, and shaping national policies, for the present and the future. The power to reduce, or remove, foreign political controls. The power to experiment with different policies, solutions, constitutions and new ideas across the whole range of self-government. The power to work towards new forms of unity within, and between, African nations. In all these ways, the political gains of independence gave another power: they restored to Africans the power to make their own mistakes in policy and government, and, therefore, the power to learn how not to make mistakes.

Cultural gains included the destruction of the colonial weapon of racism. They reinforced the right of Africans, now recognised by all the world, to stand equal with the rest of mankind after long colonial subjection. These cultural gains broke through the isolation of Africa's peoples; through their ignorance of their own continent and of the world; through all the barriers erected by colonial rule against Africa's self-expression and intellectual development.

Social gains included the opportunity to build modern services in public health as well as public education; to bring the benefits of modern science to the work of improving everyday conditions of life; to train qualified men and women for all such services; to overcome ignorance or superstition about the causes of bad health and social conflict. Not least, social gains gave the power to reduce the many inequalities suffered by women.

Economic gains included the power to build national plans for national development, to command national resources, and to own and manage all kinds of business enterprise. They also included the power to work with new kinds of economic policy, organisation, and control; and the opportunity to join, whenever desirable, with other African countries in joint plans or enterprises. Above all, these economic gains gave independent countries the power to cut down, at least to some extent, the transfer of Africa's wealth to countries overseas; and to use Africa's wealth, more and more, for Africa's own benefit.

The challenge of independence

But how far, in practice, was it possible for the new states to *defend* these gains of independence, and build them into everyday life? How far, in practice, could the new states *use* these powers for the good of their peoples?

All of the new states, in these early years after independence came, had to face the same real challenge. This challenge was how best to strengthen their internal stability, their drive for development, and their unity of action.

Yet the new states were not all in the same situation. Some of them suffered from much bigger problems than others. Some were much poorer than others. So the story of what happened to them, after independence, has greatly differed. Some have succeeded very well, others very little. Several have failed altogether.

In what follows here it is important to remember that Africa and the World are not separate from each other. On the contrary, they belong to each other: whatever happens in Africa is influenced by whatever happens in the rest of the world, and of course the same is true in reverse. The mistakes and confusions and miseries of post-independence Africa – and these have been many – have to be seen as part of the world's wider problem: how to build communities of people who work together with each other for the common good? History so far has given us no agreed answers. Meanwhile, since the ending of empires in Africa, the record in this huge continent shows repeated effort by Africans to use their new freedoms, and, whenever possible, to enlarge them.

CHAPTER EIGHTEEN
Questions about National Stability

All peoples, winning their freedom, have had to go on wrestling with the handicaps of their own history: with the legacy left to them by the past. The gains of independence, and the powers these have given, have had to be measured against the weight and drag of those handicaps. So the questions we need to ask, when looking at the years since independence, have to refer to the struggle between old handicaps and new powers.

This struggle can be examined from many points of view. We shall examine it in three main fields of effort and experiment: the struggle for political stability, the struggle for economic development, and the struggle for unity both within and beyond national frontiers. Each has a chapter to itself.

HOW MUCH INDEPENDENCE? 'NEO-COLONIALISM'

A first and general point to keep in mind is that independence could not be complete (see also Chapter 9). There were limits on the powers it gave. The width of these limits varied from country to country. What could be done within those limits also varied.

In the economic field, as will be seen in the next chapter, limits on the powers given by independence were often narrow. Each new nation, becoming independent, found itself tied to a whole system or network of economic controls and conditions. Partly these controls and conditions were exercised and imposed by the world economic system; and no country could escape from them.

Partly they were a carry-over, or a continuation, of the controls and conditions of this or that colonial system.

Other limits were in the field of culture and education. Here, too, there was a big carry-over from colonial ideas and colonial schools and teaching. We discussed some aspects of this cultural carry-over, and what was done to escape from it, in the last chapter.

There were also limits on the powers of independence in the political field, in the degree to which new nations were really free to govern themselves and settle their own affairs in their own way. Narrowest in the new nations of the former French empire, these limits were an attempt by the former colonial powers to keep an indirect control; to govern indirectly through 'convenient partners'; to undermine a radical independence of thought and action.

This attempt at continued overseas control, by indirect means, became a frequent feature of the African scene after the colonial flags were lowered. It came to be called 'neo-colonialism', or new-colonialism, meaning a many-sided attempt by outside powers to tie the new nations closely to the interests and needs of those outside powers. Sometimes this neo-colonial attempt was easy to see, as when France imposed military agreements on its former colonies, so that many of them, when becoming independent, had still to accept the presence of French troops. At other times, when economic pressures were used, the attempt was more difficult to see, as in the treatment of interest-payment on national debts to foreign lenders, or in a refusal by the 'developed' countries to agree to pay better prices for the exports of former colonies.

Some leaders of modern Africa were unable or unwilling to oppose this neo-colonialism. Others set themselves to defeat it. Their struggle for greater independence, and the struggle of the governments they led and the peoples who followed them, has held a central place in the history of the years since independence. This struggle continues.

THE LEGACY OF DIVISION

Other aspects of the struggle for a fresh start, for a greater independence of thought and action, added to the dramas of that time. We have already touched on this subject. These aspects arose from Africa's own history before colonial times, as well as from what happened in colonial history.

Africa's own history had produced many hundreds of independent communities or states. These had developed their own political systems. Often, they had built wide networks of regional trade among themselves, and had composed their own regional zones of economic co-operation to their general advantage. An example of this had been the wide 'cowrie-currency zone' of western Africa, linking many communities by common use of the imported cowrie-shell as a 'money of trade'. Earlier, another example had been the vast trading region of northern Africa linked by use of the Fatimid or Almoravid golden *dinar*, the monetary 'gold standard' of the Middle Ages that drew its indispensable precious metal from West Africa.

Colonial rule destroyed these old and often prosperous regional networks of trade and agreement, and, instead, imposed quite different ones. These new colonial networks were designed, primarily, to make African labour and land serve the interests and profit of the colony-owning powers. Colonial governments used force to do this. Afterwards, they used policies of division. They used the instrument of divide-and-rule that may be called 'colonial tribalism'.

The great struggle of the nationalists, before independence, was to overcome this 'colonial tribalism' and to unite peoples into nations. We have followed some of the achievements of that difficult but necessary struggle.

Nationalism proved strong enough to win the political unity required to end colonial rule. But nationalism in Africa, like nationalism everywhere else, has shown itself a contradictory force. It may start well, but still end badly.

In Europe, as we noted on pp. 33–34, forces of nationalism during the 19th and early 20th Centuries were strong enough to liberate the Italians and then the southern Slav peoples from various European empires. Nationalism did this in the name of equality and freedom. But the liberated Italy of 1861 soon began to use its armies to invade and dispossess Africans; and its nationalism then degraded into the brutalities of Mussolini's fascist dictatorship during 1922–45. The Slav peoples liberated from the old European empires likewise turned to quarrels among themselves and the rise of their own dictatorships. In much the same way the nationalism which gave rise to a united Germany became a disaster to the Germans and everyone else when, in the 1930s, German nationalism became nazism and launched the holocausts of the Second World War of 1939–45.

In Africa, too, the liberating force of nationalism was not long in becoming a source of conflict. Here, then, was a general problem for Africans liberated from the European empires. Nationalism brought great gains, but then asked a heavy price for them. Was this unavoidable? What could or can be done to neutralise the destructive aspects of nationalism? We may find some of the possible answers as we go along.

THREE PERIODS OF EXPERIMENT

The detailed history of the years after independence fills many books on separate national histories. Here we can try to make a summary. Generally, but above all in the countries coming out of the British and French empires, the years after independence passed through three periods or phases of effort, experiment, and renewal.

The first of these periods was rather short. It was when the new nations tried to govern themselves by the means and methods left to them by the departing colonial governments. Mostly, these means and methods were set in place on the day of independence, or shortly before that date. They were constitutions and parliamentary systems on the British or the French or some other European model. They were drawn, that is, from the history and conditions of modern Europe, amd not from the history and conditions of modern Africa.

The second period was longer. It was when the new nations found that these means and methods, these institutions of government drawn from Europe's history and conditions, did not work. Often painfully, they broke down. The reasons for these breakdowns were not in the least that Africans were less able to govern themselves, in peace and justice, than Europeans. The inherited means and methods broke down for two quite different reasons.

One reason was that these means and methods, left behind by colonial rule, proved a poor weapon against the legacy of tribalism or other divisions of the past. The other reason for breakdown was a sharp contradiction. On the one hand, the new nations took over laws and habits of colonial dictatorship. On the other hand, they acquired parliaments which were supposed to be democratic. Colonial laws or habits, and democratic laws or habits, came into conflict.

With breakdown of the means and methods of government left behind by colonial rule, there was an urgent need to fill the resulting vacuum or absence of political power. This was when one or another kind of military government stepped in.

The third period began during the 1970s. This was when new nations began to research for their own answers to the problems of government and development, and to experiment with their own ways of finding justice and peace. This remains a period, more generally, when Africa's new nations have begun to grapple with the divisive consequences of nationalism.

The whole story has been rich and various. It had indeed reflected the problems of the modern world in all countries everywhere. The influence of the colonial legacy, or of neo-colonialism, or of still older handicaps, has led to disasters and defeats. But the struggle against those weaknesses has also led to solutions of success. More and more, as Africans have come to grips with their real problems, these successes begin to reveal the work of creative minds and talents.

We turn now to some of the major situations met with after independence, and to some examples.

THE SITUATION AFTER INDEPENDENCE

Confronting regionalism, separatism

The means and methods of government left behind by the departing colonial rulers did not work. Why was that? Nigeria, Kenya, and Sudan offer three examples from the British model.

As was explained in Chapter 13, Nigeria began independence under a constitution which divided this very large country, and its very numerous population, into three regions. Each was governed by a party representing the majority people in each region: Hausa-Fulani, Yoruba, Igbo; while smaller parties represented other peoples or ethnic groups. Each region also elected members of a federal parliament based in Lagos, the country's capital; and this had power over all-Nigerian matters such as foreign policy and national defence.

There were several reasons why this failed to work. One was that each leading party and its politicians, in each region, tended more and more to govern as though, in fact, its region was a separate country. Each regional government claimed more and more power to take decisions in matters such as commerce and industry; and there were politicians who played this game in order to promote their personal careers. For these and for other reasons, there came a sharp rivalry between the regions. The project of an all-Nigerian unity began to fade.

Another reason for dispute grew out of that rivalry. Who should control the all-Nigerian federal parliament in Lagos? This became a serious source of conflict. As things turned out, the Northern Region's chief party, the NPC, dominated the federal parliament because it had more voters, and therefore more members of parliament, than two other big parties in the east and west, the NCNC and AG. So these two parties had to be 'junior partners' in a federal government dominated by the NPC, or else go into opposition. As things turned out, this put the AG into isolation.

Tensions came quickly to breaking-point. A first explosion occurred in the Western Region during 1962, only two years after independence. A split in the AG led to violent strife. The federal government under NPC control tried to end this conflict by further undermining the AG. It imposed a state of emergency in the Western Region, and ruled there through a federal administrator until the beginning of 1963. But this really solved nothing.

Regional rivalries continued to sharpen, especially after a national census of 1964. This produced returns which gave the Northern Region a voting force so big that northern control of the federal parliament seemed bound to become a fixture to the disadvantage of other regions. On top of that reason for southern dissatisfaction, the Western Region exploded again during a campaign for new general elections in November 1965. By this time there was great bitterness among large sectors of Nigerian public opinion. To make matters worse, some important politicians were widely accused of gross dishonesty and corruption. With continuing violence in the west, and more threatened elsewhere, the politicians now seemed helpless or discredited. In January 1966 the military stepped in and took over national government. For Nigeria, the first period of independence had ended.

What had happened? The answer is that the means and methods left behind by colonial government had encouraged regional rivalries, and personal ambitions, to the point where everything was in confusion. New experiments were urgently required. Nigeria must find its own way to peace and progress.

This proved difficult. A complete collapse of Nigeria into several separate nation-states now threatened. The military leaders were ready to prevent this, but they still had to lead towards long-term solutions. Inflamed regionalism in the north meanwhile brought death and persecution to Igbo living there. In response, Igbo people flocked to the shelter of their Eastern Region. There was now practically a state of war.

In May 1967 a new military president, General Yakubu Gowon, opened a new initiative. He declared that Nigeria was to be divided into twelve federated states, thus dissolving the solid blocks represented by Hausa-Fulani, Igbo, and Yoruba parties. This came too late to prevent bigger trouble. The Igbo leadership in the Eastern Region declared a separate republic of Biafra.

A bitter civil war ensued, with the rest of Nigeria united against the Igbo separatists and their people. With the additional support of the non-Igbo peoples of the Eastern Region (Biafra), Federal Nigeria won this war by the beginning of 1970; and its military leaders then built a tolerant and generous peace.

Nigeria could resume its necessary experiments in finding new means and methods of government. These were carried forward with useful success, at first under General Murtala Muhamed and then under General Olusegun Obasanjo. The Gowon plan of 1967 for twelve federated states was extended. Nigeria was divided into nineteen federated states. Each had its own government. More states were formed, but strong federal leadership continued at the centre.

Far from breaking down, Nigeria held together. Those who had prophesied disaster were shown to have been mistaken. Most Nigerians might feel dissatisfied with their politicians and their military rulers, and hope for better ones in the future. Meanwhile, as events proved, most Nigerians wanted to go on being Nigerians. They wanted to stay together in the same country. They wanted the chance to prove that they could do better in the future than they had done in the past. Bowing to this optimism, the Nigerian military stepped back from power in 1979, and parliamentary government was restored in 1980. As we shall see, parliamentary government did not last. But its failure seemed only to confirm that what could save Nigeria would not be breakdown into a cluster of little rival nations but, on the contrary, new ideas and new approaches which could underpin a more successful federation.

Success by KANU

Kenya was another country which had to find its own way to a system and constitution which fitted its own needs. Kenya was fortunate in being able to do this without violent strife. Though smaller than Nigeria, and with a much smaller population, Kenya was left with a constitution which divided the country into no fewer than seven federated regions, each with its own local government, parliament, civil service, police force, judiciary, border controls and other public services. In the circumstances, different from Nigeria's, this threatened to create the very disunity which Kenya nationalism had striven so hard to overcome. Besides this, critics saw that it would leave the richest region, centred on Nairobi, under powerful white-settler influence, and, perhaps, under white-settler control.

Accepting independence in 1963 with this British constitution, the ruling majority party, KANU under President Jomo Kenyatta, at once set about removing the regionalist threat to national unity. It introduced a new constitution with a single parliament and government for the whole country. This came into force in 1964; and Kenya could then move into a period of political renewal. Many problems of the colonial and pre-colonial legacy remained, and have since become still more difficult to solve. But the threat to the country's unity was gone.

Sudanese divisions

Another problem of regionalism and separatism, once more arising from past history and the legacy of colonial rule, brought much trouble to the republic of Sudan. Here, acute cultural differences were combined with a legacy of acute colonial division. About four-fifths of all the people of this large country were Muslims, as they are today. They live in the north, centre and west of the Sudan; and many of them speak Arabic. The remaining fifth live in the distant south. Few of these southerners are Muslims; many are Christians. They speak Dinka, Nuer, Shilluk, and other languages.

A North-South confrontation

These differences in Sudanese culture and history are very old. They go back to the early times of Islam and its penetration into the lands of the middle Nile. They were sharpened by conflict at many times in the past, and especially during the period of Egyptian control in the nineteenth century. And when the British took over, after their defeat of the Mahdia, they gradually built a colonial system which more or less completely divided Arabic-speaking Sudanese from the peoples in the far south. Instead of being able to get to know and trust each other, these two populations were kept severely apart.

When independence came in 1956, the Muslim Sudanese naturally took control because they were far more numerous than the southern peoples. They were left with institutions, with means and methods of government, which they proceeded to use. But instead of helping the southern peoples to share in government on a federal basis, the northern Sudanese sent down officials to take the place of the British.

Yet here was a case, different from Kenya's, where agreeing to some regionalism could help to avoid conflict and separation. If the southerners could run their own affairs within a federal Sudan, the old distrusts and differences between south and north might gradually be overcome.

As it was, the southerners believed they had good reason to fear northern domination. An 'army of liberation', called *Anyanya*, took the field against the central government's police and army. Only years later, in 1972, could peace seem possible. This was when, in that year, the Sudanese government gave southerners their own parliament and government. *Anyanya* withdrew its demand for a separate southern state. The way to Sudanese federal unity seemed open. Once again, after the means and methods left by colonial government had broken down, a time of experiment and renewal had proved necessary. Unhappily, this produced no success. Repeated northern failure to meet the demands for federal self-government by southern peoples has brought new warfare and huge disaster.

Facing 'élitism' and 'tribalism'

Another big problem arose, after independence came, when new national leaders lost touch with the lives and interests of their peoples. This opened a gap between the leaders, who now enjoyed power and privilege, and the mass of voters who were living in the same way as before. Into that poverty gap, many troubles flowed.

Here was another part of the colonial legacy at work. For the colonial rulers had always behaved as an élite, as a 'chosen few', who had no need or wish to keep in touch with the lives and interests of ordinary people. Taking over power by the means and methods left to them by colonial rulers, new national leaders found it easy to behave as an élite. They found it difficult to behave in a different way. All too often, they clung to power and privilege.

This problem of élitist government by a small privileged group was not of course confined to Africa. It has brought trouble to all nations everywhere. But in Africa it was linked to another part of the colonial legacy; and this made the problem worse. 'Elitism' became linked with 'tribalism' – with all that part of colonial influence which had pushed the idea of tribes. And the two together – élitism *plus* 'tribalism' – could be very destructive.

How, in practice, did this happen? Let us take a little-known example, but a very clear one: that of Somalia after its independence in 1960.

Departing, the Italians gave Somalia a parliamentary system modelled on that of Italy. This parliament was elected by 'proportional representation': meaning, in brief, that each class in society could have a party with seats in parliament. Landowners, businessmen, farmers, city workers: each could have their own party. Now this might work well in Italy, where people were divided into classes. But it could not work well in Somalia.

Nearly all Somalis were farmers or cattle people. They were not divided into classes. They were divided into clans. These clan divisions were very old, but colonial rule had deepened them. We saw in Chapter 3 (p. 24) how the colonial partition first divided Somalis into four different colonies, and then destroyed the unifying work of the Sayyid Muhamed. Repeatedly after that, colonial rule used the old clan divisions as a way of preventing Somalis from uniting together, while Somali customs of clannishness repeatedly worsened disunity.

Even so, the Somali Youth League (in practice the first Somali nationalist party, founded in 1943) was able to win sufficient unity to take power in 1960. But the constitution left to them began, at once, to make disunity. It turned all politics into tribalism. Each big clan, and then each small clan or sub-clan, used the system of proportional representation so as to form its own 'party' and send its own man or men to parliament. A reckless competition for the fruits of power and privilege was soon under way.

Five Somali parties contested the first general election at the time of independence. But by 1964, this people of only three millions had produced 21 competing parties; and by 1969 there were no fewer than 62 competing parties. That was bad enough at a time when every united effort was needed in order to overcome Somalia's desperate poverty and backwardness. But élitism, joined to this tribalism, again made things much worse.

To govern Somalia, at that time, it was necessary to know the English and Italian languages, because Somali, as we have noted was unwritten until 1973. Very few Somalis could speak European languages. Still fewer could read and write them. So the great majority of Somalis had no chance of any share in the responsibilities of public life and government.

Having all the power and privilege, a small élite at the top fought personal battles for their own interests. Whenever elections came, they went back to their clans, whether big or small, and drummed up support against their rivals. Once back in power again, they returned to their dog-fights and squabbles over sharing the spoils of office. This disunity and personal rivalry led directly to bad government and corruption.

Somali farmers and cattle folk began to hate their rulers. They began to say that independence had brought them nothing but dishonesty, lies, and broken promises. Yet nothing got better. So great was the corruption at the top that the prime minister of 1969 was believed to have paid out £500,000 from public money in order to buy the votes of newly-elected members of parliament.

The gap between these rulers and the majority of ordinary people was now wide and filled with anger. People longed for a change. It came at the end of 1969. With general rejoicing, and without a shot being fired, the system left by colonial government was swept away. A group of patriotic officers under General Siad Barre took over. Not long after, they began to experiment with new ways of governing Somalia, of promoting Somali unity of effort, of using that effort to tackle the country's real needs.

There followed a brief but hopeful period of democratic experiment. New ways of 'grass-roots' democracy were tried. Unhappily, this experiment in promoting 'people's power' was given no time to develop. In

1976 the Somali government became involved in a war against the Ethiopian empire. This happened because the Somalis of the Ogaden or eastern region of that empire – enclosed in Ethiopia by Ethiopian invasion during the partition of Africa in the 1890s – wanted to join Somalia. But this war was disastrous for Somalia; the experiment in 'people's power' was abandoned and worse times lay ahead.

Troubles in Uganda

Political experiment was needed almost everywhere. There were countries which found their way, after many troubles, to renewed stability, to new means and methods of government, to better paths for progress. There were notable successes; and we have looked at one or two of them. Other countries marked up failures; with them, the time of necessary experiment had to continue. Uganda was also among these.

We saw in Chapter 14 how Ugandan stability was undermined by internal divisions which were not overcome. After independence in 1962, these divisions continued. They even grew worse. The problems of élitism *plus* clan-ism became acute. National politics, more and more, were increasingly reduced to a destructive rivalry between personal or group interests, whether clans or not.

A determined effort to impose unity began in 1966. Prime Minister Milton Obote suspended the independence constitution of 1962, and assumed state power. In April he proclaimed a new constitution under the slogan of 'one country, one parliament, one government, one people', with himself as executive president. This was quite widely welcomed, especially by the northern peoples. But it was entirely rejected by the Buganda kingdom and its separate parliament (see p. 147). In May Obote sent in troops who occupied the Buganda king's palace. The king escaped to England, and Buganda was divided into four administrative districts. In 1967 another constitution abolished all the traditional kingdoms, and gave more power to the central government.

This could solve nothing for, once again, it was 'unity imposed from above'. Popular discontents as well as new internal rivalries soon revived. In 1969, trying to win popular support by reducing the economic inequalities between Uganda's 'haves', who were few and were mostly in the towns, and its 'have-nots', who were many and mostly in the rural areas, Obote introduced an equalising programme called'The Common Man's Charter'. This inflamed political opposition led by the 'haves'. Obote replied by banning the opposition parties. In this situation, his government decided to rely, more and more, on troops and police. This reliance on force, instead of democratic political action, proved fatal.

In 1971 President Obote was overthrown by his army commander, General Idi Amin, with the initial support of Britain and other foreign interests who feared what they saw as Obote's 'left-wing turn'. Uganda then passed under a military dictatorship. This became ever more harsh. Soon it was seen that Amin, by means of terror, could secure no more than a 'unity of silence'.

In October 1978, with none of Uganda's internal problems solved, Amin began to attack neighbouring Tanzania, to which Tanzania responded by sending troops into Uganda. Aided by these troops, Amin's surviving opponents drove him out. Their task now was to try once again for stability and united effort. But not until the late 1980s, with the successful emergence and political initiative of new groups, led by Yoweri Museveni, did light began to appear at the end of Uganda's tunnel of conflict and destruction.

Many other experiments were made. Some are very well-known. Ghana passed from multi-party rule to one-party rule under Kwame Nkrumah, then to military rule in 1966, back to civilian rule in 1969, again into military rule in 1971, and then once more to civilian rule. Why so many experiments? The failure of leaders, especially when arising from élitism or clan-ism was one explanation. But, as elsewhere in the world, this was not the whole explanation. The rest of it lay in the sheer difficulty of overcoming the divisions of the past, and of tracing a road to progress in which all could have their share.

Many lessons had to be learned after independence came. Many new things had to be understood. Seen from this angle, the time of experiment has been rich in difficult experience, and in the determination of Africans to find out how to solve their problems of community. We have looked at some of the internal costs and obstacles. There were external costs and obstacles as well.

Cases of foreign intervention

Various forms of foreign intervention, from the day of independence, had to do with neo-colonialism, or the effort to keep an indirect control in foreign hands. Some of these forms were economic, and will be discussed in a later chapter. Political and military intervention was mostly in the weakest of the new countries; or else in large states, notably Zaïre, which failed to find the way to national consensus and unity of effort. The general result of all such intervention was to inflame existing conflicts, and make stability still more difficult to reach. Sometimes, as in the case of France and the Central African Republic, foreign intervention helped local dictators into power, and then gave them enough support to stay in power. In exchange, such dictators served the interests of the intervening power and its foreign partners.

Strong countries, with patriotic leaders, could and did reduce foreign intervention. Other countries failed, and paid a heavy price. Chad was a particularly sad example. That vast country came to independence, in 1960, with fewer than four million people, mostly in the centre and south but otherwise scattered through northern plains and hills in the Sahara. Though small, this population was sorely divided. Elitism and tribalism worked against unity; but the chief division was between the (mostly Christian) southerners and the (mostly Muslim) northerners. Reversing the situation we looked at in the Sudan, independence gave control to the southerners. But this was a very limited or neo-colonial independence. France kept strict economic controls, and stationed French troops in much of the territory.

No progress was made in overcoming internal divisions. Soon after 1960, on the contrary, these were deepened by actions of the southern-led government of President Tombalbaye, strongly supported by France. Northern rebellions began in 1968, and grew rapidly into civil war. Tombalbaye tried to put down these rebellions with the help of French troops and air force. This failed. In 1975 the dictator Tombalbaye was overthrown when the French switched their support to a group of military officers. Fighting continued as before, with repeated French intervention. Meanwhile the northerners were receiving some military support from Colonel Gaddafi's Libyan government and army. Interventions worsened.

Chad became a battleground for diverse groups and interests, local and foreign. New rivals for power appeared. Divisions multiplied. In 1979 Nigeria led an attempt at mediation, but in 1980 civil war again shattered the fragile peace. As the scene of so many destructive ambitions, whether foreign or local, Chad fell into chaos, and ceased to have any claim to being a national community.

There were lesser but still serious cases of intervention. External use of white-mercenary adventurers to overthrow African governments, in the interests of this or that foreign power, became quite frequent in the 1970s. Mostly, such attempts failed: as, for example, an attempt by white mercenaries to overthrow the government of Benin (former Dahomey) in 1977, and a similar attempt to overthrow the government of the Seychelles in 1981.

The fact or threat of military intervention by forces from outside Africa remained on the scene, and sometimes grew worse. Repeated military aggression by South Africa's armed forces against Angola and Mozambique began in 1975, and was renewed, especially against Angola, in 1978 and in following years. These South African attacks by air, land and sea were clearly aimed at undermining the newly-independent republics of those two countries, and replacing their government by pro-South African puppets. These aggressions continued, as we saw in Chapter 16, and were painfully destructive. They failed to overturn the newly founded republics of Angola, Mozambique and Zimbabwe, but they raised another question. Could Africa have peace and stability as long as internal conflicts were enlarged and enflamed by external rivalries and interventions? The answer seemed increasingly to be that peace and stability can be achieved only if Africa steps outside the quarrels of the non-African world, and above all outside the rivalry between any of the Great Powers. If so, it was now increasingly argued, the right policy would be one of 'non-alignment': of joining neither the Western power-bloc nor the Eastern or any other power-bloc.

Countries in central and southern Africa now had to face great difficulties, in the economic field, caused by their support for the further liberation of southern Africa. Sanctions against the settlers' republic in Rhodesia (Zimbabwe), applied in 1966 and continued until 1980, placed a particularly heavy burden on Zambia, and, between 1975 and 1980, also on Mozambique. Zambia's economy suffered badly in those years, and there, too, setbacks in local farming and a widening city–village gap were hard to bear.

SEARCHING FOR SOLUTIONS

We can now stand back a little, and make another summary for these years to the 1990s. Many of the troubles of Africa, after independence, followed on breakdown of parliamentary and administrative institutions set in place, at the time of independence, by departing colonial rulers. Those institutions failed to meet the problems left by past history, but, especially, by the legacy of colonial history.

Often enlarged by failed leaders and foreign interventions such problems consisted of internal divisions, élitism, clan-ism, and other forms of disunity. Patriotic leaders set themselves to solve those problems; selfish or corrupt leaders simply made them worse.

To these political difficulties on the road to stability, all of which were built into the situation on the day of independence, others of an economic and social nature were added. For what the new governments were obliged to take over, as Chapter 8 has shown, was not a prosperous colonial business, but, in many ways, a profound colonial crisis. There was poverty and hunger in wide rural areas. Towns and cities grew hugely in size as rural people flocked to them in search of food and jobs, and often could find neither. If a few persons managed to make money or get good jobs, the majority did not. Even before independence, the gap in living-standards between the few with money, houses, or good jobs, and the many who had none of those good things, was wide. It was also widely resented.

Yet the few with jobs and money were precisely that small minority who, as Chief Awolowo claimed in 1947, were 'destined to rule the country', because they had the necessary education and political knowledge. They duly took over power; but the gap in living-standards between them and the majority continued to widen. As it widened, so did popular discontent. And when that discontent exploded into strife or violence, the politicians proved helpless. Then the soldiers stepped in and took their place.

However painful, these breakdowns were often unavoidable. And they had one very positive side to them: they opened the way for new experiments in searching for stability. There were many experiments, with varied failure or success. Some of these experiments were highly successful, and showed that Africans, left to themselves, could solve their problems and make progress. Other experiments were less successful, but were still useful in the lessons they taught and the experience they provided. Some experiments failed altogether. Nearly always, these failures occurred in countries subject to neo-colonial controls or repeated outside intervention.

This chapter may be rounded off by looking at the record of the military rulers.

The soldiers' record

Already by 1970, about half of Africa's then independent states were being governed by one or other kind of military rule. Why was this?

The reasons for military take-over may be divided, for the most part, into four:

1 Because parliamentary and administrative institutions – chiefly, multi-party systems – had failed to overcome a destructive regionalism; or a threat of separatism; or a collapse of political power into intrigue and corruption.
2 Because popular discontents, largely economic in origin, had reached a point of explosion that undermined law and order.
3 Because, in weak or neo-colonial countries, foreign interests or governments wanted a change of government in their favour.

4 Because of personal ambition for power and privilege, with support from this or that élitist, clan or 'tribalist' grouping.

Such reasons were not, of course, peculiar to Africa. They had led to military rule at many moments of European history. They had often produced military dictatorships in Latin America or Asia. But an examination of the African record brings out another point. There have been various kinds of military rule.

In the period examined here, there were patriotic military leaders who stepped into a power vacuum caused by the failures of civilian rule, and who then ensured the continued unity of their countries. They launched new experiments in national self-government, and were ready to hand back power to civilian rulers. Some of Nigeria's military rulers, such as Generals Murtala Muhamed and Olusegun Obasanjo, were of this type. Their aim was to 'fill the gap' until new and better forms of civilian rule could be devised.

Most military governments were of a different type. Some were imposed by men who acted for merely selfish or corrupt reasons. These men, like Amin in Uganda, had neither the personal wisdom nor the experience to bring unity and peace to their countries. Or, like Bokassa in the Central African Republic, they were militarist bullies who acted as the agents of foreign interests. Such men solved no problems. They only multiplied their peoples' woes.

In a record as complex as this, there were of course marginal cases, when useful military rule was mixed with useless military rule. Such cases have given rise to many sharp differences of opinion. Was it a good thing, for example, for the Ghanaian military to overthrow the one-party civilian rule of Nkrumah in 1966; and did that military government bring any improvement? Was it a bad thing, in another Ghanaian example, for Colonel Ignatius Acheampong to overthrow the multi-party civilian rule of Dr Kofi Busia in 1971; and did Acheampong then do better than Busia had done? How useful were the various military take-overs in Sierra Leone, or in Mali, or in Niger? These can all be examples for useful discussion against the detailed background of these countries' national histories.

Broadly, the central political problem was to get rid of the dictatorial ways of colonial government, while, at the same time, finding new ways of democratic government. How to spread the use of power among all the people? How to ensure that votes at elections became a real use of power by masses of ordinary people? How to build ways of government by which people could begin to govern themselves, rather than being governed, as before, 'from the top down'? These became critical issues.

The record suggests that military government might be positive and useful if it could prepare the way for new experiments in the search for democratic government. These positive examples are the ones that history will remember as steps toward unity and peace. But they have been rare examples. Nearly always, military government has brought disaster.

Several parties or one party?

Africans in past centuries tackled the abuse of power and privilege in several ways. They worked out a wide variety of checks and balances to control the behavior of their chiefs or kings or other leading persons. They were prepared whenever necessary – as of course it sometimes was – to act against despots, to throw down tyrants, and to punish corruption.

But the modern world called for new ways. These were the ways of democratic election, representation, and discussion within modern states different from those of the past. They in turn called for political parties.

So long as there was colonial rule, such parties all had one central aim, and were organised to get it. They were parties or movements aiming at independence. Their situation was a simple one: on their side were the people to be organised to struggle for independence, while against them were the colonial government and its forces. But the situation changed after independence. Then the sides became as many as the different and often conflicting groups of interest inside the new state.

The question then was: should each of these groups of interest have its own party, and try to reach its special aims by using that party in rivalry or combination with other such parties? Or would it be better to bring all these interests into a single party, and try to resolve their differences in that way?

Different answers were found in experiments after independence. Yet it has remained clear that the great debate is still open about which kind of system – the multi-party or the one-party – can serve Africa better. This is not the place for a full discussion of the serious and difficult questions which underlie this debate: how best to exercise political power, and ensure that there are checks and balances on the misuse of power? How best to overcome élitism, tribalism, and other handicaps? But a brief survey of experiments can be made.

Multi-party systems

We should note, to begin with, that multi-party systems were evolved in western Europe to fit a situation in which European peoples were increasingly divided into conflicting social classes. In that situation, it became generally true that middle-class (bourgeois) parties wanted a 'free enterprise' or capitalist system, while working-class parties hoped for a collective or socialist-type system. In any case, the political battle was about *alternative policies*, even if, of course, it was also about persons and personal benefits.

The problem of evolving multi-party systems in newly independent Africa was that class differences were much less deep and sharp than in Europe. This meant, in practice, that parties were seldom created to represent different class interests, and therefore different policies. Of course there were partial exceptions. The CPP in Ghana was thought to represent 'the masses', while the UGCC was thought to represent 'the chiefs'. Mostly, however, parties were created to represent different interests of a regional or similar kind, and to enable these rival groups to compete for power.

Secondly, most of the leaders and organisers of the parties and mass movements, during the 1960s, had to be persons of educational or other privilege. These persons, as Chief Awolowo had forecast in 1947, were 'the articulate minority destined to rule'. So it came about that the struggle between parties was not so much a struggle between alternative policies as a struggle between alternative persons; and elections were less about what to do with political power than about who should have the benefits of possessing that power.

Looking back over the first ten years of Nigeria's independence, Professor Billy Dudley wrote that politics in Nigeria was 'not about *alternative policies*, but about *the control over men and resources*'. That was the situation which had helped to produce the collapse of the first Nigerian federation (1960–66). The gap in living-standards between 'haves' and 'have-nots', for example, had grown ever wider, but there were no alternative policies framed to narrow this gap. So the multi-party system, however democratic it was intended to be, had failed to work.

But Nigerians still wanted to make it work. After a bout of military (non-parliamentary) rule, a renewed multi-party system was launched in 1979.

But this new attempt at parliamentary rule did no better than previous attempts. Bitter political rivalries were inflamed by corruption and the abuse of power. Five large parties contested federal elections in 1979, and the most successful of these, the National Party of Nigeria, received 37 per cent of the votes and was able to form a government, while its leader, Alhaji Shehu Shagari, at the same time won a presidential election with 5.7 million votes against his chief opponent, Chief Awolowo, who received 4.9 million votes. But the outcome was disappointing.

Continued regional and religious conflicts indicated that the federal government, found guilty of massive corruption, no longer enjoyed the prestige of popular legitimacy. Rightly or wrongly, people felt that the federal government neither belonged to them nor gave them its loyalty. More and more, it was being said, government was a 'carve-up' by political profiteers. Nigeria wanted to stay Nigeria, but not under this kind of government. Responding to disillusionment, the military stepped in once again. On 31 December, 1983, the armed forces seized power. This time their leader was Major-General Muhammadu Buhari.

He was not a success. Like other military rulers, he proved strong on discipline but weak on new ideas. This might have been all right if Buhari had shown much political skill. As it was, he was thought to have shown little. Blaming 'unauthorised foreign immigrants' for Nigeria's growing economic troubles, for which the policies of Buhari's government as well as the international situation were chiefly to blame, the soldiers in power simply expelled some 700,000 non-Nigerian Africans, including 300,000 Ghanaians. This act of desperation naturally solved nothing. Meanwhile Nigeria's economy fell more deeply into trouble with a collapse in the export price of oil; and oil by now was the government's biggest financial resource. Reacting to all this the army deposed Buhari in August 1985, and installed a new military ruler. This was General Ibrahim Babangida. He proved more successful in holding the federation together, again enlarging the number of its constituent autonomous states.

In 1989 Babangida again promised a move towards the restitution of parliamentary government. This, it was proposed, should be in a new form. There should be only two political parties so as to avoid, it was hoped, the fruitless rivalries of many parties. Veteran politicians should be excluded on the grounds that they had had their chance and had missed it. What happened next belongs to the detailed history of recent years. More important, as the debates of these years soon showed, was the question as to whether *any* imported political system could now meet Africa's needs?

So far, the answer seemed to be no. In the weakest of these new countries which had emerged from colonialism, there was little more than brutal dictatorial rule, bereft of any large ideas and barely worth discussing. Other countries devoted to free enterprise, besides Nigeria, had made do with a single-party system. In the Ivory Coast, for example, the party which had emerged on top at the time of independence, in 1960, was the PDCI, and the PDCI, under the talented leadership of Felix Houphouet-Boigny, had stayed in power ever since. This was not exactly a dictatorship, but it was far from a democracy. How then could the interests of ordinary people be protected and advanced? Or would these interests be better protected if the Ivory Coast had formed many political parties, as in Nigeria?

Here were urgent questions for discussion. The debate obviously had to continue, and it did continue.

Single-party systems

If there was much to show that multi-party systems worked badly in the circumstances of newly independent Africa, single-party systems were clearly worse. The big problem, once again, was in finding 'checks and balances' whereby the abuse of power and wealth could be stopped, or at any rate reduced. Wherever democracies have been made to work, up and down the world, the problem of 'checks and balances' has been solved – seldom completely, but sufficiently – by the rule of law resting on the force of organised public opinion.

Now this was difficult in countries emerging from the stiff dictatorships and poverty of the European colonial systems. As many examples proved by the 1980s, or even by the 1970s, the legacies of dictatorship and poverty were too much for the newly installed and therefore fragile parliamentary systems. In many cases, one-party systems took their place. But it was rapidly seen that these one-party systems could degenerate into no-party systems: into militarist or personal dictatorships that ruled by fear and persecution. Censorship of the press, arrest of critics, falsifying of elections: all such abuses became much easier once there was no legal and elected opposition. That is what happened, for example, in the Republic of Guinea under the leadership of Sékou Touré. His time in power began brilliantly in 1958, and promised great gains for the people of Guinea. But within a dozen years or so Guinea's single-party system had become a personal dictatorship, and every kind of misery followed.

Some efforts were made to prevent single-party systems from degenerating into no-party dictatorships. Kenya had provided a case in point. Soon after independence in 1963, the ruling party of Kenya, the Kenya African National Union (KANU) became the only party, and Kenya had a single-party system. Critics suffered or were silenced. Yet checks and balances were also developed. KANU candidates for parliamentary election were encouraged to compete against each other at the polls, even though these candidates continued to belong to the same party. In Kenya's general election of 1979, no fewer than 740 all-KANU candidates competed for 160 seats. The results were encouraging. Several cabinet ministers lost their seats. There seemed to be a good chance for democracy. Yet it became evident during the 1980s that real power in Kenya still remained in the hands of a small group of politicians, most of whom were also businessmen, and that these were little disposed to share it. Kenya by the end of the 1980s seemed in many ways not greatly different from a no-party dictatorship. Again, fresh experiments were clearly needed.

The search goes on

So the search for viable forms of self-government has persisted. And the history of this search is already rich in political debate. This debate is perhaps particularly interesting for Americans, whose own democracy has had to face and solve many such problems in the search for viable checks and balances against the misuse of power. But the same is true of Europe.

African countries with an anti-elitist and egalitarian type of leadership have frequently supported the advantages of a single-party system. They have argued, for example, that the important question is not the number of parties, for a many-party (multi-party) system, as the case of Nigeria has shown, can also degenerate into corruption and abuse. The important question, on this view, concerns the degree in which ordinary people can really influence their governments. If ordinary people cannot do this, then a system with many parties may be worse than a system with only one party. Why should this be? President Julius Nyerere of Tanzania summarised the answer in 1963. He said that there could be only one reason for the formation of many parties in a country like Tanzania. This reason was:

> . . . the desire to imitate the political structure of a totally dissimilar society. What is more, the desire to imitate, where conditions are not suitable for imitation, can easily lead us into trouble. To try and import the idea of a parliamentary opposition into Africa may very likely lead to violence – because the opposition parties will tend to be regarded as traitors by the majority of our people; or, at best, it will lead to the trivial manoeuvrings of 'opposing' groups whose time is spent in the inflation of artificial differences in some semblance of reality 'for the sake of preserving democracy' . . .

He argued, further, that in Tanzania:

> the only voices to be heard in 'opposition' are those of a few irresponsible individuals who exploit the very privileges of democracy—freedom of the press, freedom of association, freedom to criticise—in order to deflect the government from its responsibilities to the people . . .

Clearly, then, this whole question of party system is a complex one to which there are no easy answers. Not surprisingly, it has led to an often fierce debate. Just as clearly, this debate continues. Some of it has to do with economics as well as politics. For example: can Africa still hope to build a capitalist system, a mature system with its own sources of capital and command of its economy; and, therefore, the democracy of checks and balances that such a system, *when* mature, can underpin? Is that possible in the modern era of multi-national big-corporation finance and investment controlled from outside Africa? Alternatively, can anything useful still be expected from the ideas of socialism in a period when socialism has so obviously failed, above all in the Soviet Union, to protect citizens from terrible abuse of power?

Obviously, at this stage, there were more questions than answers. Other people in other continents faced the same difficulty. Some had pinned their hopes on the ideas of socialism, but no good had come from those ideas. Others had followed the prescriptions of capitalist free enterprise, but these prescriptions, for the ex-colonial countries, had led to repeated frustration and the failures of this or that political system. Where might salvation be found? Looking for safe means of development, what did the economists have to say?

CHAPTER NINETEEN
Questions about Development

The new nations of Africa came to independence in the midst of this deepening social crisis caused by colonialism. Their governments had to find the way to stability against new problems of rural poverty and of the rapid growth of urban concentrations of ex-rural peoples, as well as against other legacies of internal division.

Some new nations were weak in unity and badly led; they made little progress. A few were strong in unity and well led; they were able to strengthen and enlarge their political independence. Winning more freedom of action, they could search for their own solutions to national problems.

Yet the new governments had thoroughly to understand, and then try to throw off, another colonial legacy as well. This was in the field of economics: of working, earning, spending, managing the nation's wealth. And this economic legacy was heavier than the political and social legacy; it was harder to shift. Against this, too, a long struggle has had to be launched, again needing many experiments; and this struggle, too, is far from over.

Historically, Africa's economies had been small in scale. They suited the needs of many hundreds of self-supplying and mostly rural communities. There had been no industrial revolution, no reliance on the manufacture of machine-made goods, and no need for imports of food. Being self-reliant, Africans were sheltered from the shocks and strains of the world market and its fluctuating prices.

Now, in the new period of worldwide industrialism, all that was changed. There could be no going back to the past. The present and the future had to cope with new demands and new costs. But the economic legacy received by the new nation-states was precisely what was not helpful to them.

218

THE ECONOMIC LEGACY

In economic affairs, the colonial legacy had two sides. On one side, the colonial systems had continually drained Africa of the wealth produced by African labour, land, and natural resources. As earlier chapters explained, that was largely what the colonial systems were for: they helped the colony-owning powers to become richer. But this draining of resources, this wealth-transfer, did not stop with independence. It continued by a variety of means. The most obvious of these means consisted in terms-of-trade adverse to African interests. Terms-of-trade is the relationship between a country's export prices and import prices. The trend is bad for a country when its export prices fall in value, and its import prices rise in value. The difference between money paid for imports, and money received from the sale of exports, shows the measure of loss or gain. As we shall see (for example, on p. 243), Africa's loss has been large and continuous.

On the other side of the economic legacy, all the newly independent countries had to join a world, of trade and exchange, that was organised by much richer countries. In this world, formed by previous centuries, the advanced (that is, industrialised) countries possessed control of the markets in which world trade (exports and imports) was carried on. They could use their control so as to ensure that the wealth-transfer from poor to rich countries did not stop on the day of independence.

How did they do this? When independence came, the answer was unclear or unknown. For the colonial governments had never admitted to any such transfer of wealth; nor did they give the newly independent governments any useful information on the subject. So new governments had to find out, by themselves, what was really going on. They had to discover how the economic legacy worked.

The power to make this discovery was among the principal gains of independence. It enabled African leaders to 'open the account-books' of the colonial legacy, look into the confidential files of government, learn the facts. Then the new governments, having analysed the economic legacy of wealth-transfer, could try to act against it.

Methods of wealth-transfer from Africa

This transfer of wealth to the industrialised countries was not easy to see: its 'machinery', for the most part, was in files and records that were out of sight.

With close inspection, it was found to work in several ways (see also Chapter 5, pp. 50-51). First, through the exchange of African raw materials for imports of manufactured goods. Second, through the fixing of export-import prices. Third, through various forms of debt-interest paid on loans advanced by the industrialised countries. Let us look briefly at each of these. They formed an essential part of the background to post-independence economic progress and failure.

Africa's task, in the world of colonialism, had been to produce the raw materials needed by machines and factories in the advanced (that is, industrialised) countries. Consider, again, the case of cotton. If Europe had the machines and factories, it did not have the cotton: Europe had to get cotton from where cotton could be grown, for example Africa. So the British pushed the growing of cotton in Sudan and in Uganda, while the Portuguese, in another example, forced African farmers to grow it in Mozambique.

African farmers grew cotton and were paid for it; but that was where Africa's profit stopped. It was sold to foreign buyers, who took it to Europe and turned it into cloth, and then turned the cloth into shirts and other garments. These shirts and other garments were brought back to Africa for sale: usually, once again, by foreign merchants. So the value added to the raw cotton by manufacturing it into useful goods, as well as the profit made from selling these goods, went to foreign interests. Africans might produce the cotton. But Africans could have little or no share in the profits made from the added value of manufacturing and trading in that cotton.

A second way in which wealth was made from African labour, land, and natural resources, was in fixing prices. Mostly, the prices at which African products were sold for export were fixed by foreign companies backed by foreign governments. Only now and then were strong African peoples able to revolt against such prices: this happened, as we saw, in the Gold Coast 'cocoa hold-up' of 1937 (see p. 76).

But the same foreign machinery of control also fixed the prices of goods imported into Africa. Again, nothing could lower import prices except mass action: this, too, we saw in the no less famous Gold Coast boycott of 1948. In colonies outside British West Africa there was practically nothing that Africans could do to make such protests heard. Fixed by overseas interests, the price-system meant that Africans had to sell cheap and buy dear.

A third method of wealth-transfer consisted in the interest-money that Africans had to pay on foreign loans: on what is called 'debt-service'. We will come back to this point.

This legacy was especially difficult to throw off because, in many ways, it was built into the way in which newly independent countries had to work and earn their living.

EXPORT-CROPS OR FOOD?

By the 1960s, large rural populations were earning their living by growing cash crops – cocoa, groundnuts, coffee, cotton, and so on – and by selling these for export. This was a way of wealth-transfer overseas, as we saw above: it was part of the economic legacy of colonial rule. Yet the new government of Ghana, for example, could not simply say to the cocoa-farmers: 'Stop producing cocoa, start growing food.' For the cocoa farmers depended on cocoa for their livelihood. Besides this, the new Ghana government depended on cocoa exports for a large part of its revenue or income.

What that government had to do, and what it tried to do, was to cut down the size of wealth-transfer involved in exporting cocoa-beans, and to use the extra money for the national benefit. Why and how far it failed or succeeded in doing this remains a question for the detailed study of Ghana history. The big point for us, here, is that the colonial economic legacy could not be thrown off from one year to the next: it could only be reduced, or removed, slowly. But any real progress would have to depend on doing this.

Another reason why it was desirable to cut down on cash crops grown for export was the need to produce more food. Wherever cash crop production became important in an African country, shortages of local food began to be felt. This was partly because the more land and labour that was taken for growing cash crops, the less land or labour was there left for growing food. Local food shortages began to be acute, in some countries, as early as the Second World War. Even local famine broke out in the worst cases: as, for example, in northern Mozambique where the Portuguese forced farmers to grow cotton instead of food. Cotton, these farmers rightly said, became 'the mother of poverty'.

Increasing shortages of local food meant two things. There was less to eat than before, whether in villages or cities. Secondly, governments had to spend money on importing foreign food, often at high prices. So the result, by the 1960s, was that a continent whose population was still, largely, a farming population had become a continent which could no longer feed its own people. Here was another, and most serious, part of the economic legacy.

As the newly independent governments realised the seriousness of this growing short-fall in local food supplies – and it was only with independence that Africans could get at the facts – they came up against another problem of the economic legacy. Increasingly after the 1930s and the Second World War, there were two Africas, the Africa of the rural areas and the Africa of the towns and cities; and the interests of these two

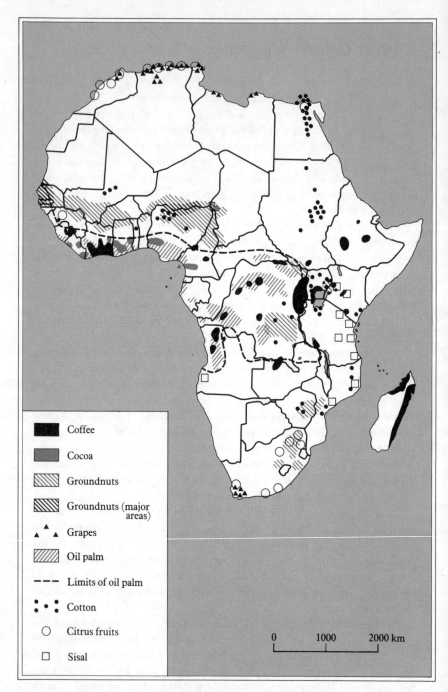

Map 10   The distribution of some important cash-crops, in 1980

Coffee
Cocoa
Groundnuts
Groundnuts (major areas)
Grapes
Oil palm
Limits of oil palm
Cotton
Citrus fruits
Sisal

0   1000   2000 km

Africas were by no means always the same. On the contrary, they have come into increasing conflict with each other.

It is easy to see why. The Great Depression of the 1930s and the strains of the Second World War had reduced large areas of rural Africa to a deepening poverty. So rural people began flooding into the towns where, after independence, political power was also concentrated. What the cities now wanted, for example, was cheap food from the rural areas; but what the rural areas expected was that independence would bring them higher prices for their produce. The two demands clashed. But the cities usually won. Not receiving higher prices, the farming peoples responded by producing less. So food imports to the cities from outside Africa had to rise, and there was that much less money to be spent on anything else. And the 'anything else', of course, included the needs of basic economic development.

Caught in this 'scissors' between the competing interests of these two Africas, governments have tried many ways to reduce urban-rural conflicts of interest. Satisfactory solutions proved hard to find.

POPULATION GROWTH AND MOVEMENT

African populations began to grow in size, ever more rapidly, after the 1940s. Scientists are not yet sure why this happened, although one reason probably lay in the spread of preventive medicine – inoculations against disease, for example – during the late colonial period. By the 1960s, most African populations were growing at an average rate of about 2.5 per cent a year. This meant that most of the new nation-states would double the size of their populations in twenty or thirty years. If Nigeria had 90 million people in 1980, as seemed likely, Nigeria will have upwards of 200 million by 2010 or soon after. The same rapid rate of growth was general throughout the continent.

This huge increase in the number of Africans could present advantages for Africa. Most African countries still had much smaller populations than countries of comparable size in other continents. Angola, for example, is more than twice as big as France, and has great natural resources in minerals and crops. But Angola in 1975, when it became independent, had fewer than 7 million people while France in 1975 had more than 50 million.

Yet doubling the number of Angolans could be good for them only on one condition; and here again was a general truth. This condition was that national skills, labour, teamwork, and planning could each year win more wealth, whether in food or other necessities, than the year before. For if the population went on growing, but the quantity of its productive or consumable wealth did not, then the population would get poorer. The average standard of living would fall, as has actually happened in most of Africa over the past twenty years; and would go on falling. A higher standard of living has to mean a better and bigger system of production and distribution, whether of food or other goods.

There was another reason why large economic changes were urgently desirable. If shortages of local food were caused by growing cash crops, they were also worsened by shortages of rural labour. We saw that the 1940s brought the beginning of a flight to the towns from villages where people had to suffer from forced labour and hunger. But once this flight began, it continued for other reasons as well. The towns grew even larger in size after independence came, because rural people, or at least rural workers, looked to the towns for a less hungry life. In Ghana by the late 1970s, for example, there was not only a shortage of local food; there was also, in the food-growing areas, a shortage of local labour. Again it was the same in many countries.

But how were these new populations of the towns to make a living, and work in ways that would increase the national wealth? Here, too, there was an absolute need to build better systems of production.

What, in turn, did this have to mean?

THE MEANING OF DEVELOPMENT

All the new governments faced this difficult question, and tried to find good answers. Many efforts were made. The story of those efforts, in detail, belongs to each new nation's separate history. Here we can offer a general guide to what was attempted, and what was achieved.

Broadly, the problem of building a better system of production was to find out how to use national resources – in people and in things – so as to produce more wealth. What could be done, in practice, was governed by two factors. One was the quantity of natural resources, especially in soil fertility or minerals, which each country possessed. Some countries, such as Niger or Burkina Faso (formerly Upper Volta), were generally poor in natural resources. The second factor was the amount of real independence which each country had won. There were rich countries, such as Zäire, that remained under strong foreign control.

But all the new countries recognised their central economic task: how best to *develop*: to build, that is, more productive systems. This required more than the development of skills, methods, and organisation of work. It called as well for a big cultural change: from habits and attitudes of work that produced goods by hand, or by simple hand-worked tools, to habits and attitudes that produced goods by machines in factories. So development could not be a simple process of ordering this or that change. It had to be a complex process in people's minds as well.

Seen in this light, the process of development had several major requirements. To begin with, the new governments had to win national control over national resources. This was difficult wherever foreign interests were deeply entrenched; and in the weaker countries it has often so far proved too difficult. Next, they had to begin to build a new national infrastructure. That means providing the basic equipment for producing and exchanging more goods, such as more and better transport and communications, and much more electric power. Further, they had to make a vast improvement in the poor systems of education and public health left behind by the colonial governments.

Then, through the process of greater control *plus* more infrastructure, they had to decide on the plan or strategy by which they were going to help their peoples to move ahead. Should this be by the methods of private enterprise, by methods of a capitalist type; or by the methods of collective enterprise, by methods of a socialist type? Was the first priority to go to helping the rural areas or the towns? To farming or to industry?

Having settled such basic questions, the new governments had then to promote new methods of production, banking, trade, and other aspects of economic life. Last but not least, each government had to decide how best to gather the national savings needed for infrastructure, industry, and public services; and how far it might have to rely on raising foreign loans for these purposes.

The strategy of private enterprise

We have touched on the matter of *alternative policies*: or, putting it in a different way, alternative strategies for economic development. In practice, of course, all the newly independent countries had to rely on a combination of different strategies. Even countries most attached to the strategy of private enterprise, like Nigeria, kept some national ownership of production and trade. Even those most pledged to the strategy of a collective or socialist type, such as Angola, left farmers in private ownership of their farms. Yet the differences between the two strategies have been real and important.

Countries following the strategy of private enterprise can, in turn, be divided into two kinds. There were weak countries under strong foreign control or influence, such as Niger or the Central African Republic, which really had no choice: they had to do whatever they were told, and, above all, make sure of not offending foreign interests. In most of the countries of the former French empire, for example, France kept control of the national currency, by means of banking operations and the so-called 'colonial franc' tied to the French franc, as well as by keeping French troops on the spot (see for example p. 255).

But other countries, smaller in number though much bigger in economic weight, were able to choose private enterprise and build national economies of that type. Notable among these was Nigeria after its first federation, which ended in 1966. Once the ravages of the civil war of 1967–69 were overcome, Nigeria moved rapidly to gain control of its national resources, and to ensure that Nigerian entrepreneurs (capitalists) were able to build up their own businesses.

National planning was geared to the needs of private enterprise while, at the same time, providing for new kinds of infrastructure. Even before the 1980s, three Nigerian national plans produced a steady expansion of wealth and economic action. New factories and industries were built. Nigeria's large deposits of offshore oil were realised at a rate which soon made Nigeria one of the world's major oil producers; and there were corresponding benefits for the incomes of all the Nigerian states, nineteen in number by 1985.

The whole economy became better balanced, and this great African federation of states was clearly on the way to becoming a structure of expanding free enterprise. Bustling cities such as Kano became the seat of new commercial companies, new factories, better roads and means of transport, comfortable hotels that were now the meeting place for countless visitors and tourists. But once again the urban-rural conflict of interests had its painful consequences. While the cities shook and boomed with profitable action, the rural areas, for the most part, fell into economic decay.

Most Nigerians still lived in the rural areas, and people in the rural areas by the 1970s had become poorer even than under colonial rule. The prices for their produce paid to rural food-growers were kept artificially low by means of national marketing boards which fixed prices for the overall benefit of city-dwellers. Urban wages were also low but became steadily higher than before; rural wages, however, scarcely improved at all.

In this situation it was hoped that policies of free enterprise could give new life to the rural areas. This meant, in the Nigerian case, that government support was given mostly to city investors who undertook to go into farming and boost farming output. But – Salisu Na'inna writing in *West Africa* (4 July 1988) –

the policy failed to admit that many of the so-called large-scale farmers often leave most of the land they control to lie fallow. They take bank loans, ostensibly to promote agriculture, and end up using the money in building dream mansions, buying expensive cars and aircraft, and organising fairy-tale type weddings.

Meanwhile little or nothing was done to help the ever-toiling peasant or small rural farmer with better prices for his produce, cheaper fertilisers, more country roads and health clinics.

Free enterprise policies in Nigeria could evidently work powerfully against any general progress. In Zimbabwe, by contrast, free enterprise was made to go together with a real concern for the interests of peasants and small farmers, and the resultant successes became impressive. In less than ten years since independence in 1980, peasants and small farmers in Zimbabwe increased their share in the country's total farming production from 10 per cent to about 65 per cent, and their crop revenues about ten-fold. Far from suffering hunger at home or relying on ever-greater imports of foreign food, Zimbabwe was able to export food, and even to make substantial gifts of food to countries hit by drought, such as Mozambique, Tanzania and Ethiopia. All this was achieved by policies in favour of the peasants: giving peasant farmers more land, guaranteeing good prices for peasant produce, installing new distribution centres for seeds, fertilisers and tools, and so on.

The Ivory Coast was another country of strong development of private enterprise, but its situation was different from that of Nigeria. On the one hand, the local position of foreign business interests was considerably stronger than in Nigeria. On the other hand, a big shortage of local farming labour could be made good only by a continual influx of migrant workers, chiefly from Upper Volta. These two factors in Ivory Coast capitalism indicated serious weaknesses and social distortions which began to be felt increasingly in the 1980s.

Kenya has been another interesting case. Generally, after independence, it went for a 'no-holds-barred' system of free enterprise. Its agricultural policies were remarkably successful in promoting new African farms on land evacuated (against compensation) by white-settler farmers in the central highlands, while its centres of urban enterprise, notably Nairobi, enjoyed an expansion comparable with some of the major cities of Nigeria.

But the problem here, as elsewhere in similar systems, lay increasingly in another kind of conflict: in a widening gap between the living standards of the few and the living standards of the many. The first went up, often steeply; the second went down, and so fast that official figures by 1987 indicated that nearly one-third of all Kenya's people were living in acute poverty. Nor was there much prospect of lessening this mass of poverty. With a rapidly rising size of population, it was calculated in 1987 that some 300,000 school-leavers every year were entering a national economy which had no hope of providing jobs for most of them.

Other countries followed various types of mixed development, some with more private enterprise, others with less. Malawi remained strongly free enterprise in its policies and system. Under the severely authoritarian hand of President Kamuzu Banda, great productive expansion was achieved by reliance on free-enterprise policies, but at the cost of cutting into the living standards both of small farmers and of wage-earners in towns. While 'middle-class' incomes rose, school and health facilities for the majority of the population failed to keep pace. Other countries have displayed much the same contradictory picture. Zambia was a mixed economy with a large element of national ownership, as in its copper mines; but, at the same time, with an expanding private sector of Zambian businessmen and of politicians in private business. Their relative prosperity was increasingly at the price of deepening rural poverty. Uganda, in its brief moments of internal peace, combined support for co-operative production with a growing private-business sector.

Thus it can be seen that successes as well as setbacks were marked up by countries following the strategy of capitalism. But all of them had to face two central problems of private-enterprise development. One of these was the general failure to expand farming output and productivity. Even Kenya, in spite of some notable successes (see p. 239), failed on this front. Its farming output grew through the 1970s at a yearly rate of about 2.5 per cent. This was a very positive achievement. But Kenya's population grew still faster; and, to feed it, there had to be higher imports of expensive foreign food.

The second big problem in the private-enterprise systems was the poverty-gap – the difference in living-standards between the minority of people who had good jobs and property, and the majority who had neither. Inequalities of this kind were not new. They had existed even in the distant past. But now they grew much bigger than before; the poverty gap became steadily wider. It was soon a major cause of discontent, and therefore of instability. But it was not, of course, limited to private-enterprise systems in Africa: its dangers and disadvantages have occurred in such systems everywhere.

The need for better solutions

Many Africans felt that the free-enterprise (or capitalist) solution to their problems of development went against the expectations of anti-colonial freedom. This kind of solution, they found, tended more and more painfully to help the lucky few at the expense of the hungry many. It worked to continue and even to enlarge the social inequalities of the colonial period. Unchecked, it was seen to promote individual greed and social immorality, precisely those human evils against which Africa's traditions of community life had stood firm. With all this, the free-enterprise solution seemed to lead to strife and still greater poverty. Was there not a better way?

The answer in the outside world had been socialism in different variants, all of which derived from the thinking and analysis of Karl Marx during the middle years of the nineteenth century. These variants ranged from a mildly liberal reformism at one extreme to a harshly revolutionary change of existing society at the other. Yet they were all applied in European, and later Asian, societies which had already built, or were engaged in building, economies of capitalism: economies, that is, of mature free-enterprise, economies based on an industrial revolution.

Could any of these non-African models be useful in an Africa yet to enter an industrial revolution, and, therefore, yet to develop sharply opposed social classes? During the early successes of the anti-colonial struggle, many Africans thought that the answer was yes, or could become yes. Broadly, two trends developed. One has proved of no historical interest. Proclaimed especially in Senegal and Kenya, this was a so-called 'African Socialism' that was merely a mask for no-holds-barred capitalism. Under 'African Socialism', existing inequalities grew worse.

A second trend, sincerely meant, evolved here and there but notably in Tanzania (mainland Tanganyika as it was called in the colonial period) under the leadership of President Julius Nyerere. Increasingly after 1967, Tanzania took the opposite road from Kenya. Explaining why in 1971 during a review of the Tanzanian scene, Nyerere pointed out that since independence there had been 'an increase in the amount of inequality between citizens'. Apart from this widening gap between 'haves' and 'have-nots', with the second far more numerous than the first, there was waste of public resources. Tanzania, he concluded, was 'beginning to develop an economic and social élite' – a 'chosen few' – 'whose prime concern is profit for themselves and their families, and not the needs of the majority for better basic living standards'.

After 1967 the ruling party, Tanzania African National Union (TANU), and its government began to seek other ways of development. Their aims now were to close the gap between the few and the many, to bring the interests of village people into line with the interests of towns-people, and to 'develop Tanzania without dividing it'. Important among their initiatives was the policy of *ujamaa*, a Swahili word meaning togetherness or neighbourliness. A big programme was launched to gather scattered hamlets and homesteads into *ujamaa* villages. These were to be provided with primary schools, health clinics, better and more farming tools, and even tractors. Foreign banks and other companies, at the same time, were taken into national ownership.

These *ujamaa* initiatives ran into big administrative problems in the late 1970s. But, no less serious, Tanzania now began to suffer increasingly from adverse terms-of-trade, as well as from steep rises in the price of oil. World recession worsened these setbacks. Many development projects had to be abandoned. But much of this appeared to have arisen, also, because too much power was retained at the centre of affairs – in the cities of government and bureaucracy – and too little was devolved to the rural areas. The city-*v*-village contradiction, in other words, was not being resolved.

The countries emerging from liberation wars against the Portuguese empire meanwhile embarked on other experiments of a socialist nature. They also began to develop some specifically African solutions, notably the policy of 'people' power' or 'people's participation' (see Chapter 18) that had done so much to help them win their liberation wars. But in the principal countries where this policy was tried, notably Angola and Mozambique, these failed to prosper after independence.

The policy itself was found to be good and sound. There were two reasons for its failure. The chief of these consisted in the aggressions and violent subversions initiated, and kept going, by *apartheid* South Africa. South Africa-sponsored banditry ruined large areas of Angola and Mozambique, and for the time being defeated every effort to build anew. But there was a second important reason here why 'people's power' failed. This was that both countries followed the advice of the European 'communist bloc', and chiefly of the USSR. The effect of this advice, which proposed a 'giant leap' into industrialism in countries with very little or no industry, was to enlarge the power of the 'centre' – of the towns, of the State bureaucracies – to a point where the peasant farmers of the rural areas felt themselves neglected or forgotten. The enthusiasm and participation that they had given so fully during the liberation wars fell away; and this rural discontent was ruthlessly exploited by South African subversive movements such as UNITA in Angola, and RENAMO (or MNR) in Mozambique. In other words, State-power policies advocated by the 'communist bloc' worked in practice against 'people's power' policies, and failed.

This failure of 'communist-bloc' policies became clearest in the one country which accepted their full doctrine. This was Ethiopia. Under Mengistu Haile Mariam, onwards from 1977, a more and more centralised

State-power regime proved unable to resolve Ethiopia's biggest problems, notably the demand of large dissident nationalities for rights to local self-government of their own. Paradoxically, as we have seen, Ethiopia's attempt to install a Stalinist model of society was made at the very time when new Soviet leaders were trying, in the USSR, to reform that model in favour of democracy.

In face of these setbacks and disasters, Africans who pinned their faith to alternative solutions saw increasingly that any successful solution would have to be adjusted and applied to the real and actual circumstances of Africa and its legacies, and not to any theory and practice imported from outside Africa. How this was to be done would have to remain a problem for the 1990s. Meanwhile it was clear that many thoughtful Africans believed that it *would* have to be done.

Much pointed to this. Even in free-enterprise Nigeria, 1987 had seen the emergence of a government-sponsored programme called 'Mamser,' mass mobilisation for self-reliance, social justice, and economic recovery, the aim being (in the words of Mamser's chairman, Dr Jerry Gana) to create 'a new political culture that could sustain a stable democracy in Nigeria'. This was clearly at least a gesture in the direction of the policy of 'people's power' even if sceptics, by 1988, were arguing that the in-built centralism and bureaucracy of Nigeria would be likely to defeat Mamser's objectives. Meanwhile the Nigerian Federation grew stronger with administrative decentralisation, and, in 1988, consisted of 21 constituent States, afterwards increased to 30.

Elsewhere there were other such pointers. The island republic of Cape Verde, which had shaken free of the Portuguese empire in 1975, was well advanced in the building of a grass-roots democracy based on structures of 'peoples' power'. They were not aiming at socialism, but they were also not aiming at an unrestricted capitalism. They set themselves to eliminate, as far as might be possible, every form of *systemic* exploitation: every way in which the poverty of the many has to derive from the privileges of the few. Only in this way, Cape Verdean political thinkers argued, could their newly formed nation grow strong in unity of effort.

Were they right about this?

'We had to carry our people with us', in the words of one of their political thinkers, speaking in 1986,

> in an enormous effort at self-realization and common purpose. It was completely obvious that any policy at the cost of the majority – a terribly impoverished majority in 1975 – would bring failure. There could be no case for trying to adopt – as Europe adopted for its own self-development – the policies of capitalism: policies to benefit the few on the argument that later on they would benefit the many. We couldn't have accepted that. We were bound to look to

the interests of the vast majority of our people (in B. Davidson, *The Fortunate Isles*: see Notes on further reading, p. 286).

Cape Verde might be small and apparently weak in its fight against the giant of poverty. Was David any different when he overthrew Goliath?

A deepening crisis

But the 1990s would inherit huge new difficulties. Years of upheaval in Africa, eruptions of bad government, failed experiments, were already combining with world recession to deepen a profound crisis of poverty and hunger. In strong contrast with the hopes of the earlier independence years, the crisis now was seen to threaten every chance of improvement. Meanwhile the warning signs had already become visible during the 1970s.

In April 1981, for example, the hard-working and hard-headed Nigerian executive secretary of the UN Economic Commission for Africa, the Nigerian Dr Adebayo Adedeji, warned that: 'With deteriorating economic prospects and a generally bleak outlook for growth, no continent has been worse hit than Africa. In the poorest or least-developed countries, people are as badly off as they were in the 1970s.' There was even much to suggest that they were worse off. Adedeji added that: 'With drought in the Sahel countries and escalating drought situations in East and Central Africa, many countries face imminent economic collapse.'

This tough realism was among the gains of independence. But the struggle against poverty, it was now very clear, was going to prove more difficult, even much more difficult, than the struggle against colonial oppression.

NATIONAL PLANNING AND INFRASTRUCTURE

Yet much was achieved in the early years of independence. In order to tackle problems of development effectively, the new nations had in any case to discover the real facts of their national situation. For example, what was the size of their populations? The colonial governments had merely guessed the answer. Now it was necessary to do better than guess. This called for detailed counting of people in national censuses. Or again, what natural resources in minerals and other wealth could the new governments command? The colonial governments had seldom known, or had kept their knowledge to themselves. Geological and other scientific surveys were necessary.

Armed with these kinds of vital information, the new governments could begin to make national plans. Centrally, such plans had to answer two big questions. How much money could the national economy command for its daily needs, and how much for its development? How should available money best be spent?

The first question concerned the amount of money for public purposes that could be found from taxation and foreign aid. The second required agreement on a list of priorities for spending that money: in the queue of things that each nation needed, which should come high on the list? Was it more useful to build a new port here, or a new river-dam there, or a new mine somewhere else?

Several priorities were generally agreed. One of them was to improve national infrastructure: that is, the basic equipment needed to expand the production of wealth, such as better roads, more railways, new deep-water ports, dams for the production of electric power. Here, much progress was made.

Colonial Africa had only a primitive infrastructure of modern equipment. There was, for example, a shortage of modern sea-ports. Ghana had only Sekondi for the export of minerals and cash-crops; Nigeria had only Lagos. There were few major sea-ports elsewhere along the western coast, or along the eastern coast except at Mombasa and Maputo. But independence soon improved this situation. New ports were built at Tema in Ghana, at Abidjan in Ivory Coast, and elsewhere in the west. There was also improvement of existing ports such as Dar es-Salaam in Tanzania.

Existing railways were improved, and some new ones built, notably from the coast of Tanzania to the capital and centre of Zambia. Great efforts were successful in producing electric power from major dams. One was at Akosombo on the Volta river of Ghana. Another was at Inga on the lower Congo river in Zaire; there, the steep fall of the river can produce, in theory, as much electric power as it used in all of Britain. A third was at Aswan in Egypt. A fourth was the great Kainji dam in Nigeria; even by 1975, before completion of the whole project, Kainji could provide Nigeria with twice as much electric power as the country had formerly possessed. Electric light for towns and even villages, as well as power for industry, began to become available as never before.

Other priorities were the provision of public-transport services, whether by buses in towns, or between towns, or by new ferries and modern vessels along the coast and between islands. Outlying areas began to be linked to the modern world for the first time in history.

The detail of all this development of infrastructure is part of the history of each new nation. Here we have indicated some of the many forms it has taken in the years of independence. These improvements in infrastructure opened the way for the beginnings of industrialisation: that is, for the production of goods by machinery instead of by hand. Africa began to be less dependent on the outside world for everyday things that people need. African factories began to make shirts, shoes, and other things which, formerly, had to be imported from overseas.

Another priority of national planning was to press for more home-grown food, partly to feed expanding populations, and partly to cut down on the expense of buying foreign-grown food. Little progress was made in this direction; sometimes, none at all. Several obstacles stood in the way. One was lack of good communications, and also lack of labour, in the rural areas. Another, as we have seen, was the tendency for the interests of people in towns, with their civil services and middle-class needs, to take priority over the interests of the people of the rural areas. This tendency increased the pressure for more cash-crops for sale overseas, so as to pay for imported goods and luxuries wanted in the towns. The problem here was that more cash-crops for export generally meant less home-produced food.

Countries with valuable minerals, requiring little or no rural labour, had a better chance of avoiding this second obstacle. They depended less on the export of cash-crops. In 1978, for example, Zambia could rely on copper for 93 per cent of its export earnings. Oil provided 90 per cent of Nigeria's export earnings, and 79 per cent of Gabon's, while diamonds provided 41 per cent of Botswana's, and 67 per cent of Sierra Leone's. Other countries were less fortunate in their natural resources. In that same year of 1978, for example, The Gambia had to rely on groundnuts for 76 per cent of its export earnings. Mali's export earnings were 47 per cent from cotton; Malawi's 56 per cent from tobacco; Rwanda's 72 per cent from coffee. This continued reliance on cash-crops made it hard to enlarge the quantity of labour and land for producing home-grown food.

The study of Africa's drive for modernisation of its infrastructure, and for the building of new economies of wealth, is complex and often contradictory. It was increasingly realised, in the years of independence, that if Africa had great economic problems, Africa also had great economic resources. The challenge to governments and planners was how best to turn those resources into new sources of wealth: this is a challenge which has been sometimes met, and sometimes not. One other example may be usefully considered: the infrastructural development of the river Nile for land-irrigation and electric power.

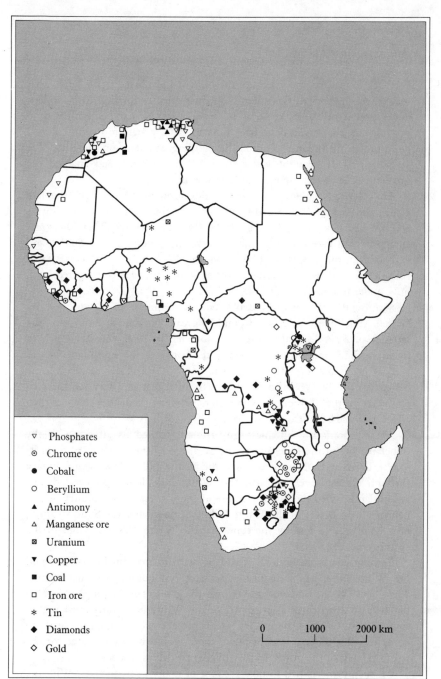

▽	Phosphates
⊙	Chrome ore
●	Cobalt
○	Beryllium
▲	Antimony
△	Manganese ore
⊠	Uranium
▼	Copper
■	Coal
□	Iron ore
*	Tin
◆	Diamonds
◇	Gold

Map 11 Main areas of mineral exploitation in Africa, in 1980. (See p. 242 for oil.)

The example of the Nile

Far back in history, the waters of the Nile had produced fertile land. That was where the ancient Egyptians built their great civilisation. But modern development of the Nile, so as to bring water to parched soils and to provide electric power, dates back only to 1925, when the British colonial government of Sudan promoted the building of a dam on the Blue Nile at Sennar. This brought water to the Gezira region, and enabled the growing of long-staple cotton for factories in Britain.

The Gezira scheme was a major development success. By the late 1950s, the Gezira cotton-growing area of irrigated land was as big as 800,000 hectares, and supported 100,000 tenant-farmers. Then the great enterprise was taken over by the independent government of Sudan, and extended further. A second dam on the Blue Nile, at Roseires, was completed in 1966. This added another 40,000 hectares of irrigated land, now under full national control.

Meanwhile, the newly-independent government of Egypt, led by Gamal Abdel Nasser, decided to build a great Nile dam at Aswan, on the frontier of Egypt and the Sudan. Completed in 1968, this did much to improve the irrigation of land along the banks of the Egyptian Nile, as well as providing Egypt with electric power. Sudan also received some benefits from the Aswan dam, thanks to an agreement between the two countries on the division of Nile waters between them. Lesser dams then added to these benefits.

At this point the Sudanese government turned its attention to the upper reaches of the Nile, where the great river flows northward from its source in Uganda. Here it is called the White Nile. Flowing northward through almost level country, the White Nile long ago created vast swamplands called the Sudd. Because of the flatness of the country, about half of all the water of the White Nile that flows into the Sudd swamps, near Mongalla, is lost by the time that the White Nile flows out of the swamps, near Malakal.

Cutting canals through the Sudd, so as to reduce this loss of water in the White Nile, had long been discussed; but nothing had been done. Then, in 1978, the Sudanese government began to cut the Jonglei Canal, a big one, so as to carry a large part of the White Nile northward with a smaller loss of its water. This great project would require years to complete, but then, it was planned, there would be more water for the parched lands to the north. Meanwhile, great delays ensued.

All such projects had to take account of many consequences. With the Jonglei Canal, for example, care would have to be taken to protect the grazing pastures of the cattle-raising peoples of the southern Sudan. If too much water was kept for the parched northern lands, these southern pastures would suffer.

Big dams created big lakes upstream: above Akosombo in Ghana, on the Zambezi river between Zambia and Zimbabwe, again on the Zambezi above Cabora Bassa in Mozambique, and elsewhere. These could provide new fishing industries. But they also meant that many people had to leave their homes. The creation of Lake Nasser above the Aswan dam, for example, meant that local farmers and their families had to be re-settled on irrigated land elsewhere. Dams also caused other problems, such as the silting-up of the lakes they made, the blocking of these lakes with weed, major new dangers from parasites (such as the infestation of the big Ghana lake, above Akosombo, by the bilharzia snail), and the difficulties of fish-refrigeration and transport. The long-term outlook, in spite of setbacks, was for more power and more irrigation: for new sources of wealth. But, again, a sometimes crushing price has to be paid in ecological degradation.

Farmers aren't fools

National planning for more productive farming suffered, for a long time, both from the colonial legacy and from experiments that failed. Broadly, the reasons for failure have been two-fold: first, too much reliance was placed on the advice of foreign experts who did not understand the real problems; secondly, there was a failure to consult African farmers on what best to do.

Severe famine in the West African grassland countries of the Sahel, during 1968–1974, showed an extreme case of failure. One of the countries to suffer worst was Niger. In 1974 its production of food-crops, chiefly millet and sorghum, was only about half of what had been produced in 1969–70. Between 1970 and 1974, on top of that, nearly 40 per cent of all the country's cattle were lost. Famine came, and people died.

Drought was the cause: but sufferings from drought were increased by failures of policy. The Niger government had encouraged farmers to use more land and labour for growing groundnuts. So there was less of both available for growing food. When drought struck, food reserves were small or non-existent. Meanwhile the same enlargement of groundnut production had pushed Niger's cattle-raising people to the northward Their herds were packed into smaller pastures. These pastures were soon over-grazed. When drought came, the cattle died; and then the people.

By 1980, many governments were revising their plans for rural development. They were turning away from experiments and policies which had failed. In countries such as Sierra Leone, for example, the large-scale use of tractors was seriously questioned. Generally, it was seen that much more attention must be paid to the knowledge and skills of African farming communities. The big questions now became: How do farming communities think they can best be helped? What solutions do *they* recommend?

Hardly anyone, up to now, had bothered to ask them. Great numbers of highly-paid foreign experts had come to Africa to tell peasant farmers how to farm in Africa's difficult ecology: with its irregular or tumultuous rainfall, with its often thin soils, with its varieties of climate, and so on. Africa's farmers had faced these difficulties since long before any Europeans or Americans first appeared in Africa. But the possibility that Africa's farmers might therefore know the right answers a lot better than foreign experts seems seldom to have crossed the minds of those experts, and of the governments who employed them.

At last, it was beginning to be understood that Africa's farmers could overcome the problems of food shortage, now as in the past: but only if they were helped to do what *they* wanted to do, and not what foreign experts told them to do. Let the experts and the governments first listen to the farmers, and then work to meet the farmers' needs; and progress could be made.

Secondly, let the governments and their agencies pay better prices for peasant produce, and the results could be sensational. That was proved by the Zimbabwe 'farming miracle' that followed independence. In 1978, two years before independence and freedom from white-settler rule, Zimbabwe's black farmers produced 518,000 tons of maize (corn). In 1981, only one year after freedom from white-settler rule, those same farmers produced 1,054,000 tons of maize. In 1985 they went better still, and produced 1,780,000 tons of maize: more than three times as much as seven years earlier.

And why? The prices paid to these farmers tell their own story. In 1978 the white-settler government paid black farmers $53 per ton of maize. In 1981 the newly independent government paid them $120 per ton, and, in 1985, $180 per ton. But much more than better prices was involved in scoring this success for higher farming output. The farming policy of the white-settler government had given every priority to the interests of large commercial farms run by white settlers. It had ignored the needs of small peasant farms. The newly independent Zimbabwe government sharply reversed this policy. It strongly believed, to quote Zimbabwe President Robert Mugabe, 'that the rural population is the backbone of a country's agriculture'.

To give an example [said Mugabe], prior to 1980 peasant farmers had virtually no access to farm credit. By the end of the 1984–85 farming season, the number of loans extended to small farmers had risen to 70,000. (At the same time) we reduced costs to the peasant farmer by making sure he is within a maximum radius of 20 kms from a marketing depot.

And it seemed clear that this policy, if adopted by other countries, could have the same kind of success.

In this struggle for more food, some successes were meanwhile scored with new varieties of seed. Kenya, for example, made a breakthrough with the use of hybrid-maize, capable of yielding a bigger harvest. Kenya's farmers were shown the advantage of hybrid-maize by pilot projects and farms. They rapidly adopted it. By 1975, as much as 30 per cent of all Kenya's maize-growing land was being planted with hybrid-maize seed. This 30 per cent was already yielding as much as 56 per cent of Kenya's maize harvest. An intelligent use of science was linked to close co-operation with farmers. The result was more food.

There were other such successes. One of a different kind was scored by the island republic of Cape Verde. Very poor when independence came, its people are farmers who live on nine volcanic islands off the coast of westernmost Africa. Their biggest problem was the loss of rare but tumultuous rainfall, bouncing down steep hillsides into the sea. After centuries of colonial neglect, the independent government set out to change this.

Cape Verdeans were led to rebuild their country so as to conserve rainfall, and store water. They made a start in 1977, only two years after independence. By 1980 they had built 7,200 stone dykes and about 2,000 km of retaining walls so as to save rainfall. By 1986 they had planted their bare hillsides with more than nine million drought-resistant trees; and this very desirable afforestation was continued year by year. There therefore began a good improvement in the natural condition of their rocky islands. More was achieved in half a dozen years of independence than in four centuries of colonial rule.

Whose development? The debt burden

The notion of 'foreign aid' is a very modern one. It originates from the imperialist-colonialist division of the world into 'rich countries' and 'poor countries' It means the aid in cash or in credits, or in goods such as food, that the industrialised countries extend to their former colonies. It may be given free, or, as in most cases, it has to be paid for by the countries that get the aid.

'Foreign aid' started in a very small way in the 1930s, and became important only late in the 1950s. Presented often as generosity by the 'developed' countries, it has as often been a compensation to the former colonies for the wealth sucked from them by the 'developed' countries: a necessary compensation if the poor or 'under-developed' countries are to become profitably productive. Foreign aid has in fact served the interests of the rich countries as well as of the poor.

In colonial times there was almost no foreign aid. There was only a little money, given mostly by the British and French governments, to help the colonial economies to export more wealth. After 1945, the same two powers put much more of their own taxpayers' money into enlarging the colonial economies. Sometimes this had very wasteful results, as we saw with the Tanganyika groundnut and The Gambia egg schemes (see p. 83). Little of it, in any case, was aid for African development. Most of it was aid for the enlargement of wealth-transfer from Africa to countries overseas. Beginning in the 1950s the government of the USA and its official agencies have given or lent a great deal of money and other help to many African countries. This was supported by the American people. Usually, however, it was not understood by the donors that the benefits of foreign aid went both ways. For what would have happened to the interests of the donor countries if the receiving countries had gone bankrupt because aid had been denied to them? The question is one more subject for useful discussion.

After independence came, the new governments nearly all had great need of foreign aid. Very few of them had been left with any reserves of capital (money to spend on development). Ghana was an exception, having reserves of capital built from selling cocoa. But most, like Zambia, had very small reserves because profits from mining minerals had always gone overseas. Tanzania, for another example, had almost no reserves. So foreign aid was necessary. It came from many countries, with the USA high on the list. After about 1960, aid also came from the USSR and other communist countries.

The problem for the new governments was how to use this aid to the best advantage. Much of it continued to enlarge the transfer of wealth overseas. But more of it began to be used to help Africa's own development. Yet this aid, even when well used, was found to have other disadvantages. Little of it was given. Most had to be paid for at high rates of interest. Indebtedness to foreign lenders soared alarmingly.

Africa desperately needed aid in money from outside Africa if its problems were to be solved. But simply throwing money at these problems proved no solution. As well as policy changes inside Africa, some of which we have discussed, there was need for a major change in the 'international economic order': in the relationship, that is, between the industrialised countries and the former colonial countries. Above all, this meant that the industrialised world should agree to raise the prices that it paid to African exporters, and lower the prices that it demanded from Africa's importers: in other words, there must be a big improvement in Africa's general terms-of-trade (see also p. 243).

Of this, meanwhile, there was no sign. Yet a good many African governments had reached the point where they could no longer pay the interest on their foreign debts. And who can be surprised? In 1985 Africa's total foreign debt exceeded double the value of all its export earnings; in 1987 it exceeded three times the value of its export earnings. This meant that Africa's export earnings were going increasingly, and sometimes overwhelmingly, into paying the interest on foreign debts. This had to be the direct road to deepening 'under-development'. The crisis of Africa's economies could plunge to catastrophe.

In this situation the big financial institutions of the industrialised world, notably the US-managed International Monetary Fund (IMF), responded by insisting that African countries should further tighten their belts, devalue their currencies, spend less on social welfare, abandon many development projects. These demands were usually accepted. Yet any general improvement had still to follow. Meanwhile the poor got poorer.

The amount of aid, furthermore, had already begun to shrink, especially after the industrialised donor countries moved into economic troubles of their own, late in the 1970s. Two conclusions began to be drawn. One was that foreign aid could still be useful, and even necessary, provided that it really went into new infrastructure and social improvement. The other was that it was dangerous to rely on foreign aid. Either this aid meant more wealth-transfer overseas, in debt-service payments, or else it failed to arrive.

In some countries, this led to policies of self-reliance in an effort to maximise local production, and to cut down on borrowing abroad. Mostly, the nominally independent countries found such policies too difficult. They slipped even more deeply into a more or less helpless dependence upon the industrialised countries. Sometimes, as in the countries of the Sahel, they entered a time of disaster.

But the strongly independent countries, large or small, began to make some progress towards self-reliance. Those with oil or other valuable minerals naturally found this easier. Nigeria was an example. In Nigeria's first national development plan, half of the total new investment came from foreign aid or foreign investment. In the second national plan, only a fifth came from foreign sources. In the third, almost all the money came from Nigeria's own resources. All this was some compensation for Nigeria's agricultural failures.

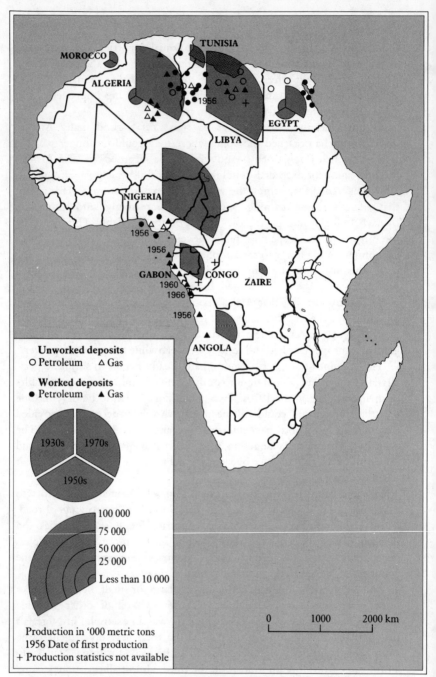

Map 12 Petroleum and gas production in Africa, up to 1980. Prospecting is currently being undertaken in many countries

A bitter lesson about export prices: failure of UNCTAD

The colonial legacy in the economic field left material and cultural backwardness; it left a continuous transfer of wealth to industrialised countries overseas.

We have briefly reviewed the principal efforts that were made, after independence, to overcome this backwardness, and to end or at least reduce the transfer of wealth. Some of these efforts worked; others failed. But much, in any case, was learned and understood. Above all, it was increasingly seen that Africans must solve their own problems of development: nobody else was going to do it for them.

This was a hard truth best proved, perhaps, by the failures of world-wide negotiation for the improvement of prices paid for African exports of crops and minerals. During the 1970s a series of meetings known as UNCTAD (United Nations Conference on Trade and Development) set out to win agreement for better or more stable prices. They achieved little or nothing. The following table shows the huge fall in effective purchasing power of export commodities that African commodity producers in fact experienced in the 1970s.

What commodities could buy in 1975 and in 1980

	Barrels of oil	Capital (U$)
Copper		
(1 tonne could buy)		
1975	115	17,800
1980	58	9,500
Cocoa		
(1 tonne could buy)		
1975	148	23,400
1980	63	10,200
Coffee		
(1 tonne could buy)		
1975	148	22,800
1980	82	13,300
Cotton		
1975		
1980	119	18,400
	60	9,600

Even if the above table were brought up to date, it would only show that Africa's exports have continued to be able to buy less and less imports. With some partial exceptions, African export-commodity prices went on declining in value after 1980. Some years have been appalling in this respect. At the 7th UNCTAD conference, in 1987, aimed at getting a better deal for the ex-colonial countries, it was revealed that the fall in African export prices, during 1986 alone, had cost the black continent no less than 19,000 million dollars, at a time of deepening poverty and famine. Meanwhile the cost to Africa of manufactured imports had risen by 14 per cent in 1986 over the level of 1985. The black continent was getting visibly poorer year by year. But the 'developed' world once more failed to make good this underlying injustice embodied in the 'world economic order'.

At the root of the problem

Africa was decolonised into a world already divided into two very different parts. That division belonged to the epoch of imperialism which is now drawing to an end. One of these two parts was, or is, the 'developed' world. This refers to all those countries, mostly in northern Europe and America (or, here and there, in the Far East), that have gone through industrial revolutions and reconstructions, and so have been able to build wealth and power by the use of machine-made and advanced technologies, and now, of course, more and more by the use of electronic systems. These are the countries which include all those that have possessed direct or indirect empires in the recent past. They have commanded the ways in which our world is organised. They have had the final say in deciding who wins and who loses. This part of our world is called the North.

The other part of the world into which Africa was decolonised is called the South: broadly, all those countries that were colonies of the North up to the later years of the 20th century. As we have shown, the South has had to accept the conditions imposed by the North: not least in terms-of-trade which have tended to bring wealth to the North but poverty to the South. This is why the 'developed' world of the North has failed to correct the underlying economic injustice in what is known as the 'world economic order'.

None of this was clearly understood at the time of decolonisation, and the not understanding of it led to many illusions about rapid national development in the newly-independent countries. Now it was increasingly seen that Africa must find its own way out of this inheritance of poverty and injustice. As thoughtful persons saw this truth, they began to think back to the old ideas and aspirations of African unity.

Long before, during the early 1960s, Africa's prophet of modern unity, Kwame Nkrumah, had written a book called *Africa Must Unite*. He argued that steps towards an all-African unity were necessary to defend

Africa's independence and build a better life. Only unity could give the strength to achieve those ends. His was a vision of continental unity ahead of its time. Yet if continental unity remained too difficult, why not now make a start with regional unity?

The question began to be asked again as the high hopes of prosperity for some fifty new nation-states, each separate from the others within its former colonial frontiers, began to fade. Perhaps the old idea of unity could after all become the key? So let us turn back to the history of Pan-Africanism. Here too, after many setbacks, some promising experiments seemed on the way.

CHAPTER TWENTY
Questions about Unity

Grim crisis during the 1980s cast a sombre light over the real achievements and gains of independence. That kind of shadow was nothing new in the ups and downs of any continent's long-term history. But now in Africa this crisis seemed as new as it was generally unexpected, no doubt because of the high optimism of the earlier independence years. The white man's world tended to bewail the fate of the black man's continent while forgetting the catastrophes through which the white man's world had itself been obliged to pass, during the Second World War, less than fifty years earlier.

The best thinkers in Africa, meanwhile, began to strike a new note of self-criticism: Africans should stop blaming their troubles on other peoples, and look to their own faults and failings.

For this self-criticism there were powerful reasons. One example among many may be enough to show this: the bloodstained story of the little East African republic of Burundi, where anti-colonial liberation and nationalism, far from becoming a source of progress and unity, led to years of mass misery and death. Burundi became independent (from Belgium) in 1962. Its Tutsi minority, about one-sixth of the population, seized all power, privilege and top jobs, denying these to its Hutu majority, about five-sixths of the population. Hutu protests in 1972 were put down with the massacre of about 100,000 Hutu people. (See also p. 158.)

In 1976 Tutsi army officers declared that Burundi had become the victim of 'multiple clans of egoist politicians greedy for personal power and benefits', but these officers proved no better than the Tutsi politicians they condemned. Hutu protests against the discriminations they suffered continued to be met by mass shootings. In 1988 many more thousands of Hutu peasant farmers and their families were massacred by Tutsi troops.

Burundi's rulers had evidently done their best to justify the worst things about 'savage Africa' ever said by the white man's world.

Elsewhere it was different. Nigerians had healed the wounds of their civil war of 1967–70. But many ethnic tensions still remained, and national unity could still appear fragile. The Nigerian historian G.O. Olusanya was speaking a general truth when he said, in a lecture of 1977, that in his own country there was still a lack of unity among Nigerians:

> Anyone who takes the trouble to monitor opinion, not only through the pages of newspapers but through contact with people, would realize that there are deep fissures within the body politic which do not provide confidence for the future.

But Professor Olusanya spoke also for the future of this new Africa of independent nations. He spoke for the confidence with which Africans could begin to solve their problems of unity.

We have looked at these problems of building unity *inside* new nations. We have studied efforts and experiments to overcome the legacies of division. We have seen that further efforts and experiments would be needed. But other problems of unity were now coming into the foreground of discussion. These were the problems of building unity *between* new nations.

New questions were being asked. Could the new nations defend themselves, and make progress, if they stayed in rivalry with one another, or even in conflict? Were the frontiers of the new nations, the old colonial frontiers, to act as barriers against solidarity and common action? Or were these frontiers to be down-graded, gradually, so as to become a liberating framework for regional and, later on, even for continental co-operation? If so, how could this be done? And in what ways, then, could new nations gain from joint planning, development, diplomacy?

To see why such questions came into the foreground, we need to turn again to the history of Pan-Africanism. In earlier times, during the colonial period, the ideas of Pan-African unity were far from the reality of daily life. Few persons knew about them; fewer supported them. The main task for the nationalists then, as people rightly saw it, was to free each country from its colonial system. The building of intra-African unity, of unity between Africa's nations, had to remain a task for the future, even the distant future.

But now, in and after the 1980s, this second task came closer. The ideas of unity between nations, of regional unity or even of still wider unity, began to seem usefully possible. Let us see how the history of the last thirty years has prepared the way for this.

A NEW VISION AND UNDERSTANDING

In Chapter 4 we left the Pan-African story far away in New York, at its fifth Congress of 1927 (see p. 33). A sixth Congress was held in Manchester, England, in 1945. With this Congress of 1945, attended by some of the future leaders of independent Africa, including Jomo Kenyatta and Kwame Nkrumah, Pan-Africanism came alive with a new strength of purpose.

A new vision of unity in independence began to develop in the years after that. A new understanding of the need for that unity began to spread. Here are two statements, among many, which define this vision and understanding as they now grew stronger.

The first is by President Julius Nyerere of Tanzania, in his book called *Africa's Freedom*. 'Only with unity', he wrote, 'can we ensure that Africa really governs itself. Only with unity can we be sure that African resources will be used for the benefit of Africans.'

The second is by the Nigerian historian Adekunle Ajala in his book called *Pan-Africanism*. 'Africa has many untapped resources', he wrote, 'and is majestically situated between East and West. With a population of 350 millions [but many more today] it exceeds those of the USA and USSR. There is therefore nothing to prevent a united, stable, economically strong and highly-industrialised Africa from competing with them in world politics.'

The road to these new ideas about the need for all-African unity and progress was long and difficult. It passed through several stages.

Early experiments

Africa's nationalists, before independence, had to put the building of national unity before any thoughts of building international unity. Yet Pan-Africanism was not forgotten, and the great unifying example and federal experience of the United States of America continued to be an inspiration. That was shown as early as the 1920s by the four-colony National Council of British West Africa (see pp. 35–36). Later, as independence came nearer during the 1950s, Pan-Africanist ideas took shape in other regional forms. None of them succeeded, largely because the struggle for national independence had to take, and keep, first place. But they deserve to be remembered.

In French Africa, for example, there were the efforts of the anti-colonial RDA, in its various territorial sections, to form two big independent federations, one for (ex-French) West Africa, and the other for (ex-French) Equatorial Africa (see Chapter 12). These efforts failed because

France was against them, as were some leaders such as Félix Houphouët-Boigny of Ivory Coast and Hamani Diori of Niger.

But the 'federalists' went on with their campaign. Before independence, new national assemblies (parliaments) in Senegal, Sudan (now Mali), Dahomey (now Benin), and Volta each voted in favour of federal unity between them after independence. Dahomey and Volta pulled out of the plan under French pressure. That left Senegal and Sudan. In 1959 their assemblies voted to form a federal state called Mali. But this federation was prepared only 'at the top'. Too many differences still separated the two countries. The Mali federation fell apart in 1960.

When Ghana became independent in 1957, its leader Kwame Nkrumah at once threw his support behind a strong campaign for Pan-African progress. He declared then that Ghana's independence would be 'meaningless, unless it is linked up with the total liberation of Africa'; and this liberation, in Nkrumah's mind, was in turn linked to the ideas of Pan-African unity. In 1958, when Guinea became independent, its leader Sékou Touré shared Nkrumah's convictions. So the two new governments at once declared a Ghana-Guinea Union, soon joined by Mali (former Sudan). This union was only on paper. It could not be a real one, given problems of geography (the two countries have no common frontiers) and other problems but was designed to point the way ahead.

The same linking of the ideas of freedom and unity – of *uhuru na umoja* in Swahili – were held by leading nationalists in the British East African colonies. A programme for *uhuru na umoja* was discussed, at a meeting in Mwanza (Tanzania) during September 1957, by 21 nationalist delegates. A second meeting, again at Mwanza during December 1958, decided to form the Pan-African Freedom Movement of East and Central Africa (PAFMECA).

At first, PAFMECA aimed only at common action for the national independence of these colonies. Later, the aim was broadened to one of East African federation between Kenya, Tanganyika (later Tanzania), and Uganda, together with any others that might want to join later. A third meeting, at Mbale in Uganda during October 1960, brought more nationalists from other countries. PAFMECA was widened to PAFMECSA (Pan-African Freedom Movement of East, Central and Southern Africa). Its aims were to work for independence, and for regional unity.

No progress was made on agreement for federation; and then, after independence, PAFMECSA was dissolved at the same time as the formation of the Organisation of African Unity in 1963 (to be discussed later in this chapter). Efforts at East African federation were nonetheless continued. There was some progress towards regional planning and development within a new framework called the East African Community. But once again, as with the Mali Federation of 1959–60, the difficulties were too great; the plan for East African federation failed. Economic disagreements between Kenya and Tanzania were the principal causes of this failure.

Another attempt at regional unity aimed at a federation of the three countries of the (North African) Maghrib: Morocco, Algeria, and Tunisia. Again it was chiefly the rivalries between political projects that brought failure.

With these failures the project of regional unification vanished from practical affairs. The new nation-states had in any case first to establish their existence and capacity to survive. Not until many years later did it begin to be accepted that the weakness deriving from the extreme disunity of Africa's new nation-states might be fatal to any further progress. Then it would begin to be found, as this chapter will show, that united effort could after all be possible as well as desirable.

The All-African People's Conferences: towards the OAU

These conferences began in 1958 under the leadership of Kwame Nkrumah and independent Ghana. They had two aims: to support the anti-colonial struggle in every part of the continent, and to strengthen the ideas of Pan-African unity.

The first conference organised by Nkrumah was a meeting at Accra, in 1958, between the eight states then independent: Egypt (United Arab Republic: UAR), Ethiopia, Ghana, Liberia, Libya, Morocco, Sudan, Tunisia. 'For the first time in the modern world', wrote the Pan-Africanist historian V. Bakpetu Thompson in his book *Africa and Unity*, 'leaders of independent African states met to discuss common problems, with a view to working out common policies concerning political, economic, cultural and social matters.'

A second Accra conference followed in December 1958. This was a meeting not of governments but of nationalist parties. Delegates came from all parts of Africa, whether or not these were independent countries, except from French Africa and Northern Nigeria. An All-African People's Organisation (AAPO) was formed with headquarters in Accra. It called for all-African liberation and steps towards an eventual Commonwealth of Free African States. Anti-colonial and anti-racist, AAPO was a channel through which the old ideas of Pan-African unity might develop in new forms and with new force.

Other AAPO conferences were held in Tunis in 1960, and at Cairo in 1961. An All-African Trade Union Organisation was launched. Referring to this in 1963, Nkrumah argued that:

the development of a united African trade union movement will give our working classes a new African consciousness and the right to express themselves in the councils of world labour, unfettered by any foreign view.

These AAPO conferences, and other meetings of that time (including a second conference of independent states, then numbering twelve, at Addis Ababa in June 1960), were, in fact, useful steps towards a continent-wide organisation. Finally, this took shape at Addis Ababa in May 1963: 31 out of the 32 African states then independent (only Morocco failing to attend) agreed to form the Organisation of African Unity (OAU).

Non-alignment, Bandung, the United Nations

Several ideas powered the formation of the OAU. One of them was that Africa's independent nations must remain outside the 'big-power blocs' into which the rest of the world was mostly divided. Otherwise, Africa's nations would soon lose their new-found independence. This was the idea or policy of *non-alignment*. Africans, it said, must stand firm on their own ground. They must become able to resist outside pressures.

Non-alignment as a world movement took shape first at a meeting in Bandung, Indonesia, during 1955, attended by representatives of 17 Asian governments and of 6 African governments (Egypt, Ethiopia, Liberia, Libya and the non-yet-independent governments of Ghana and Sudan). Later, most independent African governments joined the movement. Its aims were to defend newly won independence; advance the interests of the poorer countries of the world; and assist in settling conflicts between them.

Non-alignment thus aimed at sheltering Africa from the bruising consequences of being trapped 'in the middle' of the so-called 'East-West' conflict: of the rivalry, that is, between the two great-power blocs led by the USA and the USSR. This aim had little success; and yet the Non-Aligned Movement, as it has been called, has proved useful to the new nation-states. It has helped to give them solidarity between themselves. It has encouraged them to think about their own solutions to their own problems.

A different source of co-operation has been of great value in these years. As African colonies won their independence, each new state became a member of the United Nations. Their delegates naturally worked together in the General Assembly of the UN, and in its various committees. Soon they formed an important grouping. This encouraged them to act together, and to pursue a common diplomacy on matters of concern to them.

But conflicts of opinion also divided the new governments. Different groupings took shape. One was the Casablanca Group, formed in January 1961 by the heads of state of Egypt, Ghana, Guinea, Mali and Morocco, together with representatives from Libya and the provisional independent government of Algeria (independent only in 1962). They wanted to urge common action to help patriotic nationalists in the Congo (Zaire) against breakaway secessions such as that of Tshombe in Katanga (Shaba). They wanted rapid progress towards an all-African organisation of unity.

A second grouping, known as the Monrovia Group, was formed in May 1961 at a meeting between the leaders of Liberia, Nigeria, and Togo. They were more conservative, and doubtful of rapid action for unity. They were joined by a third grouping, the Brazzaville Group. This consisted of representatives of former French colonies still under powerful French influence and indirect control. Generally, the Brazzaville Group would do no more than talk about all-African unity.

Though divided by differences of opinion, leadership, and personality, the two big groups, those of Casablanca and Monrovia, were both in favour of working for unity, while the third group, that of Brazzaville, was too weak to be able to stop them. So a compromise was possible. Out of this compromise there came the Organisation of African Unity (OAU), a major success of Africa's modern history.

PAN-AFRICANISM AND THE OAU

The launching of the OAU in 1963 marked up a success for three reasons, each of them good for Africa's progress:

1 This launching proved that the new African states were going to begin their independent life, after the colonial period, with a determined effort to work together for common interests.
2 The OAU gave the new states their own means of settling disputes; of shaping joint policies; of combining in defence of African independence; of continuing the struggle for liberation.
3 Once launched, the OAU gave the old Pan-Africanist ideas a basis in reality. In doing this, it could point the way to overcoming the destructive rivalries of nationalism and the consequent quarrels between nation-states.

The 31 heads of state who signed the Charter of Unity at Addis Ababa pledged that the OAU would:

1 Work for unity and solidarity among Africa's nations.

2 Plan and act together for a better life for Africa's peoples.

3 Defend the sovereignty, independence, and territorial integrity of Africa's states.

4 Get rid of all forms of colonialism in Africa.

5 Work for common action with nations outside Africa, having due regard to the Charter of the United Nations and its Universal Declaration of Human Rights.

Other provisions of the OAU Charter affirmed the principles of:

1 Equality of all the member-states with each other.

2 Non-interference in the internal affairs of member states.

3 Respect for the existing frontiers of member states.

4 Peaceful settlement of all disputes between member states.

The Charter condemned all forms of political subversion and assassination. It pledged the member states to work for the liberation of African peoples still under colonial rule, and in South Africa. It declared the loyalty of member-states to the policy of non-alignment.

How was all this to be attempted? Meeting that question, the Charter provided the necessary political organisation. This consisted of an assembly of heads of state and government; a council of ministers appointed by the assembly; a general secretariat, based in Addis Ababa; and a commission to settle disputes. Money to run this organisation came from member states, each of which was asked to contribute on the same scale as its contribution to membership of the United Nations. A distinguished Guinean, Diallo Telli, became the first secretary-general.

The Charter had to be a compromise between various opinions, chiefly those of the Casablanca and Monrovia Groups. Some leaders, notably Nkrumah, wanted to go much further, and begin to provide Africa with its own continent-wide parliament and government. Others, such as Abubakar Tafawa Balewa of Nigeria, thought that it was far too early for any such steps.

Generally, this compromise was successful. The Monrovia and Casablanca Groups were dissolved. The continent now possessed its own international forum; and this forum won the loyalty of all the states which became independent after 1963.

A start was made towards economic co-operation in the shape of an African Development Bank, formed in 1964 with the aim of channelling investment of African capital into a wide variety of enterprises. Other gains were in the settlement of frontier conflicts (see pp. 256–257). A special committee was formed to support the liberation movements in colonies not yet free, and to supply these movements with money and arms if wanted. A large majority of member states combined to oppose racist South Africa. This majority defeated a policy of 'dialogue' with South Africa, put forward by Ivory Coast, Malawi, and others, on the grounds that dialogue indicated acceptance and recognition of racist South Africa. The same majority insisted on a policy of boycotting South Africa as far as this might become possible.

Refugees were another of Africa's problems, after independence, in which the OAU could help with various forms of action and relief. In 1964 the OAU set up a special commission to work on refugee problems together with the UN High Commission for Refugees. In 1968 all member states signed a convention, or agreement, aimed at helping refugees, while, at the same time, preventing refugee problems from growing into inter-state conflicts. Such action proved very necessary. In 1976 the UN High Commission estimated that about one million Africans had fled from their own countries into neighbouring countries, some for political or social reasons, many others to escape from wars. Later, refugee numbers increased again, and OAU help had to continue.

Such gains and actions of the OAU were valuable. They reduced a number of troubles. They prevented others. But there were obvious limits on what could be done to build unity of policy and work. These limits could not be avoided. Like the world-wide UN, on which the OAU was partly modelled, the OAU was an assembly of heads of state or government. The OAU could only go as far as those national leaders wished or were able.

This being so, the OAU was unavoidably an organisation controlled 'from the top' of the new states, and not nourished 'from the base'. Further unification of Africa's peoples, through political parties and their elected delegates, was in no way possible yet. Until that could happen, the power of the OAU would have to stay within very narrow limits. As a sympathetic critic in the *Ghanaian Times* noted as early as 1963, the aims and means of the OAU Charter would be able to 'become a reality only if the masses of Africa are mobilised for action.' No such mobilisation was possible in these years and the OAU's value greatly dwindled.

OCAM, THE ARAB LEAGUE

Meanwhile, even within these limits, the OAU proved useful.

Two large difficulties were usually overcome in the course of its conferences and resolutions. The first of these difficulties lay in the fact that the earlier division between 'moderates' and 'radicals' continued to exist. The other difficulty was that the all-African scope and nature of the OAU sometimes came into conflict with regional opinions and disputes.

Such difficulties were unavoidable. They help to explain why the meetings of the OAU have been at times reduced to little more than empty talk, or even to the echo of voices and interferences from outside Africa.

The first difficulty consisted, really, in a strong neo-colonial presence. This came from leaders, such as the Abbé Fulbert Youlou of Congo-Brazzaville – now the People's Republic of Congo – or President Philip Tsiranana of Madagascar, who both closely reflected the policies of France. Other leaders of influence, notably President Houphouët-Boigny of Ivory Coast, were independent-minded; but they also believed that their countries should accept French leadership.

Others again, including some of the spokesmen of important former colonies of Britain, were much inclined to listen to the wishes of the USA or Britain, whenever any serious dispute arose. In those opening years of the OAU, for example, Nigeria scarcely possessed a foreign policy of its own. Over against these 'moderate' leaders were a number of 'radicals', notably Nkrumah of Ghana, Ahmed Ben Bella of Algeria (removed by Algerian military action in 1965), and Sékou Touré of Guinea. In between the moderates and radicals were many small states which lacked the power to take an effective independent line.

Some regional organisations or groupings also made it difficult for the OAU to work well. This trouble came chiefly from former French colonies which had formed the Brazzaville Group. They now formed a body of twelve states known as the Afro-Malagasy Union (in French, UAM), whose members were – Cameroun, Central African Republic, Chad, Congo-Brazzaville, Dahomey, Gabon, Ivory Coast, Madagascar, Mauritius, Niger, Senegal, Upper Volta.

All the UAM states had great dependence on France; generally, they were all neo-colonial states. They maintained a special relationship with France, even though this went against the OAU Charter. In 1965 they went further. Together with Congo-Kinshasa (Zaire) and Togo, they formed a 'mini-OAU' of their own, the Afro-Malagasy and Mauritius Joint Organisation (in French: OCAM).

This dependence continued. In March 1981, for example, the Nigerian political scientist Yusufu Bala Usman pointed out that most of the then existing governments of Central Africa:

> were installed and are maintained by French military presence. The government of President Ahidjo of Cameroun was installed and is maintained by this presence. The government of President Bongo (of Gabon) was installed by French paratroopers who up to this day occupy the country. The government of President Mobutu has been maintained by a series of military interventions by NATO (the Western military alliance), spearheaded by France, since it was installed.

And he went on to list other such cases.

So long as OCAM aimed at direct rivalry with the OAU, there was bound to be trouble. But gradually, after 1970, its main action was transferred to the economic field. It formed joint OCAM enterprises for postal travel, airlines, other matters. These had to be accepted by the OAU, given the reality of French presence and, now, the arrival of the European Economic Community of which the OCAM states, as well as some of the non-OCAM states, became associate members.

The Arab League was another regional organisation with which the OAU had to come to terms. Founded in 1944 by Egypt, Iraq, Lebanon, Syria and Jordan, the League was later joined by African states which had an Arab-speaking or Muslim majority (Libya, Tunisia, Algeria, Morocco, Sudan, Somalia), as well as by other Arab states in the Middle East. Aimed at strengthening the security of these states, it rapidly became a forum for discussion between their governments, and a means of common action, especially against Israel and in defence of the Arabs of Palestine (see p. 67). Generally, the member-states of the OAU supported the aims of the Arab League.

Frontier conflicts

The new states gathered in the OAU had to inherit some frontier disputes. Most of these were successfully settled by OAU diplomacy.

A small war broke out in October 1963 between Morocco and Algeria. It concerned a frontier area of Algeria that was claimed by Morocco. Acting as mediator, the OAU was able to bring about a cease-fire, and, in February 1964, an agreement for peace. Each side gained something, and agreed to co-operate in the economic development of mineral deposits at Tindouf in Algeria. But this failed to satisfy Morocco. OAU peace efforts had to continue. They were crowned with success by a new agreement of May 1970. Other disputes of this kind were settled; and the OAU proved a valuable instrument of peace.

Some large disputes could not be settled. One of these consisted in Moroccan (and, at first, Mauritanian) efforts to share out the ex-Spanish Sahara, and prevent the formation of a republic of the Western Sahara by its liberation movement, POLISARIO, which had Algerian and other African support. After a while Mauritania withdrew from this conflict, but fighting between POLISARIO and Morocco continued; and the OAU remained divided.

Another and bigger conflict concerned the frontiers of the Ethiopian empire, built by the Emperor Menelik at the time of the colonial partition. As mentioned in Chapter 10, the Somali people of the Ogaden province of the Ethiopian empire continued to press for their right of self-government or independence, and were strongly supported by the Republic of Somalia next-door. Fighting broke out in 1976 and led to an Ethiopian victory with the support of Soviet tanks and Cuban troops.

The former Italian colony of Eritrea, as we saw in Chapter 10, passed first under British military government, in 1941, and then, in 1952, became a federated state of the Ethiopian empire. In 1962, however, Ethiopia reduced Eritrea to a mere province or colony of the empire. To this the nationalists of Eritrea replied with guerrilla warfare until their victory in 1991. After 1974 a number of other minorities in Ethiopia, such as the Oromo, also began to revolt in order to win local powers of self-government. Here again a divided OAU proved powerless to help.

NEW MOVES FOR REGIONAL CO-OPERATION

Generally, by 1980, it had become clear that the OAU could be useful and effective within small limits, but that no real progress could be made outside those limits. What other road towards common action might now be open? Some important answers were already on the scene. These were echoed and reinforced during a 1980 meeting of African heads of state in Lagos, the capital of Nigeria. This emphasised a new interest in promoting economic co-operation between OAU member states.

Earlier efforts at economic co-operatin between states, or between groups of states, had failed for several reasons, sometimes because they were tried too soon. But with the experience of more years of independence, and with a better understanding of Africa's real problems of development, it was now seen that co-operation was increasingly desirable. Africa could face disaster unless much stronger systems of production and or productivity of goods, especially of food, were installed and made to work. We have examined the reasons for this (see Ch. 19, *Questions about development*).

Stronger systems of production and productivity called for new policies and plans inside independent states. But they just as surely called for co-operation between these states. New efforts and experiments began to be made. Here we can mention two of them.

In 1975, fifteen West African states signed the Treaty of Lagos. This formed the Economic Community of West African States (ECOWAS). The founding members were Benin, The Gambia, Ghana, Guinea, Guinea-Bissau, Ivory Coast, Liberia, Mali, Mauritania, Niger, Nigeria, Senegal, Sierra Leone, Togo, and Upper Volta; in 1977, the Republic of

Cape Verde also joined. They pledged themselves to work together to promote more trade between them; to co-operate in various fields of enterprise; and to aim at self-reliance in regional development.

An important point about ECOWAS is that it has linked strongly independent states which had come out of the British empire, and later out of the Portuguese empire, with much less independent states of the former French empire. This helped to reduce the strength of neo-colonial influence and financial control. The prospects were strengthened for African autonomy of decision about African needs and problems. Another important point is that ECOWAS has helped to build a common front of African self-defence in respect of the European Economic Community and of other outside groupings.

Progress towards the major aims of ECOWAS, embracing sixteen countries containing some 160 million West Africans of many languages and loyalties, had to be slow. Creating a 'common market' among all these people could not be easy. A customs union between the states was deadlined for 1990 but could not yet be realised. Meanwhile there had been continued effort and some useful minor progress. In November 1984, for example, the ECOWAS governments agreed, in what became known as 'the Lomé Declaration' after the city in which it was hammered out and signed, that they would adopt a joint programme of economic effort and construction throughout their region. They pledged themselves to a common economic strategy, to the formation of an ECOWAS monetary zone aimed at promoting financial stability, and to stronger attempts at reaching the unifying goals of their Community.

A further move of the same nature, as yet less advanced than ECOWAS, emerged in southern Africa during 1980. Nine states decided to find ways of helping each other and working together for their economic benefit. These were Angola, Botswana, Lesotho, Malawi, Mozambique, Swaziland, Tanzania, Zambia and Zimbabwe. Potentially rich because of its many natural resources, the whole region still laboured in poverty: if they could combine their efforts, as for example in building better roads and railways to connect them, and better ports to link them with the outside world, these nine states could look to the future with confidence. They began to make initial progress in these ways.

But they had one great and common enemy. This was the aggressive power of *apartheid* South Africa, whose leaders still intended to dominate the whole southern sub-continent. On the other hand, once there could be a democratic South Africa freed from *apartheid* and its violence, the riches of an industrialised South Africa could become available for the benefit of the whole region. During the 1980s the nine SADCC states (SADCC means Southern African Development Co-ordination Conference, in fact a standing body drawn from all nine countries) could do little more than defend themselves against *apartheid* threats and aggressions. But they tried increasingly to defend themselves by joint action. Very important in this respect was the aid in troops and arms given by Zimbabwe and Tanzania to Mozambique in defence of Mozambique against South Africa-backed terrorism and subversion. On a longer perspective, the SADCC states prepared themselves for a time when they could work together with a liberated South Africa.

CHAPTER TWENTY ONE

Towards Africa's Reconstruction: Summary and Overview

The story of Africa during the past 90 years or so, the story of modern Africa, is one of difficult survival in the face of mortal dangers, and of stubborn struggle for peace and progress. As these chapters have shown, mighty storms have struck at the black continent and driven it through a time of tremendous change. This time of change has probed every aspect of life with revolutionary impact, and creativeness unknown to any earlier time.

As the 20th Century approaches its end, our history has measured the losses of the colonial period; the gains of the struggles for independence from colonialism, the achievements made in overcoming legacies of poverty and racism imposed by imperial systems of European rule. We have looked in detail at the problems of building post-colonial stability; at the problems of economic development; at the problems of forging unity among peoples of different languages and traditions. We have noted defeats as well as victories, failures as well as successes. We have watched the unfolding of a complex tapestry of human effort.

Today the black continent at last comes nearer to being able to command its own destiny within the modern world.

Beyond many sorrows, this is a story of profound change.

That is the most important conclusion to be drawn from our study of history. The myth of 'black inferiority' is shattered. Emerging from long and painful struggles, the black peoples in all their diversity and vigour stand forth now within their own cultures, and with confidence in their own abilities. All the world is richer for this.

But we have also seen that this great gain was hard to make and hard to defend. In this respect the concluding years of the 20th Century have again brought a time of trouble. And the trouble seemed to threaten everything that Africa had achieved for itself. Africa found itself in a crisis of poverty and conflict, a crisis in some ways more dangerous and destructive even than the long crisis of imperialist dispossession a hundred years earlier. Africa is not alone in this respect. And yet Africa's crisis of hunger and poverty struck at many of her peoples, while, after 1985, medical science revealed that Africa was now the victim of a new and terrible epidemic, that of AIDS; and against AIDS there would then be no sure defence and no cure.

Yet Africa's long history, generally, had not been one of great poverty and crisis. The old states and kingdoms of the past, sometimes of the distant past, had certainly had their own problems, but generally they had fed their people well. They had flourished with their farming production and their networks of internal trade. Their communities had functioned, their systems had worked. Why then should modern Africa be struck down by a crisis in which communities are torn apart, and every system of government seems to fail? What reasons were responsible for this?

We have looked at some of the reasons in the history of the years since the beginning of independence from colonial rule. Partly they arose from a common heritage in human frailty, greed, lack of foresight into the destructive consequences of get-rich-quick policies. Wide forests have been destroyed, perhaps forever. Broad grassland plains have withered under drought and over-grazing. Partly these reasons for failure lay in bad government, irresponsible leadership, habits of waste and idleness.

Looking at these results of independence during the 1980s, however, wise thinkers in various regions of Africa began to say that these internal reasons for failure, and for the arrival of crisis, were not enough. Other continents and peoples were in sore crisis too. Simply blaming African bad government was not convincing. It was merely looking at the surface of events. To get at the roots of Africa's trouble, a deeper analysis must be applied. These roots, it began to be said, were not to be found primarily in human failure. Humanly, Africa had not failed. On the contrary, the years of post-colonial independence had raised an abundant harvest of African talent in many fields, whether industrial or scientific, organisational or administrative, artistic or commercial.

The roots of trouble were not to be found in human failure, but in institutional failure. Above all, they were to be found in the methods and means and systems of government or development which Africa had used in its new-found independence.

How else can we explain why the huge country of Zaïre, for example, had possessed 88,000 miles of good all-season motor road at the end of the colonial period, but only 1,200 miles in the middle of the 1980s after more than 20 years of independence? How else could it have come about, by 1990, that the once famous country of Liberia was far sunk in misery and conflict? And these were only two examples, among many others in various regions of Africa, of tragic decline and deterioration in public life.

RE-THINKING THE NATION-STATE: TOWARDS A CULTURE OF RESTITUTION

There came a recognition, generally among African thinkers and historians, that their continent was somehow on the wrong track. For they knew, from their studies and meditations, that Africa within its own history, before the colonial dispossessions, had not been deep in continental crisis. Africa then had possessed solutions to its own problems. This was not to say that pre-colonial Africa had been a time of glory, a time of unbroken peace and reconciliation: of course not. History here has been as much a story of struggle as anywhere else in the world. But Africa's own development had nonetheless produced Africa's own solutions.

So what had been these solutions? What principles of pre-colonial state-craft had protected the old states of Africa from institutional decline, from self-destructive conflict, from dictatorship and the sins of greed?

Universities and other schools of higher knowledge, in independent Africa, had begun to produce new generations of trained scholars and specialists from about the end of the 1960s. Increasingly, these scholars turned their minds and skills to this central problem of institutional decline. By the 1990s there was available a new body of thought. Conclusions began to come to hand.

Some reasons for institutional decline were obvious, quite apart from human frailty and failure. One of these, the most obvious of all, lay in the system of world trade into which Africa had been decolonised: as we have seen, within this world system Africa was obliged to continue to export wealth to 'the North', to the 'developed' countries, whether by pressure of the terms-of-trade or by debt service or by other economic means. Another obvious reason for decline lay in destructive foreign interventions or foreign-inspired banditries, notably in countries such as Angola and Mozambique.

But now it was increasingly seen that these obvious reasons for Africa's crisis were enlarged by the very nationalism, or nation-statism, which the pioneers of anti-colonial liberation had used as their necessary instrument of change. Instead of building new states from the foundation-culture of Africa's pre-colonial states, Africa had tried to build new states from the foundation-culture of colonial states, a very different thing. So independence had not been able to join Africa to its own history and tradition. Independence, in practice, had come to mean a continuation of Africa's subjection to others, it had come to mean another period of alienation from Africa's living roots and self-belief.

This was not a case for blaming the pioneers of anti-colonial liberation. They had done their best. But it *was* a case, as more and more African thinkers began to say during the sad years of the 1980s, for re-thinking the chief and central structure on which independence had rested. This structure of ideas and of power-distribution was easy to see and define. It consisted in the kind of state that had emerged from the colonial state at the time of independence: a kind of state that claimed to be an African independent state but was, in practice and in power-distribution, closely modelled on the colonial state. In fact, as we have seen, the fifty-odd colonies into which the imperialist powers had divided Africa became, after these powers withdrew or were driven out, fifty-odd African states within the same frontiers as before, and governed, often and essentially, in the same ways as before: except, of course, that the governors now were no longer European, but African.

The pioneering leaders of independent Africa, back in the 1950s, had seen the danger in this kind of state: it meant, they said, that Africa might be exchanging direct colonial rule for indirect colonial rule, for what these leaders defined as 'neo-colonial' or new-colonial rule. If that happened, then the further development of an independent Africa would be in peril, and might become impossible. In earlier chapters, notably in relation to the West African colonies of France, we have traced the ways in which this peril became real.

Sharp analysis of this new-colonial state showed where the problem lay. All the real powers of government were concentrated 'at the top', so that the structure of government was dictatorial. In colonial times these supreme powers were held by European governors. The governors, one or several men in each colony taking orders from London or Paris or some other European capital, controlled all executive decisions. They ensured that these decisions were carried out 'down the line of command'. Now it was seen that much the same was happening in the newly independent states. African presidents or military dictators had taken the place of the old colonial governors. But the peoples still found it hard to make their voices heard. Sometimes they found it impossible.

Out of this situation, bad government had come. The widening conclusion of the 1980s, accordingly, was that this new-colonial kind of state had to be reformed. Said a prominent African thinker, Professor Lamin Sanneh, speaking for this conclusion in 1988: 'Political renewal in

Africa must begin with curtailing the power of the state'.* Many by this time agreed with him. The dictatorial system of the new-colonial state must be transformed into a democratic system. Power to make and execute policy must be devolved from central government to local government: from 'the top' to the 'grass roots'. It would be good to form new and even many political parties, but this would not be enough: they might become no more than as many pressure-groups that would continue to keep the monopoly of power in their own hands. The reform of the new-colonial state that was required was therefore a reform which would enable electors to share in power, to *participate in power*.

A WIDE DEBATE

But could it be done? The debate on this question spread out from universities and colleges. It became a matter for wide public discussion. And in this debate there were many sceptics who said that the idea was good but could never be put into practice. This, they said, was because the few who held power at the top would never share their power – with its privileges, with its hands on money and land – among the many 'at the bottom'. And the dictators who now ruled in a number of African states certainly seemed to prove that this was true. They held on stubbornly to all the power they had. They sent their police or troops to silence any persons 'at the bottom' who tried to get hold of a share in power.

Yet Africa has never been short of brave and thoughtful persons and protesters. There were those, now, who said that Africa's history had useful lessons to teach in this tough debate about power-sharing. For Africa's history could show that democratic forms of power-sharing had stood at the centre of statecraft in centuries before Africans, during colonial rule, had lost the ability to rule themselves. Therefore what was needed, in this profound social and political crisis at the end of the 20th Century, was to look again at the old principles of pre-colonial statecraft, and consider whether they could have some useful application in reforming the rigid centralisms of the new-colonial state. What lessons, in short, could be learned from the living history of Africa's self-development in the past? Perhaps a culture of restitution might after all be possible?

* When speaking at a seminar organised by Northwestern University, Evanston: proceedings edited by John O. Hunwick, and published as *Religion and National Integration in Africa*, 1992.

LEARNING FROM SELF-DEVELOPMENT

It is an old and true saying that you cannot develop other people, you can only develop yourself. Other people either develop themselves, or they do not develop at all. Peoples in Africa, before the long colonial interruption, had developed themselves. From this self-development had come a rich variety of social and political systems: self-governing communities, complex patterns of trade and of production for trade, valuable techniques like the skills of tropical agriculture, metal-working, textile weaving and so on.

History also showed that this self-development, in all its complexity, had derived from indispensable principles of statecraft. Communities which upheld these principles had been able to succeed and prosper. Communities which ignored or denied these principles had failed and fallen into confusion.

These pre-colonial principles were concerned with preventing the abuse of executive power; with ensuring that power was shared across the community in question; and, to safeguard this participation, with upholding the rule of law.

Every successful community in old Africa had operated in one way or another on these principles of statecraft; and such communities had been many. These were the truths that the colonial powers, and their ideologists, had always denied. Colonial ideologists had said that black people had never known how best to govern themselves: white people must do it for them. Such was the ideological basis of colonialism. And the same idea, however muted, was also the basis of what Africans were now calling 'new-colonialism'. Learning from self-development therefore had to mean, among much else, recalling the pre-colonial principles of African statecraft.

African thinkers began to do this. And it proved to be no good dismissing these thinkers as 'mythmakers' or 'romantics' or persons who did not understand the world they were living in. For these persons were qualified and highly realistic. Among them, for one example of many, was the African economist and thinker who led the United Nations Economic Commission for Africa throughout the 1980s, Professor Adebayo Adedeji. His name was known and respected wherever African affairs came under serious discussion throughout the world. What Adedeji was now saying, in these last years of the 20th Century, was that in no way should Africa try to 'return to the past'. Even if that could be possible it would do no good; and in fact it was impossible, because no people can ever return to their past. But Africa should reconsider the traditions of its past, recall its old principles of statecraft, discuss how these might still be a source of wisdom and self-rescue from the crisis of the times.

When at home in the ancient Nigerian state of Ijebu, which is a country situated near the Nigerian city of Lagos, Professor Adedeji is also recognised as something else. He is the Asiwaju of Ijebu, in traditional usage the chief executive officer of Ijebu state, a kingdom founded several centuries ago under its traditional king, the Ajuwale of Ijebu. And although these traditional titles no longer confer any official power, they still stand for a living history of self-development, a history both real and respected by the people of this old state. Ijebu had been one of the famous and successful states of the numerous Yoruba people of southern Nigeria. And it was famous and successful, Professor Adedeji argued, because it was 'homogeneous, cohesive and united'.

For this state of Ijebu, founded sometime in the 16th Century, was 'a society where the monarch reigned rather than ruled, where there was decentralisation of power, public accountability, and economic and political empowerment' of the people. Needless to say, none of this was done to perfection, for humanity can never be a perfect organ; but it was done with sufficient success to guarantee stability of government and progress in self-development. Professor Adedeji wears his title of Asiwaju as a reminder of that notable success in African self-government.

As these ideas came under debate, especially in response to the crisis of the 1980s, other examples of past wisdom were remembered and examined. Among the states of the Yoruba, in south-western Nigeria, there had been the important state of Oyo. This had flourished for some 200 years before the colonial invasion. At first glance, invading Europeans had thought Oyo was a form of centralised dictatorship under its undoubtedly powerful monarch, the Alafin. They were encouraged in this opinion by the fact that the Alafin was flanked by a hierarchy of prestigious chiefs who were aristocrats like himself. These men assembled, whenever important public decisions had to be taken, in an Oyo state council called the Oyo Mesi. It looked as though they were accustomed to carve up executive power among themselves, and abuse this power to their own advantage. And this, the evidence suggests, is just what they did whenever they got the chance: this, after all, was bound to be the nature of aristocrats.

But then, as study of Oyo continued, it was realised that there had come into operation a principle of statecraft, whereby public controls were applied to this expected abuse of executive power by those who held such power. Expected abuse: because this principle of statecraft took it for granted that men and women with power would abuse it unless they were prevented from doing so. The political thinkers of old Oyo, as you see, were anything but romantic about their fellow citizens; and the hard wisdom in this attitude may be less surprising when you remember that Yoruba history began to unfold very many centuries ago. A means of controlling persons with power had long been found necessary, and had long been devised.

Their means of control, as it evolved before modern times, was the Ogboni. This was not some kind of 'secret society' of mysterious or magical purpose. On the contrary, the Ogboni was a public and popular means of keeping rulers in check, being open to wide membership and endowed with appropriate authority. It appears to have worked well as a means of popular control of the use or abuse of executive power. Its operation was aimed at ensuring a large degree of public accountability of the rules to the ruled. This helped the Oyo state to be seen and accepted as legitimate in the eyes of its citizens, and to the extent that this was so the rule of law was in safe hands.

Mechanisms like these, in short, limited the central powers of the state. They placed a protective shield between the state and its citizens. To the outside eye, of course, these mechanisms were hard to see and harder still to understand; and the European invaders, bursting in with their guns and gunboats, saw in organisations like the Ogboni nothing but the rituals of an unregenerate barbarism. It would be many years before such opinions were revised. When they were revised, respect for the achievements of old Africa could begin to take the place of contempt.

These are powerful and important aspects of Africa's history, but we cannot go into them here. Suffice it to say that states such as Ijebu and Oyo, where popular participation in the exercise and control of executive power was applied and maintained, were not rare exceptions: rather they were examples of what was usual. The principles of statecraft to which they stayed loyal were also present and at work, if under different appearances, in other African communities whose histories have become known and studied: for example, in the states of the Akan, of the Mossi, of the Hausa, of the Swahili, and of others up and down the continent. These showed stability and developmental success over a long period, even while it is also true that some of their neighbours along the coastland were drawn into the overseas slave trade, after about AD 1600, and made subject to that trade's violence and moral degradation.

What we are generally seeing, however, is not the evidence of any kind of pre-colonial Utopia or 'Golden Age'. We are seeing the presence of a stable developmental success in societies which had understood how to match power with responsibility, and authority with the control of authority. There is no need to fall into the propagandist error of supposing that in this old Africa all was good and as it should be, nor that violence and barbarism were always absent, nor that everyone was safe and happy. But what is just as certain is that this old Africa, generally in terms of civility and everyday social behaviour, lived better than the Africa which emerged from colonial dispossession. What we need to do, accordingly, is not to imagine a 'Golden Age' before colonialism, for no such age ever existed, but to ask an absolutely central question. If old Africa could successfully develop itself over the centuries of the past, why should this self-development have stopped?

INVASION AND DISPOSSESSION: COLONIAL REALITY

The colonial invasions of Africa during the 19th Century were carried out by old-fashioned methods, guns that were far from reliable, and numbers of troops that were seldom large. They were able to succeed because invaders from Europe came from countries that were more or less industrialised, whereas industry in Africa, though widespread and often profitable, was still at the stage of handicraft production. African communities often defended themselves from European invasion, but the invaders invariably had better guns and stronger organisation. So almost the whole continent was taken into European possession. A network of entirely new frontiers between peoples, and sometimes through the middle of peoples, was drawn across the map by Europeans. These Europeans claimed, and were increasingly able to exercise, every power of public government and decision. African self-development had to stop. All this was done by the beginning of the 20th Century.

This physical and political dispossession involved more than African loss of control over territory. The colony-building invaders wanted far more than that. They wanted control of the lives of the peoples whom they had enclosed within their colonial frontiers. Above all, they wanted control of the labour-power of these peoples. Africans were accordingly stripped of their powers of self-development. Henceforward they were to do as they were told, and obey the dictates of their conquerors. Chiefs and kings might continue to exist, but they too would have to become agents of colonial power. Every concept of self-development, accordingly, had to be set aside, or, at best, reduced to helpless rituals of ornamental folklore. There would have to be new development; but this must be along European lines and in line with European interests.

The guiding thought of the colonialists was that history in Africa *could now begin*. Whatever had developed through the centuries before colonial dispossession, it was affirmed and taught, had not been history, or else it had been history of no meaning or value for this dispossessed Africa. Entering the modern world by way of the disaster of colonial dispossession, Africa was expected to develop as part of European history.

What did this mean? It meant, so far as most Africans were concerned, that physical dispossession by colonial enclosure was to be accompanied by mental and moral dispossession. As this process of alienation gradually took shape and purpose, the result for a great many Africans was a deep and necessarily wounding loss of self-confidence, a psychological loss that was also a loss of self-respect. In the long epoch of modern imperialism, Africans at best were to be cast in the rôle of second-class citizens of an outside world which believed that it possessed 'all the answers'.

A DISTANT BUT INSTRUCTIVE PARALLEL

Having taken possession of Africa in the 1880s and soon after, the dispossessors were bound to assure themselves, if only for their own peace of mind, that they had also acted for the benefit and eventual welfare of the peoples they had dispossessed.

Left to their pre-industrial and pre-scientific primitivism, said the colonialists, Africans could never have modernised their communities, their ideas and beliefs, their ways of self-government. Colonialism might be a rough and tough business; never mind, foreign rule was what Africa needed if any real progress were to become possible. The Africa of a century ago, it was said, was lost in the futile ties of a bygone age, unable to help itself.

The study of history cannot deal with 'might-have-beens'. We can only guess at what might have happened, or failed to happen, if imperialism had not stepped upon the stage. But if we do make that kind of guess, we can usefully look back for guidance at what educated Africans were thinking about their countries' future, for example in the 1860s, before the full-scale arrival of imperialism. Those educated men and women, few though they were, saw quite clearly that the outside world, beyond the oceans, was about to descend on Africa with a mighty impact. To absorb the impact, Africa would have to change, Africa would have to modernise.

In 1867, for one example, the Fanti people (of Ghana today, or what was then known as the Gold Coast) called their leading men together and devised a new constitution, a new set of rules and laws for self-government. This reinforced a famous Fanti self-defence alliance known as the Bond. It provided for a modernising reform of government which should nonetheless be based on Fanti historical experience. As we know, British imperialist armies arrived instead, and the Fanti, like their neighbours, lost all command of their own future.

But could their plan, left to itself, have led to real progress? The Fanti thought so, and in later years their thinkers and writers would point to a distant but instructive parallel: the experience of self-modernisation launched in Japan during that same year of 1867. This was the period of rapid modernisation of Japan that was ushered in by the Meiji emperor and his government. Those Japanese saw very well that foreign imperialism was about to descend upon Japan with a mighty impact. Japan must therefore modernise, and fast: otherwise Japan would forfeit its independence, would become the vassal of foreign powers, would lose its place in the world.

As we know, the Japanese of the Meiji period were able to keep their independence and modernise: for various reasons of their own, the Western powers which had threatened Japan turned away from any project to subjugate Japan. But the Africans had no such luck. In those same last years of the 19th Century, the whole of West Africa – and then the whole of the continent – was made subject to Britain, France, Germany, Portugal, Spain and finally Italy. Reflecting on this disaster to their plans and hopes, the thinkers of the Fanti – and they were not alone in this respect – clearly saw this painful contrast.

Thinking back to the intention of their plan, the Fanti historian Mensah Sarbah wrote: 'Fanti patriots, and the Japanese emperor with his statesmen, were both striving to raise up their respective countries by the proper education and efficient training of their people. The same laudable object was before them both. The African's attempt was ruthlessly crushed and his plans frustrated.'

A hundred years ago Mensah Sarbah and his friends believed that Africans could have developed their own means of modern development if they had been given the chance. Were they much too hopeful? We don't know: racist colonialism came instead, and killed off that chance. But even if Africa had been spared racist colonialism, was there ever a real possibility that Africa would have been left to evolve on its own? Given that opportunity, would Africans then have been able to resist and survive the corruptions and self-destructions of the 20th Century? These are 'what-if?' questions, but they are worth thinking about. For it looks very much as though the route to real development for Africa is opened, now in our own time, only with an end to imperialism.

FROM DISPOSSESSION TO 'TRIBALISM'

As it turned out a hundred years ago, the big question for Africans was: How can we defend ourselves in this time of imperialist dispossession? They could no longer seek to modernise, for they had lost all power of public decision. Imperialist racism was running high, and insisted that all the powers of public decision should be in the hands of the invaders. Chiefs and kings might survive, but only upon condition of obedience to the imperialist rulers. And the main concern of these rulers was not to modernise Africa; it was to extract from Africa whatever wealth could be found there, whether from mines in the subsoil or from the labour of African farmers.

In these circumstances men and women had no state-power to defend themselves. They were driven to rely upon their individual resources. There reappeared, and became strong, an old means of self-defence that had flourished in the evil times of the slave trade. Families banded together to help each other, and made alliances with neighbouring families against other families or clans. Each family or clan then struggled for its separate interests in a kind of destructive 'free for all'. Now, once again, old structures of clan or family loyalty grew strong. The Europeans called it 'tribalism'. They saw it as a proof of African backwardness.

This weapon of 'tribalist' self-defence was to become destructive to all community values, and to grow ever more destructive as the helpless colonial years continued. It killed off all scope for community progress by the very fact that it divided communities against themselves and within themselves. In the 1990s, for example, this 'tribalism' proved able to ruin whole peoples and wreck their hopes of any kind of progress, as for example in the terribly self-destructive case of Somalia.

In fact, ethnic or tribal loyalties had very little to do with this disaster. We can better think of this 'tribalism' as a kind of 'clientism'. 'Strong men' fought other 'strong men' by promising favours to those who supported them in elections or other bids for personal power. No rule of law, however sensible, was able to control this 'clientism'. Society simply fell apart. When economic crisis struck Africa ever more severely in the 1980s, little was left for several African countries save the rule of the gun. All too often, the institutions of civil government collapsed into dictatorship. But dictatorship, here as elsewhere in the world, relied on militarism. And militarism, in turn, relied on the massive import and use of firearms. These, unhappily, the industrialised powers were willing and even eager to sell for use in Africa.

At this point everyone had to suffer except the favoured few who had seized power. Rampant in Africa even by the 1970s, militarism wasted huge resources in buying arms and paying for inflated armed forces. One very painful case was Ethiopia under its successive forms of dictatorship up to the beginning of the 1990s. Vast areas of Ethiopia, a major African country, began to suffer famine. Yet spending on arms for war and oppression continued to soar. In 1974, for example, the dictatorship in Ethiopia spent $103.4 million on arms and armed forces: this was about $3.60 for each person then living in Ethiopia. By 1979 this war-ravaged and very hungry country was spending $526 million on self-destructive arms and armed forces. This was about $17.40 per inhabitant. The state and government of Ethiopia, in other words, had become the enemy of its people. Ethiopia was by no means the only country where this happened.

There were other pressures for 'short-term gain', very understandable in a continent reeling from its poverty and yet out of sight of any better future. For example, independent Africa inherited many natural riches; among these were its great forests of valuable hardwood timber. When the independent states fell ever more seriously into debt to foreign banks, as they did after the 1970s with recession spreading on every hand, the pressure to pay the interest on these foreign debts also grew. This had to mean higher exports. In the case of the tropical forests, for example, each year of the 1980s (and subsequent years) has seen these superb forests of hardwood destroyed over vast areas so as to export more timber. And yet these forests cannot be made to live again. With their trees felled for 'short-term gain', their friable soils leach away under the pelting of tropical rainfall. Replanting hardwoods becomes ever more difficult or impossible.

All this, of course, can be seen as part of the bitter price that the modern world exacts from those who want to join it. In 1985, for example, it was said that about 30 per cent of the population of Nairobi, the capital city of Kenya, were living under conditions of acute poverty. One hundred years or so earlier, the same had been true of the great European city of London. And today, how many hungry people are there in the midst of America's wealth and comfort?

Is the black continent also bound to pay this kind of price? In the midst of Africa's modern miseries of 'clientism' – of the money-rivalries called 'tribalism' – what answers to this question can be heard? What lessons are being drawn from Africa's long history of pre-colonial self-development: from the self-development of these black peoples who, back in the past and skilfully, had discovered how to tame their continent and make it prosper?

QUESTIONS OF RELIGION

Here we are back to the central problem: how to steer Africa out of this crisis of the late 20th Century? Much advice came from the world outside Africa, from the 'developed world'; but much of this advice seemed contradictory, and little of it useful. The socialism of the East had collapsed. The free-enterprise capitalism of the West might work well in the West, or well enough, but in Africa it had helped to induce the very crisis it had promised to avert. In this 'ideological void', where should Africans look for salvation?

Wise persons in this troubled Africa looked back on their history, and, not least, on all those efforts and experiments embarked upon by Africans since the termination of colonial rule. What people in crisis clearly needed, according to the record of the history we have traversed in this book, was a lamp of loyalty to show the way ahead, a guide to common action that is also useful action. Where could this lamp and guide be found?

Africans in their own history had looked to God for the answer to this question. They had looked to their various interpretations of religion. They had seen that spiritual wisdom had come down to them through those whom they considered to be their divinely-appointed ancestors: those were the spiritual powers who could point the way ahead, who could reward living people who followed that way, or who could punish those who failed to follow it. As it fell out in old Africa, spiritual powers for blessing or for punishment were in the possession of extended families, of what the scientists have called 'segmentary lineages' or their equivalents. So while they were unifying for members of those lineages, they could also be divisive in relation to other lineages.

These lineage loyalties – often wrongly called ethnic loyalties – have remained powerful in modern Africa, sometimes helpful in their unifying effect, sometimes destructive in their divisiveness. The great universalist religions of Christianity and Islam, each in its own way superseding the older loyalties of ancestral belief, have won countless converts, and have continued to win new converts. But the spiritual power of the ancestors has not been forgotten.

Over past ages, Christianity and Islam – sometimes in conflict, sometimes not – offered their divinely-empowered promises of salvation. The records of Christianity in Africa, after all, go back to the earliest years after the Crucifixion, while the records of Islam in Africa begin with the earliest years after the life of the Prophet Muhammad almost 14 centuries ago. Here we cannot follow this rich and varied history of religion. But we may usefully note, so far as Africa is concerned, that the moral and political beliefs of Islam played a leading role in the formation and government of ancient states in the grassland countries, and continued to do so during later upheavals.

Whether through its historic brotherhoods or *tariquas*, such as the Qadiriyya and the Tijaniyya, or in famous schools of Islamic learning in cities like Timbuktu and Djenne, African Islam upheld and defended the teachings of the Prophet Muhammad, and of the Sharia that is believed by Muslims to be the constitutional and legal system divined by God. In the troubles and confusions of the modern world, accordingly, there have been many Muslims in Africa who believe that salvation must lie in a strict return to the ancient beliefs and practices of Islam. This current of thought among Muslims became ever more influential after the 1960s while converts to Islam continued to grow in number: by the 1990s it seems that about half of all Nigerians, for example, have joined Islam. And as troubles multiplied, this loyalty to Islam acquired an increasingly special form, an 'extremist' form known as Fundamentalism: a 'return to the foundations of Islam'.

This had strong appeal in a world that seemed to have turned away from morality and honest government. It was advanced as offering hope and comfort to the poor and anxious, especially to the poor and anxious of the new cities and huge urban conglomerations; and these poor and anxious, now, were very many. But this Fundamentalism, as a politically-directed movement with aims in this world rather than in Heaven, rapidly took the road of a violent intolerance. It began to spurn the traditional civilities of Islam, and return to the hostilities of the *mujahiddin*, the warriors of Islam in times of *jihad* or 'holy war' of forced conversion.

Political Islam, in this form, soon had violent results. It is easy as well as painful to see why. To Fundamentalists, the law of a Muslim country must be a strict interpretation and application of the law of Sharia. As Professor Abdullahi An-Naim has taught us, Sharia is Islam's comprehensive and systematic legal code, developed by Muslim jurists of the 8th and 9th Centuries (AD), and derived by them from the Quran and from the Sunna of Muhammad. But in all that time since then, great controversies and schisms have divided Muslims as to what lawful behaviour really is or should be. Since then, too, Muslim authorities have introduced many reforms of their law, many tolerances, many reconciliations with fellow-citizens who are not Muslims.

Yet modern Fundamentalism has set its face against these reforms and tolerances, and has insisted, for example, that the extremely harsh punishments laid down in the Sharia code, long ago in medieval times, such as the amputation of the right hand for theft, severe lashing or even stoning to death for fornication or adultery, be still applied. 'Other aspects of the penal law of Sharia', adds Professor An-Naim, 'would be unacceptable to non-Muslims as well. For example, most jurists (according to the law of Sharia) would not allow the Muslim murderer of a non-Muslim to be executed'.

In other words, in a Muslim state subject to the law of Sharia, justice for non-Muslims cannot be at all the same thing as justice for Muslims. This means that Fundamentalism, wherever it rules (as in the Sudan during the 1980s), has to lead towards violent conflict, and fails to be the means of solving the problems of modern life.

Christianity in sub-Saharan Africa can be seen to have suffered, on a small scale, from the same kind of Fundamentalist (but Christian) affliction and intolerance, and may again be understood as a product of poverty and despair. As with Islam, according to Professor Don Ohadike of Jos University in Nigeria, when speaking at a seminar in 1988, 'the unity of Nigeria has been disturbed by the activities of Christian fundamentalists. There are now (i.e. at the end of the 1980s) over one thousand independent Christian sects in Nigeria, many of them exhibiting fundamentalist traits'. The older Christian Churches were meanwhile reported to be losing members to these Fundamentalist movements, the latter being characterised by their innovations in modes of worship and of evangelicism. Some of these Fundamentalist Christian movements claimed inspiration from the USA. This attraction owed much to the glaring contrast between American wealth and African poverty as portrayed in motion-pictures, television and so on. The American brand of Christian Fundamentalism, according to Professor Ohadike, could gain wide acceptance in Nigeria 'because of the present economic difficulties'.

The religious solution to Africa's social crisis, in this dimension, thus appears as the product of crisis and not as its solution. Notably in the Islamic northern provinces of Nigeria, various kinds of Muslim Fundamentalism appeared to be powerful only in the power to destroy. 'Between eight and ten thousand people were killed in the first seven years of this decade (of the 1980s)', notes Professor Ohadike, 'as a result of religious disturbances in Nigeria'. Many others lost their property and their livelihood, for the same reason, elsewhere in Africa.

TOWARDS AFRICA'S SOLUTIONS?

So which way to turn?

By early in the 1990s it became increasingly clear that thinking

Africans, women now as much as men, were asking themselves this question and beginning to find new answers. Conclusions began to emerge. Religion in all its spiritual power, whether in African ancestral terms or in those of Christianity or of Islam, would remain a dominant inspiration, moral and social, for a majority of people. But religion in its directly political guise, its 'fundamentalist' urgings, could offer no exit from crisis; it would be more likely to deepen conflict and disunity.

Above all, there must be political renewal. In country after country, men and women gathered in meetings and demonstrations. They defied government repression. They demanded an end to bullying, dictatorship, bureaucratic arrogance and other political miseries. They campaigned for restoration of the rule of law. They asked for the realities of self-government. They insisted that without these realities no democracy was possible.

But how to secure these realities of self-government?

To this, too, new answers could now be heard. The Nigerian political scientist Claude Ake was one participant in widening debate who summarised these answers. The central failure of African politics, on this view, was the rigid centralism of the nation-states created at the time of decolonisation. Ake considered that 'development strategies in Africa, with minor exceptions, have tended to be strategies by which the few use the many for their purposes. They are uncompromisingly top-down. There is not, and has never been, popular participation in political and economic decision-making'. As we saw near the beginning of this chapter, this was criticism of the post-colonial nation-state as a basically anti-democratic institution. It was the criticism strongly stated by a former Nigerian Head of State, Olusegun Obasanjo, at a conference in 1990: 'The bald fact', said Obasanjo, 'is that in Africa we have squandered almost 30 years with ineffective nation-building efforts. Our policies were far removed from social needs and developmental relevance.'

To reform this kind of nation-state, and make it work for its citizens, there must therefore be devolutions of executive power in favour of widespread political participation in the use of power. 'The centrality of popular participation and the human factor', concluded Professor Adebayo Adedeji a year later, was now generally agreed to have become 'the only viable developmental paradigm of Africa'. Without the application of this paradigm of popular participation, this pattern and thought of democratic action, there could be no effective reform of the neo-colonial state.

This was the situation in which people began to reflect on their precolonial history, and on the principles of pre-colonial statecraft with which, as we have seen, Africa in the past had built successful independent states. Obviously there can be no going back to the past. But the wisdom of the past, it was argued, may be helpful in finding good ways ahead.

It was recalled that the principles of old Africa's success in self-development had been, as we have noted, three in number. First of all, the community whether small or big had to live according to its own specific charter of rules and laws. These rules and laws could not be just anyone's invention. They had to be the outcome of a community's adjustment to the place and circumstances in which the community lived and worked. They had to derive from a long and often difficult process of experiment: of 'trial and error', and therefore of repeated effort. They had to arise from an intimate knowledge of local ecology and environment: for example, what soils and rainfall were necessary to the cultivation of this or that vegetable or food-bush?

This body of local knowledge was generally ascribed to the wise teaching of revered ancestors, and seen as having come ultimately from the source of all power, which is God. So the laws and rules for self-development, in those old states, were embodied in Africa's many religions, it being believed that persons who broke the rules and laws, and thus hurt the community, could be punished by God as well as by citizens. All this expressed the principle of Africa's rule of law.

But these rules and laws could not be imposed 'from the top down'. They and their application were, and had to be, the work of 'power-sharing' among the people, or, as Africans have often expressed it, of 'people's participation'. Kings and generals would no doubt try to be tyrants: before long, as countless historical examples can show, tyrants were obliged to bend to the will of the majority, or else they were thrown out. All this was the opposite of colonial and neo-colonial experience. It embodied the principle of Africa's diffusion of executive power.

A third principle was devoted to providing safeguards against the abuse of executive power. In the successful states of pre-dispossession Africa, the ideal was a community in which a system of compensatory arrangements, a system of 'checks and balances', should see to it that executive power, the power of government, was always distrusted: that executive power was kept under a people's control by sharing it out among citizens. So religious powers were balanced against economic powers, central powers against local powers, collective powers against individual powers, and so on. The aim, as with the Ogboni among Nigeria's Yoruba people, was to prevent misuse of power by those to whom power had been entrusted.

Of course this did not spell any kind of perfection. The ideal was not reached: no more here than anywhere else in human history. But the developmental success to which these principles gave rise was the result of finding Africa's solutions to Africa's problems. The same approach, it was now being said in Africa's end-century crisis of poverty and confusion, could once again be possible and useful. This was a conclusion that men and women now argued for in many African countries and circumstances. Imported solutions had been tried. Mostly they had failed. Or else these solutions had merely served the interests of persons and peoples, outside Africa, who had little or no concern with the interests of persons and peoples inside Africa. Such solutions, said King Mosheshoe of Lesotho at an international seminar in 1985, had been 'a bonanza for the transnational corporations and for consumers in the industrialised countries'; but they had done 'very little to improve the living standards of most people in Third World countries.'

This democratic monarch went on to emphasise what others had been saying. Africa needed 'to develop open and participatory forms of economic and political planning': forms within which 'people can take part in public debate about the main production and development issues, and then have a direct say in the final decision'. Securing this might be a long and difficult struggle. But it would be a struggle in which the civic achievements of African history could have their weight of example and encouragement.

Africans, and peoples everywhere concerned with Africa, must therefore look again at Africa's history, and evaluate its positive as well as its negative record. They must re-examine its civic achievements. They must reject the sense of inferiority imposed by colonialist dispossession. This might not be easy. But it would have to be done. 'So great and pervasive has been the down-thrusting of colonial rule,' recalled Professor Adebayo Adedeji, writing in the November 1992 *Bulletin* of the newly-formed African Centre for Development and Strategic Studies, 'that many Africans and most non-Africans have persistently denigrated the pre-colonial historical achievements of the continent; its arts, customs, beliefs, system of government and the art of government. Indeed', he continued, 'the tragedy has been that when the opportunity came to cast aside the yoke of colonialism, no effort was made to reassert Africa's self-determination by replacing foreign institutions and systems of government, and the flawed European models of nation-states, with rejuvenated and modernised indigenous African systems that the people would easily relate to, and would therefore be credible.'

Looking ahead to the 21st Century, this whole approach to Africa's problems reflected a new vision of the future, the vision of a further and effective decolonisation: a decolonisation, this time, of minds and attitudes such as could promote a decolonisation of institutions. As our tumultuous 20th Century came to a close, the prophecy and promise of this vision might well find a widening acceptance.

Key periods and events

Readers will have found a very large quantity of dates, referring to events and persons, in successive sections of the text. Besides these, an outline sketch of some of the important periods and dates in the making of modern Africa may be useful:

1884–5
Imperialist powers meet in Berlin to agree on the partition of Africa where, so far, they have only a few colonies. This is the so-called 'scramble for Africa' conference. The European powers agree, in effect, to invade and parcel out Africa without fighting each other.

1885–1901
Many colonial invasions. By 1901, most of the colonial frontiers are fixed by agreements between the invading powers.

1901–14
Chief period of installing colonial power by military means. The invading powers defeat continued resistance, and extend their control. Railways are built so as to export minerals and other wealth.

1914–18
First World War between the imperialist powers. Although able to keep the peace between each other in the Africa they have invaded, they fail to keep it in Europe. Defeated, Germany loses its colonies to Britain, France and Belgium. These transferred colonies are called 'mandates' of the newly-formed League of Nations; the practical difference between colonies and mandates proves very small.

1919–29
Colonial governments continue to extend their control, act against further resistance, and develop civil services.

New mines are opened by large companies of one or another colonial power, notably for copper and gold.

Huge development of systems of migrant labour.

A few more railways are built, mostly again by forced labour.

Settlers continue to take land from Africans, notably in Algeria, Kenya, Northern Rhodesia (Zambia), Southern Rhodesia (Zimbabwe), Angola and South Africa.

Early attempts at national liberation, notably in Morocco and Somalia, fail against overwhelming colonial military strength.

Early forms of African nationalist protest, principally in West and North Africa, gain some ground.

Various other forms of popular resistance develop, notably by religious types of organisation.

1929–35

Africans face consequences of the Great Depression, which brings a general collapse of the imperialist economies.

While the colonial powers introduce new forms of 'imperial protection' of their interests, African nationalism begins to grow. It begins to make demands for anti-colonial independence.

In some colonies, African workers begin to unite for better wages and less bad conditions of work.

1939–45

Second World War. Most colonial powers are weakened. USA becomes super-power. USSR, having defeated nazi Germany's invasion of Russia and other Soviet lands, enters fully into world councils.

United Nations is founded at end of war as successor to League of Nations. League mandates are re-constituted as 'UN trusteeship territories.'

1945–52

Encouraged by the Atlantic Charter of 1941, which has promised that every people shall be free to choose its own government, Africa's nationalists strengthen their demands.

Parties formed by the 'educated few' begin to develop into mass movements of nationalism. First breakthrough comes in 1951, when Ghana's Convention People's Party is able to win internal self-government for Gold Coast (Ghana), and when leading parties in southern Nigeria soon after achieve the same progress.

Most colonies are now in conditions of profound social crisis, deepened by forced labour in Second World War, and 'flight to the towns'.

1953–60

Nationalism continues to grow stronger.

Onwards from 1956, more and more colonies win their independence. In 1956, moreover, a British-French-Israeli invasion of Egypt, at Suez, is frustrated and fails.

Widespread colonial warfare breaks out in settler colonies, notably Algeria and Kenya, which nonetheless become independent in 1962 and 1963.

In South Africa, meanwhile, 1948 has seen the coming to power of the extreme racist Afrikaner National Party, and the launching of full-scale *apartheid* (racist persecution and exploitation).

1961–80

Drive for independence continues, notably in East and Central Africa, with success.

1963

Organisation of African Unity (OAU) is founded.

1965–85

White settlers in Rhodesia (Zimbabwe) rebel against Britain in 1965, declare their independence, and intensify their racist system. Zimbabwe African resistance replies with counter-violence. Africans win in 1980. Zimbabwe becomes independent.

Meanwhile, in Portuguese colonies, nationalists lead counter violence which begins in Angola in 1961, in Guinea-Bissau in 1963, in Mozambique in 1964. They win these wars, make their countries independent by 1974–75, and, in so doing, cause the overturn of Portuguese dictatorship in Portugal itself.

Racist repression in South Africa grows worse; many kinds of African protest there are met by government violence, but are not silenced.

From 1975 the racist regime in South Africa wages wars of aggression and subversion against Angola and, soon, against Mozambique. Their object is to recover South Africa's former position of dominance in the sub-continent. They fail but do great damage to Angola and Mozambique.

All efforts to bring about the end of South Africa's illegal occupation of Namibia, and so set that country free, continue to be frustrated by the racist regime's determination to retain control of Namibia. But international pressure against the racist regime also continues to grow.

Drought and warfare bring famine and disaster to much of the Horn of Africa, especially Ethiopia. In 1974 a revolution in Ethiopia overturns the imperial government and promises democracy. Military leaders soon undermine the promise; notably, they refuse to decolonise Eritrea (annexed to the Ethiopian empire in 1962) or to meet the demands of major nationalities, notably Tigray and Oromo, for autonomous self-government. By 1985 the Eritreans begin to win their struggle for post-colonial independence and in 1990 their victory is complete. Other historic nationalities assert their presence.

Elsewhere Africa wrestles with its legacy of partition by Europe. In

1985 a general crisis of poverty threatens the whole continent, and earlier hopes of rapid development are dismayed.

1986–1989

With their potentials still far from clear, these years remain dominated by the continent's deepening crisis of poverty and debt. On the positive side, however, it is at last widely understood that the existing world economic order, above all in relations between North and South, bears a heavy responsibility for this crisis.

The colonial legacy continues to make political trouble. But there are gains. In southern Africa the racist regime of South Africa fails, once more, to overthrow the independent regimes of Angola and Mozambique. It appears that South Africa may also make concessions to the independence of Namibia. In the Horn of Africa the Eritreans reach the threshold of independence from Ethiopian imperialist annexation.

Movement towards the internal reorganisation of a number of states, along the lines of power-decentralisation and democratic participation, continues to win ground, while the sterility of bureaucratic centralism becomes more evident. All this promises to open a new period of constructive experiment.

There is corresponding development in the field of culture. African writers and musicians, painters and other artists win new recognition, express a new self-confidence, find avenues of success.

1990

With Namibian independence (March 1990), and that of Eritrea in 1993, the long process of formal decolonisation comes to an end. As it does so, many political and economic institutions of this decolonised Africa, institutions derived largely from the colonial epoch, increasingly fail or collapse. A widespread crisis of civil society begins to be apparent.

Independence dates

	Date of Independence	Independence won from	Population★
1950s			
Egypt (UAR) process beginning in	1952	Britain	39,000,000
Ghana	1957	Britain	8,800,000
Guinea	1958	France	5,500,000
Libya	1951	Italy	2,257,000
Morocco	1956	France	16,700,000
Sudan	1956	Britain	14,500,000
Tunisia	1956	France	5,570,000
1960s			
Algeria	1962	France	16,000,000
Botswana	1966	Britain	750,000
Burundi	1962	Belgium	3,750,000
Cameroun	1960	France	6,539,000
Central African Republic	1960	France	1,850,000
Chad	1960	France	4,100,000
Congo (People's Republic of)	1960	France	1,400,000
Benin	1960	France	3,150,000
Equatorial Guinea	1968	Spain	300,000

	Date of Independence	Independence won from	Population*
Gabon	1960	France	1,100,000
Gambia, The	1965	Britain	540,000
Ivory Coast	1960	France	6,673,000
Kenya	1963	Britain	13,399,000
Lesotho	1966	Britain	1,250,000
Madagascar	1960	France	8,500,000
Malawi	1964	Britain	5,400,000
Mali	1960	France	6,108,000
Mauritania	1960	France	1,400,000
Mauritius	1968	Britain	856,000
Niger	1960	France	4,900,000
Nigeria	1960	Britain	92,000,000
Rwanda	1962	Belgium	4,700,000
Senegal	1960	France	4,800,000
Sierra Leone	1961	Britain	3,100,000
Somalia	1960	Italy and Britain	3,340,000
Swaziland	1967	Britain	526,000
Tanzania (Tanganyika, 1961) (Zanzibar, 1963)	1961	Britain	15,155,000
Togo	1960	France	2,228,000
Uganda	1962	Britain	11,549,000
Upper Volta	1960	France	6,147,000
Zaïre	1960	Belgium	24,902,000
Zambia	1964	Britain	4,981,000

1970s

Angola	1975	Portugal	6,761,000
Cape Verde	1975	Portugal	300,000
Comoros (without Mayotte)	1975	France	260,000
Djibouti	1977	France	210,000
Guinea-Bissau	1974	Portugal	750,000
Mozambique	1975	Portugal	9,200,000
São Tomé	1975	Portugal	75,000
Seychelles	1976	Britain	55,000

	Date of Independence	Independence won from	Population*
1980s			
Zimbabwe	1980	Britain and white settler regime	6,290,000
Sahrawi Democratic African Republic. (Formerly Spanish Sahara, the Sahrawi Republic was formally proclaimed in 1976, but recognised by the OAU only in 1982.)	1982	Spain	193,000 *(1988 official estimate)*
1990s			
Namibia	1990	South Africa	1,252,000 *(1988 official estimate)*
Eritrea	1993	Ethiopia	3,500,000
Already independent			
Ethiopia			24,470,000
Liberia			1,600,000
South Africa (only its racist regime being independent)			25,466,000

* 1975 approximate estimate. Many of these population totals are open to doubt. In general, throughout the continent, average populations in 1990 appeared, from often inadequate evidence, to be growing at the rate of about 2.5 per cent annually. While these population totals are out of date, and doubtful in any case, I have kept them in this latest edition as a guide to approximate comparisons.

A few notes on further reading

Books about modern Africa are many, so the student should seek guidance on those that may best help in this or that aspect of history. Here are some to choose from:

GENERAL HISTORIES

Crowder, M. (ed.), *Cambridge History of Africa: c.1940–c.1975* Vol. 8, Cambridge: University Press, 1984.

Davidson. B., *Africa in Modern History*, London: Penguin, 1978, and, as *Let Freedom Come*, Boston: Little Brown, 1978.

Davidson, B., *The African Genius*, Boston: Little Brown, 1969, and, as *The Africans*, London: Penguin, 1969.

Hargreaves, J.D., *Decolonization in Africa*, London and New York: Longman, 1988.

COUNTRY HISTORIES

Ajayi, J. F. A., and Crowder, M. (eds), *History of West Africa*, Vol. 2, London and New York: Longman, 1974.

Arnold, G., *Modern Kenya*, London and New York: Longman, 1981.

Davenport, R., *South Africa: A Modern History*, London: Macmillan, 1978.

Davidson, B., *The Fortunate Isles: A Study in African Transformation*,

Trenton N.J.: Africa World Press, and London: Hutchinson-Radius, 1989. (About the Cape Verde republic.)

Iliffe, J., *A Modern History of Tanganyika*, Cambridge: Cambridge University Press, 1979.

Isichei, E., *A History of Nigeria*, London and New York: Longman, 1982.

Karugire, S. R., *A Political History of Uganda*, Nairobi and London: Heinemann, 1980.

Liebenow, J. G., *Liberia: The Quest for Democracy*, Bloomington: Indiana University Press, 1987.

Munslow, B., *Mozambique: The Revolution and Its Origins*, London and New York: Longman, 1983.

Roberts, A., *A History of Zambia*, London: Heinemann, 1976.

Vatikiotis, P. J., *The Modern History of Egypt*, London: Weidenfeld, 1969.

MORE SPECIALISED STUDIES

Ajala, A., *Pan-Africanism*, London: Deutsch, 1974.

Asante, S. K. B., *Pan-African Protest in the Ethiopian Crisis 1934–1941*, London and New York: Longman, 1977.

Ayandele, E. A., *The Educated Elite in Nigerian Society*, Ibadan: Ibadan University Press, 1974.

Bender, G. J., *Angola under the Portuguese*, London: Heinemann, 1978.

Bermen, B. and Lonsdale, J., *Unhappy Valley: Conflict in Kenya*: Book 1, *State and Class*; Book 2, *Violence and Ethnicity*, London: James Currey Ltd, 1992.

Coleman, J. S., *Background to Nationalism* (about Nigeria), Berkeley: University of California, 1971.

Davidson, B., *The People's Cause: A History of Guerrillas in Africa*, London and New York: Longman, 1981.

also, *The Black Man's Burden: Africa and the Curse of the Nation-State*, New York, Times Books, London: James Currey Ltd, 1992.

Dudley, B. J., *Parties and Politics in Nigeria*, London: Macmillan, 1968.

Gifford, P. and Louis, W. R. (eds.), *Decolonization and African Independence*, New Haven and London: Yale, 1988.

Hanlon, J., *Beggar Your Neighbours: Apartheid Power in Southern Africa*, Bloomington: Indiana University Press, and London: Currey, 1986.

Hopkins, A. G., *An Economic History of West Africa*, London and New York: Longman, 1973.

Hoskyns, C., *The Congo since Independence*, Oxford: Oxford University Press, 1965.

Hunwick, J. O. (ed.), *Religion and National Integration in Africa*, Evanston: Northwestern University Press, 1992.

Isaacman, A. and B., *Mozambique: From Colonialism to Revolution*, Boulder: Westview, 1983.

Kilson, M., *Political Change in Sierra Leone*, Cambridge: Harvard 1966.

Langley, J., Ayodele, *Pan-Africanism and Nationalism*, 1940–1945, Oxford: Clarendon, 1972.

Lemarchand, R., *Political Awakening in the Belgian Congo*, Berkeley: University of California Press, 1964.

Leys, C., *Underdevelopment in Kenya*, London: Heinemann, 1975.

Magubane, B., and Mandaza, I. (eds), *Whither South Africa?*, Trenton N.J.: Africa World Press, 1988.

Markakis, J., *National and Class Conflict in the Horn of Africa*, Cambridge: Cambridge University Press, 1987.

Marks, S. and Trapido, S., *The Politics of Race, Class and Nationalism in 20th Century South Africa*, London and New York: Longman, 1987.

Martin, D. and Johnson, P., *The Struggle for Zimbabwe*, London: Faber, 1981.

Middleton, J., *The World of the Swahili*, New Haven and London: Yale, 1992.

Sandbrook, R., and Cohen, R. (eds), *The Development of an African Working Class*, London and New York: Longman, 1975.

Seidman, A., *Money, Banking and Public Finance in Africa*, London and New Jersey: Zed Books, 1986.

Stichter, S., *Migrant Labour in Kenya*, London and New York: Longman, 1982.

Suret-Canale, J., *French Colonialism in Tropical Africa* 1900–45, London: Hurst, 1971.

Van Onselen, C., *Chibaro: African Mine Labour in Southern Rhodesia 1900–33*, London: Pluto, 1976.

CRISIS AND RECESSION STUDIES

Barratt Brown, M. and Tiffen, P., *Short Changed, Africa and World Trade*, London: Pluto Press, Boulder, Colorado: with Trans-National Institute, Amsterdam, 1992.

Brett, E. A., *Colonialism and Underdevelopment in East Africa*, London: Heinemann, 1973.

Carlsson, Jerker (ed.), *Recession in Africa*, Uppsala: Scandinavian Institute of African Studies, 1983.

Davidson, B., *Can Africa Survive?: Arguments against Growth without Development*, Boston: Little, Brown, 1974, and London: Heinemann, 1974.

Fieldhouse, D. K., *Black Africa 1945–1980: Economic Decolonization and Arrested Development*, London: Allen Unwin, 1986.

Harrison, P., *The Greening of Africa*, London: Paladin, 1987.

Lawrence, P. (ed.), *World Recession and the Food Crisis in Africa*, London: Currey, 1986.

Richards, P., *Indigenous Agricultural Revolution in West Africa*, London: Century-Hutchinson, 1985.

Shepherd, G. W., *The Trampled Grass*, Westport: Praeger, 1987.

Timberlake, L., *Africa in Crisis: Causes and Cures of Environmental Bankruptcy*, new edn., London and Toronto: Earthscan, 1988.

TARIKH

The following issues of *Tarikh*, an occasional series of publications, published for the Historical Society of Nigeria by Longman, between 1965 and 1982, cover in greater detail some of the themes and issues raised in this book –

Tarikh 8 *France in Africa*

Tarikh 11 *Indirect Rule in British Africa*

Tarikh 12 *Independence Movements in Africa 1*

Tarikh 13 *Independence Movements in Africa 2*

Tarikh 19 *Protest against Colonial Rule in West Africa*

Tarikh 22 *White Society in Africa*

Tarikh 23 *Pan-Africanism*

Tarikh 24 *Portugal in Africa*

Tarikh 25 *Grass Roots Leadership in Colonial West Africa*

Tarikh 27 *Germany in Africa*

Index